PARTNERS IN BANKING

(*Color photograph by Taylor & Dull, Inc.*)

1818–1968

BROWN BROTHERS

HARRIMAN

(*Courtesy of Philadelphia Museum of Art.*)

Above: a painting of the four Brown brothers (l. to r.—George, John A., William, and James) as they might have appeared about 1860, grouped below a portrait of their father, Alexander Brown, founder of the fortune which led to the development of the international banking business of Brown Brothers & Co. and related firms. The painting, which hangs in the partners' room of Brown Brothers Harriman & Co., was done by Thomas C. Corner in 1916–17, and is a duplicate of one he did in 1903 for Alex. Brown & Sons of Baltimore, based on photographs and other pictures of the five men.

At right: Auguste Rodin's sculptured portrait of Edward H. Harriman, founder of the Harriman family fortune, made from photographs in 1909, after Mr. Harriman's death.

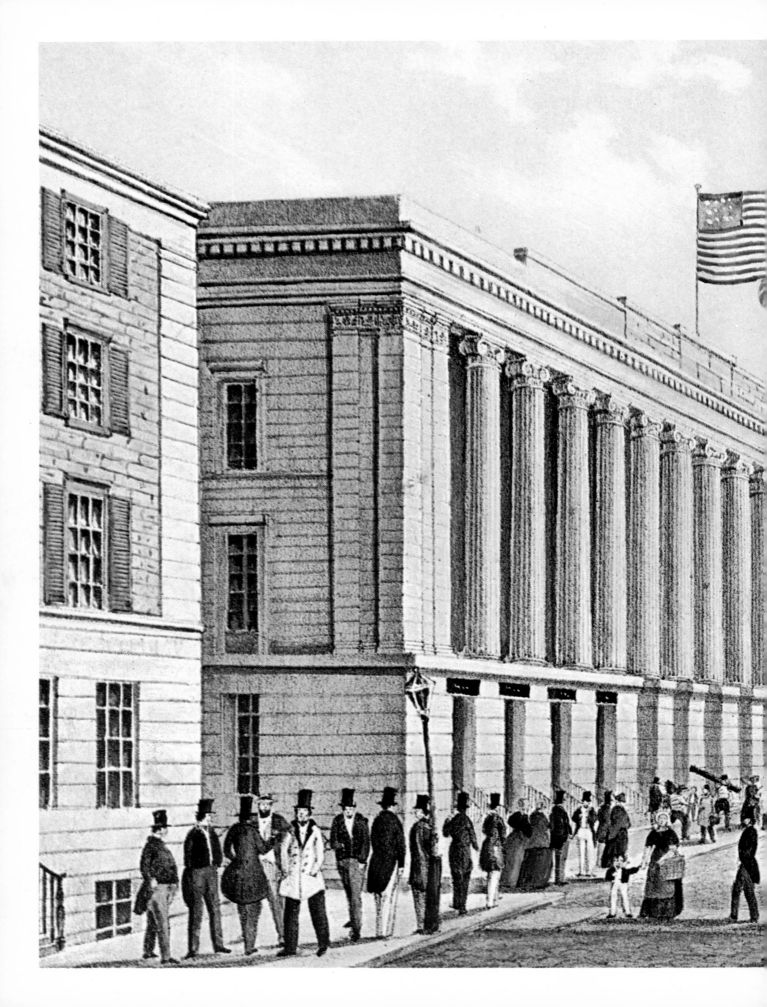

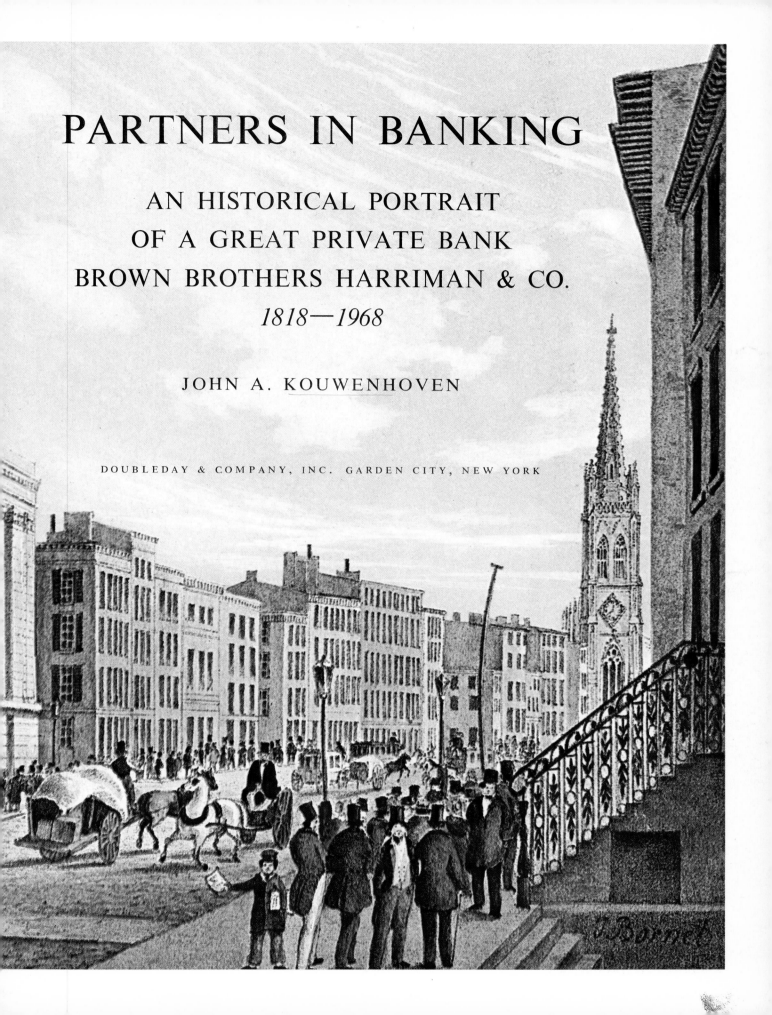

PARTNERS IN BANKING

AN HISTORICAL PORTRAIT
OF A GREAT PRIVATE BANK
BROWN BROTHERS HARRIMAN & CO.
1818—1968

JOHN A. KOUWENHOVEN

DOUBLEDAY & COMPANY, INC. GARDEN CITY, NEW YORK

The photograph at left shows a portion of the Historical File of Brown Brothers Harriman & Co., and gives some idea of the kind of documentary source material which has been indexed and arranged in connection with the preparation of this book. Standing against the wall is an 1856 Brady Imperial Photograph of James Brown, founder of the New York firm of Brown Brothers & Co. On the table there are various items ready to be filed in the cabinets at right: miscellaneous clippings, some Brown Brothers & Co. bills of exchange of the 1830s, the stock certificate book of the Wall & Hanover Street Realty Co., an 1838 parchment deed and an 1864 map of the 59 Wall Street property on which the bank has stood since 1843, and a recent issue of the firm's "Institutional Investment Guides," showing one of the charts prepared for the bank's institutional clients. On the floor are some of the old wooden chests and tin boxes in which were found copies of the partners' hand-written correspondence from the early 1800s to the late 1890s, and (open at left) the leather-bound first letter book of Brown Brothers & Co. At lower right is one of the nine leather-bound volumes of Mrs. John Crosby Brown's "Brighthurst Chronicles," open at a watercolor drawing of a family birthday party, and two of the thousands of photographs in the files, including one showing E. H. Harriman with a group of railway men in San Francisco about 1908. (*Color transparency by John T. Hill, taken February 28, 1967*)

Library of Congress Catalog Card Number 68–25592. Copyright © 1968 by John A. Kouwenhoven

All Rights Reserved. Printed in the United States of America. First Edition

The scene used as background for the title page (over) is reproduced from part of a color lithograph showing the south side of Wall Street, New York, as it looked about one hundred and twenty years ago. The building, part of which is shown at extreme left, on the southeast corner of Hanover Street, had been owned and occupied by Brown Brothers & Co. since 1843. The firm still occupies this corner. The entire lithograph, including its ornamental borders, is reproduced and described on page 84.

PREFACE

Brown Brothers Harriman & Co. is in many ways a unique institution. It is the only large commercial bank in the United States which is owned and operated by a partnership instead of by a corporation. It is the only large bank which owns a seat on the New York Stock Exchange. It is the only bank headquartered in the nation's financial capital which is authorized to carry on its banking business across state lines and can therefore offer complete banking services in Philadelphia and Boston as well as New York. It is the largest private bank on the North American continent, and by far the oldest. It is the only private bank whose history has been interwoven—always interestingly, and sometimes momentously—with the development of the nation's commerce and industry for more than a century and a half.

It is therefore appropriate, I think, to specify that this historical portrait is the result of a unique arrangement between the bank, the publisher, and the author. The Brown Brothers Harriman partners, by financing the four years of research upon which the book is based, and by agreeing in advance to purchase a substantial number of copies for distribution to friends and clients of the firm, have in effect underwritten the publication. But the book is in no sense an authorized history of the bank, for whose contents the firm is responsible. I planned and wrote it under a standard contract with my publisher for a book to be published on their regular trade list. No representative of the bank read the text or saw the completed layout until the printer's proofs were submitted for a final check, in hopes of minimizing the number of factual errors that seem inevitably to occur in works of this kind. Individual partners and executives of the bank did, at my request, read early drafts of several captions dealing with technical matters, and patiently helped me to clarify and rewrite them. But I alone am responsible for the opinions and judgments that are expressed in the text, or implied by the selection and arrangement of material.

At no time has anyone at Brown Brothers Harriman & Co. tried to influence the form or content of the book. On the contrary, I have had unrestricted access to the firm's historical records, including private and confidential correspondence, diaries, accounts, and other papers. Since June 1964 I have been employed by the bank part time as Director of the Historical File, to supervise the assembling, preserving, and organizing of whatever historical documents happen to have been kept in the vaults, closets, and filing cabinets at the bank's various offices, or in warehouses, or in the possession of the families of former partners and employees. There are blanks in the record; accident, and the haphazard decisions that businesses and families are likely to make when storage problems arise, have caused the destruction of much that would be interesting to us now. But much of great interest has survived, as the informal sampling in these pages suggests, and is being put in shape for use by qualified students of economic and financial history. Taken together with the hundreds of large volumes of manuscript records deposited some years ago by Brown Brothers Harriman & Co. in the New York Public Library and by Alex. Brown & Sons of Baltimore in the Library of Congress, and with the records preserved by Brown, Shipley & Co., Ltd., of London, the Historical File will provide an unparalleled record of one of the nation's oldest financial institutions.

In planning the book, I have been aware that my freedom of access to these records imposes serious obligations upon me—obligations to respect the privacy of individuals and to honor the integrity of the bank's confidential relationships with its clients. But I have not been aware of any obligation to speak well of people I do not respect or to suppress or minimize evidence of activities that were

1

in my judgment either unsavory or inept. If, therefore, the combination of pictures and text which follows conveys the impression of an honorable business run by honorable though fallible men—sometimes courageously against tough odds, sometimes rather placidly, and sometimes with creative elan and a readiness to pioneer—that is because the firm's uncensored records seem to me to justify that impression.

JOHN A. KOUWENHOVEN

September 11, 1967

CONTENTS

PARTNERS IN BANKING

One

THE BEST OF THE OLD AND NEW

On the evening of December 11, 1930, a group of reporters crowded into the library of Thatcher M. Brown's residence at 775 Park Avenue in New York City. They had been tipped off that Mr. Brown, one of the senior partners in the old and respected private banking house of Brown Brothers & Co., would have an important announcement to make.

A tall, rather scholarly looking man, with graying hair and a broad, comfortable mustache, Mr. Brown peered smilingly at his guests through round, horn-rimmed glasses. Few of them would have recognized him if they passed him in the street, for he was not well known outside of banking circles and the boards of the charitable and educational institutions on which he served.

Standing next to Mr. Brown was a younger man whose handsome face was already familiar to the reporters—William Averell Harriman, eldest son of the great railroad organizer and financier Edward Henry Harriman. A well-known sportsman (he had been coach of the Yale crew while still an undergraduate, and was one of the nation's top-ranking polo players), Mr. Harriman was also known as an able businessman. He was a director of a number of corporations, including his father's Union Pacific Railroad, had built ships for the U. S. Merchant

THATCHER MAGOUN
BROWN (1876–1954).
From a snapshot
taken about 1934.

(*Courtesy of Thatcher
M. Brown, III.*)

W. AVERELL HARRIMAN
(1891–   ), from a
photograph taken
March 23, 1929,
by Bain News Service.

(*Culver Pictures, Inc.*)

"All the News That's Fit to Print."

The New York Times.

Copyright, 1930, by The New York Times Company.

VOL. LXXX....No. 26,620. **** NEW YORK, FRIDAY, DECEMBER 12, 1930. TWO CENTS In Greater New York | THREE CENTS Within 200 Miles | FOUR CENTS Elsewhere Except 7th and 8th Postal Zones

THE WEATHER

Cloudy with rain today; tomorrow cloudy and colder.

Temperatures yesterday—Max. 47, min. 40.

U. S. Weather Forecast—For details see Page 51.

BANK OF U. S. CLOSES DOORS; STATE TAKES OVER AFFAIRS; AID OFFERED TO DEPOSITORS

ACTION BY CLEARING HOUSE

Twenty-three Members Willing to Lend 50% on Accounts.

$160,000,000 IN DEPOSITS

$1,500,000 of City Money and $164,927 Postal Savings—Garment Funds Tied Up.

CROWDS AT OFFICES CALM

McFadden, Fearing Effect Abroad, Explains Institution Has No Government Connection.

The Bank of United States, a commercial bank with sixty offices in the city, closed its doors yesterday morning and placed its affairs in the hands of the State Banking Department.

While officials of the institution issued a statement expressing hope of an early reopening, leading banks of the city took steps to provide temporary relief for the depositors by offering to lend them 50 per cent of the amount of their deposits.

The institution, despite its name, had no connection with the Federal Government. Deposits at the time of the closing were approximately $160,000,000.

The suspension of the bank followed a night in which representatives of the Federal Reserve Bank of New York and of the principal banking institutions, together with Superintendent of Banks Joseph A. Broderick, had made strenuous efforts to save the institution. On Wednesday evening disturbances had occurred at several branches of the Bank of United States and deposits had been heavily withdrawn. It was recognized that unless relief measures were adopted a run on the bank would have developed yesterday morning.

Ask Broderick to Take Charge.

The meeting of the bankers, which was held at the Federal Reserve Bank, lasted until 4 o'clock yesterday morning, at which time, no practical plan for immediate relief having been agreed upon, directors of the Bank of United States adopted the following resolution:

Resolved, That, Whereas rumors have been circulated which have caused abnormal withdrawals of deposits and it is feared that if the bank is opened Thursday morning these withdrawals may continue; that there will be in more than one of the branches of the bank large numbers of persons seeking withdrawals of their deposits which may result in disorder, and it is desired that all depositors be treated equally and the assets conserved for their benefit; and

Whereas the directors feel that in view of conditions it would be unwise to continue to receive and pay out moneys, that the officers of the bank be, and they are hereby authorized to advise the Superintendent of Banks of the State of New York that they believe it to be for the best interests of the depositors of the institution that, because of the emergency, he take possession of the assets of the bank in accordance with the banking law of the State of New York, with the hope that a speedy and satisfactory reorganization can be effected, the bank reopened and the moneys due to depositors paid at the earliest possible date.

The resolution was made public at 9 A. M. by Mr. Broderick, who announced at the same time that he had taken possession of the business and property of the bank, pursuant to the provisions of Section 57 of the banking law. Fred W. Piderit, an examiner in the Banking Department, was appointed Special Deputy Superintendent in charge, and the department's corps of examiners set to work immediately to determine the position of the institution.

Mr. Broderick explained the task of examination was a large one as each branch must be examined separately and completely. The last examination of the bank made by the department required three months, it was said, and was completed last September. In recent weeks the department

Continued on Page Two.

23 Clearing House Banks Offer Loans to Depositors

The New York Clearing House Association issued the following statement yesterday:

TO DEPOSITORS OF BANK OF UNITED STATES.

The undersigned, being all of the members of the New York Clearing House Association, will lend to depositors of the Bank of United States, at 5 per cent interest, up to 50 per cent of their net balances properly authenticated.

Bank of New York and Trust Company.
Bank of Manhattan Trust Company.
Bank of America National Association.
National City Bank.
Chemical Bank and Trust Company.
Guaranty Trust Company.
Chatham Phenix National Bank and Trust Company.
Central Hanover Bank and Trust Company.
Corn Exchange Bank Trust Company.
First National Bank.
Irving Trust Company.
Continental Bank and Trust Company.
Chase National Bank.
Fifth Avenue Bank.
Bankers Trust Company.
Title Guarantee and Trust Company.
Marine Midland Trust Company.
Lawyers Trust Company.
New York Trust Company.
Commercial National Bank and Trust Company.
Harriman National Bank and Trust Company.
Public National Bank and Trust Company.
Manufacturers Trust Company.

BIG BANKING HOUSES DECIDE ON MERGER

Brown Brothers & Co., W. A. Harriman & Co. and Harriman Brothers & Co. to Unite.

BUSINESS IS INTERNATIONAL

To Be Brown Brothers, Harriman & Co.—All but One of Old Partners Continue.

Announcement was made last night of the consolidation of Brown Brothers & Co., W. A. Harriman & Co., Inc., and Harriman Brothers & Co., effective on Jan. 1. These are all international banking houses with connections extending throughout the United States and several foreign countries. The new organization will be known as Brown Brothers, Harriman & Co.

The announcement was made last night by the banking groups involved. The combination will bring together three of the most important financial organizations in Wall Street, and under the arrangement that has been agreed upon the Harriman and Brown interests will continue to operate in their respective fields.

The announcement set out that the fusion of interests in the special type of service which private financial houses render will effect a combination of resources and facilities with growing requirements of modern business. Brown Brothers & Co. have been engaged in the private international banking field for nearly 100 years, while the Harriman firm was among the first to see the opportunities in this field following the World

Continued on Page Six.

EINSTEIN ON ARRIVAL BRAVES LIMELIGHT FOR ONLY 15 MINUTES

Submits on Ship to Rapid-Fire Interview by 50 Reporters Flanked by 50 Camera Men.

JESTS, BUT FINALLY FLEES

With Wife Acting as Buffer, He Escapes Reception—Praises America in Statement.

TOURS CHINATOWN IN CAR

Tomorrow German Scientist Will Be Officially Received at City Hall.

Professor Albert Einstein, whose mind works in terms of immeasurable time and space, arrived in New York yesterday and granted a fifteen-minute interview.

Surrounded by a small mob of reporters, publicity men, photographers and movie operators in the drawing room of the liner Belgenland, which brought him here from Antwerp for his second visit to the United States in ten years, he was called upon within the brief quarter of an hour to define the fourth dimension in one word, state his theory of relativity in one sentence, give his views on prohibition, comment on politics and religion, and discuss the virtues of his violin.

He was also requested to answer many other questions, some of which he took seriously but most of which he parried with a jest. He faced the interview bewildered but with good nature.

Taken on deck from the drawing room to pose before the photographers, the shy and retiring scientist tried hard to oblige the camera men but after another fifteen minutes of "torture" finally lost patience, threw up his hands and dashed toward a companionway.

Reminded of Punch and Judy Show.

He said the interview reminded him of a Punch and Judy show and, later, characterized the whole proceeding as "eccentric." Smiling most of the time the whimsical smile of one who knows the difference between eternity and the immediate moment, the scientist submitted to the questions during the allotted fifteen minutes. He then rose, terminated the interview and walked away, followed by Mrs. Einstein and a group of friends.

The worst part of his experience was yet to come, however, as he was led on deck to be photographed. His long gray hair flying in the wind, his brown eyes reflecting resignation, he steeled himself for what to him was obviously unpleasant and he did not conceal his satisfaction when it was over. He then retired to the drawing room for the first of two radio broadcasts from the ship.

In these messages and in a statement prepared for the press Einstein declared he was glad to be in the United States again, paid a warm tribute to the achievements of American science, hailed America as the citadel of democracy and expressed the hope that this country would take the leadership in the solution of the international economic depression and in strengthening the foundations of world peace. In these messages he managed to introduce a serious note to the reception.

Professor and Mrs. Einstein are bound for the California Institute of Technology at Pasadena, where the German scientist will do some work in cooperation with Professor Robert P. Millikan and will also

Continued on Page Sixteen.

Herbert Hoover 3d Sends Word to Santa Via Talkie Camera to Bring Police Uniform

Special to The New York Times.

WASHINGTON, Dec. 11.—President and Mrs. Hoover's grandchildren, Peggy Ann and Herbert Hoover 3d, today settled, at least so far as they are concerned, the momentous questions as to what they want Santa Claus to bring them for Christmas. They conveyed their wishes to Santa Claus by way of the microphones of the sound news reels.

Despite their tender years—Peggy Ann is barely more than 4 years old and Herbert has not yet reached the age of 3—they were forced to bow to public demand and pose for pictures in the south grounds of the White House early today. They lost no opportunity to let it be known what they wanted for Christmas.

Herbert, it was revealed, wants a policeman's uniform, including badge and stick, the same as he has seen since coming to the Executive Mansion last Sunday to join his grandparents. And, too, he wants an engine.

"A big one or a little one?" little Herbert was asked. After eyeing his interrogator somewhat with disdain, little Herbert replied, "A big one."

Peggy Ann asked that Santa Claus bring her a doll, and "a very big one," at that. Then, apparently remembering it might get lonely by itself, she put in a plea for some smaller ones. In addition, she wants a wagon. Herbert opined that he would like a wagon also.

Peggy Ann and Herbert, with their mother, Mrs. Peggy Hoover, and their grandmother, posed at length for the cameramen. The two children made their initial appearance on tricycles.

Their six-month-old sister, Joan, failed to get in the picture. So Santa Claus may have to guess what she wants.

Doak Moves to Deport Alien Gang Leaders; 'All Resources' Put Into War on Underworld

Special to The New York Times.

WASHINGTON, Dec. 11.—In an effort to rid larger populated centres of the United States of gunmen and gangsters the Department of Labor has undertaken a thorough investigation into the history of leading underworld figures with a view to their eventual deportation, William N. Doak, the newly appointed Secretary of Labor, declared today.

"We are going into the gangster problem with all the resources at our command," he said. Many gangsters with millions and millions of dollars behind them, he said, had been able to employ high-class counsel who had been successful in preventing many deportations.

In conducting its investigation, Mr. Doak said, the Department of Labor is planning to ask Congress for increased funds to enable it to enlarge its staff of investigators. The problem of gangsters in American cities is being stressed by the entire department, he said.

To rid cities of "undesirables," he said, a searching investigation is being made of leading gunmen and gang figures in Chicago and elsewhere and a careful check of their careers is being made in an effort to establish grounds for actual deportation.

He emphasized, however, that deportation can only be accomplished when proved warranted through due process of law, and said such proceedings are extremely involved and often very lengthy.

With these difficulties in mind, Mr. Doak said, the department would ask Congress for other funds to set up adequate machinery to hear the cases, so that the procedure might be speeded "all along the line."

Asked to reveal the names of some of those against whom action may be taken, Mr. Doak said he was not at liberty to disclose the names of gang leaders under investigation.

He intimated, however, that the list of Chicago's "public enemies," recently made public, includes several of the names which the department is tracing.

BRODSKY TO TESTIFY ON INCOME TODAY

Magistrate Is Summoned to Public Hearing—Crain Agrees to Defer "Frame-Up" Cases.

TAX FRAUDS ARE HUNTED

Federal Agent Confers With Kresel on Judges' Accounts—Bondsman Is Held.

Magistrate Louis B. Brodsky will be the first witness today at the sixth public hearing in the Appellate Division's investigation of the inferior courts, according to an announcement late yesterday by Isidor Kresel, special counsel to Samuel Seabury, the referee. Mr. Kresel intimated that the day might produce some "surprises."

The magistrate, who as the Democratic standard bearer in the three-cornered Congressional contest in the Seventeenth Congressional District was defeated by Mrs. Ruth Pratt, his Republican opponent in the last election, will be questioned, it was understood, about his finances and the sources of his income.

Frequent withdrawals and deposits of large amounts are shown in his bank records, it was reported. He was questioned privately about the matter early in November, at which time he said that his real estate activities accounted for the frequent turnover of his capital.

Brodsky Is Surprise Witness.

The announcement that Magistrate Brodsky would be the subject of today's hearing came somewhat as a surprise because it had been indicated that Magistrate Henry M. R. Goodman, who was summoned from the bench for questioning Wednesday afternoon, would be the chief witness this morning.

It had been feared in some quarters that the closing of the Bank of United States, of which Mr. Kresel was a director, might demand so much of his time that the present inquiry would be slowed up. The special counsel, however, denied this and declared "nothing will be allowed to interefere with this investigation."

Reports of large incomes enjoyed by magistrates, policemen and court officers have attracted the attention of the Federal authorities, it became known when Hugh McQuillan, chief of the Special Intelligence Bureau of the Internal Revenue Department, and his chief assistant, Arthur Murphy, called at Mr. Kresel's office for a conference on evidence of income tax frauds.

Crain Defers Prosecutions.

District Attorney Crain, at the request of Harland B. Tibbetts, chief assistant to Mr. Kresel, deferred his projected questioning of John C. Weston, the process server, who admitted that while assigned as prosecutor to Women's Court he collected $20,000 in bribes from twenty-odd lawyers practicing there. Mr. Tibbetts explained in a letter that the Appellate Division's investigators were not yet through with Weston.

Other developments of the day included the arraignment of four more policemen on charges of conducting themselves in a manner "unbecoming an officer," the opening of a campaign to maintain public confidence in the Police Department and the holding of John Steiner, a bondsman, for trial in Special Sessions on a charge that he exacted an illegal fee for a bail bond.

Lieutenant Peter J. Pfeiffer, suspended supervisor of the vice squad of the Sixth Division, and owner of a house in the Bronx which produced a comparatively large income for him and his wife, according to his testi-

Continued on Page Eighteen.

ARMY RULE RENEWED AS CUBA RIOTS GROW

Washington and Havana Hear President Will Resign—He Denies It.

NEW BACKING FOR STUDENTS

Business Men Support Foes of Machado—Call for United States Cruisers Rumored.

By The Associated Press.

HAVANA, Dec. 11.—Amid new disorders by students and with rumors buzzing through the city that he soon would resign, President Machado today suspended constitutional guarantees throughout the whole of Cuba.

This is tantamount to martial law and is similar to the suspension decreed in Havana and environs which ended last month. Both were authorized by Congress after much debate, but whereas the first decree was confined to the capital and for only twenty days, the suspension invoked today will run for sixty days over the entire island.

Student activities not only continued but increased meanwhile, and the sound of firing was heard in the streets as police attempted to break up demonstrations. Numbers of business and professional men, graduates of the National University, pledged their support to the rioting undergraduates.

Follows Cabinet Meeting.

The President's action followed a secret meeting of the Cabinet, at which United States Ambassador Harry F. Guggenheim was reported to be present, and it was known that important developments were expected.

Havana at the same time was swimming in a flood of rumors. There were numerous reports that the President would resign, another that he already had placed his resignation in the hands of the Supreme Court and still another that Ambassador Guggenheim had summoned two United States cruisers from the naval base at Guantanamo. All were denied.

Two hundred physicians, representing the Cuban Medical Federation, voted tonight to "strike" if the government makes good its threat to imprison professors of the National University who support the student leaders of recent disturbances. The doctors said they would neither answer sick calls nor issue prescriptions.

Resignation Rumor Flatly Denied.

The President made a direct reply tonight to the rumors which said he would quit.

"I have not resigned," he declared, "and I am not thinking of resigning. I see no reason for giving consideration to such a move on my part."

Concerning the lifting of guarantees, Dr. Ricardo Herrera, President Machado's secretary, explained:

"It is merely a means to insure peace in Cuba during these weeks when trouble seems to have increased. The President is determined that order shall prevail."

Six students were reported injured in the clashes today. As before, the declaration of suspension of guarantees seemed to exercise an immediate pacifying effect and no disorders were reported afterward.

Although the military was not ordered out, some of the most vital rights enjoyed by Cubans under their Constitution were taken away. The privileges of free speech, free press, assembly and habeas corpus are among those which Cuba is destined not to enjoy again until after Feb. 8, 1931. Censorship was not invoked.

The decree ordering the suspension

Continued on Page Seventeen.

DRY CHIEF TO AVOID HOLIDAY RAID FLARE; AIMS AT BIG SELLERS

Woodcock Drops Mobilizing of Agents to Search Drinkers at Resorts in Wet Cities.

BARS "FIRST-PAGE STUNTS"

He Reveals New Policy Centring on "Commercial Violators" as Way to Solve Problem.

DRY STRATEGY SESSION SET

Enlarged Board Will Reconvene to Complete Program—Wets Adopt Dispensary Plan.

Special to The New York Times.

WASHINGTON, Dec. 11.—No "first page" or other "spectacular stunts" will be indulged in by prohibition agents on Christmas or New Year's Eve, Colonel Amos W. Woodcock, Director of the Prohibition Enforcement, declared today.

Abandoning the old practice of mobilizing agents in New York, Chicago, New Orleans and other "wet" spots, garbed in evening clothes to enter hotels, restaurants and other public places and search of patrons for pocket containers of liquor, he said that instead the agents would be ordered to concentrate upon the detection of commercial violators, the large-scale sellers of liquor.

This does not mean that some night clubs and other places where the proprietors are themselves vendors will not be watched. Colonel Woodcock said that there would be no let-up in the effort to arrest and prosecute such offenders, because they were of the "commercial" class.

To Put Pressure on Traffickers.

Colonel Woodcock made it clear that, in his opinion, there was just one way to enforce prohibition and that was to checkmate the traffickers in liquors.

The new policy which the government was putting into effect, he said, was to put an end to the commercial phase and the rest of the problem would take care of itself.

Asserting that using up "government" time chasing the little fellows who "buy" would not go very far in solving the problem, Colonel Woodcock added:

"The policy is a steady pressure all the time against the traffickers and nothing spectacular at any time.

"Aiming at those who sell liquor, I want the prohibition enforcing forces to direct their efforts against the commercial, not the non-commercial, violators."

Colonel Woodcock also announced that he had adopted an "efficiency system" to file a complete history of the activities of all prohibition agents. On the basis of this, he added, "merit" would govern in making promotions. He cited the case of two agents in Oklahoma who subdued a band of armed bootleggers without the firing of a shot. His commendation of the agents has been made a part of their file record.

The system is similar to that of the army and navy. Colonel Woodcock hopes that it will mean weeding out every man who does not measure up to the new standard of merit fixed for the service.

Dry and Wet Programs Evolved.

WASHINGTON, Dec. 11 (AP).—Wet and dry advocates left the capital today after winding up national con-

Continued on Page Twenty-two.

Mellon Asks Corporation Gift Exemption; Bill Advances Plan as Aid to Employment

Special to The New York Times.

WASHINGTON, Dec. 11.—Following a request by Secretary Mellon, Chairman Hawley of the House Ways and Means Committee introduced a joint resolution to authorize corporations to deduct contributions to unemployment relief and other charities in computing their income taxes during the period from July 1, 1930, to June 30, 1931, as a further emergency measure in meeting the present economic situation.

In his recommendation for this legislation, contained in letters to Vice President Curtis and Speaker Longworth, the Secretary of the Treasury pointed out the exemption of gifts by individuals and said:

"A number of inquiries have been made by unemployment relief organizations with a view to ascertaining whether gifts made by corporations to those organizations may be deducted in computing net income for income tax purposes.

"There is no provision in the law which would permit corporations to make such deductions, though courts have held that contributions by corporations to hospitals or to charitable and educational institutions, from which they or their employes derive direct benefit, may be deducted as 'ordinary and necessary business expenses.'

"The Bureau of Internal Revenue feels that while contributions to emergency relief funds or to such organizations as community chests would undoubtedly contribute to the public welfare and as such would be beneficial to the corporations, nevertheless the benefits to be derived by the latter or their employes would not be sufficiently direct as to bring them within the terms of the law as at present interpreted.

"In view of the existing emergency and the fact that corporations as well as individuals should be encouraged to contribute liberally to relief organizations, I believe that it would be advisable, for the time being, to allow corporations the same deductions as are allowed to individuals in respect of gifts made exclusively for charitable or unemployment emergency relief purposes."

HOOVER DEMANDS SUPPORT AND PARTY SENATORS AGREE; EMPLOYMENT BILL PASSED

Smith Urges Gifts for Jobless As Price of Happy Christmas

With a choking voice, former Governor Alfred E. Smith appealed to all New Yorkers yesterday to give aid to the unemployed, so that they may enjoy their Christmas dinner with a clear conscience. He was speaking at a luncheon at the Hotel Astor at which trade groups of the commerce and industry subcommittee reported to the Emergency Employment Committee that additional contributions of $1,215,950.04 had brought the fund's total up to $6,275,000.

"New York has set great standards," said Mr. Smith. "It has always been known for its ability to rise to any situation. The emergency now confronting us will have to be met. Let's put every bit of our energy in it so that when we sit down to our Christmas dinner our inner conscience may say, 'You deserve this—you deserve all the joy and happiness you have'."

HOOVER'S AUTHORITY CUT FROM JOB BILL

Senate Eliminates Executive Power to Shift Money Among Works Projects.

ADDS $8,000,000 TO FUNDS

Amendments to $118,000,000 Measure May Cause Delay—Wagner Urges His Plan.

Special to The New York Times.

WASHINGTON, Dec. 11.—The Senate today passed the $110,000,000 House bill for emergency unemployment relief, but only after adopting several amendments, including an additional $8,000,000 in appropriations, and the deletion of the section giving to the President authority to reallocate the funds provided.

The bill was so changed, particularly through the elimination of the Presidential authority, by an amendment proposed by Senator Robinson, the Democratic floor leader, that uncertainty was aroused as to whether conferees of the Senate and House, who will be appointed to iron out the differences, will be able to reach an immediate agreement.

No other disagreement with the principle of the bill was manifested, and it was adopted without a record vote, only, however, after the conditions which have led to the necessity of such legislation were strongly denounced in a speech by Senator Wagner of New York.

Wagner Criticizes President.

Senator Wagner criticized the administration particularly for putting forward only emergency relief measures, and for the statement in the President's message that "it is as yet too soon to constructively formulate" permanent measures to circumvent unemployment. The President, Senator Wagner added, had previously made repeated recommendations for

Continued on Page Four.

PRESIDENT WARNS WATSON

Danger of Treasury Raids Calls for Solid Front, He Declares.

ACTIVE DEFENSE NEEDED

Payne of Red Cross and Woods Will Testify on Relief at the Executive's Suggestion.

SOME SENATORS RESENTFUL

Say White House Should Cooperate, but Agree in Parley to Take the Offensive.

Special to The New York Times.

WASHINGTON, Dec. 11.—President Hoover, aroused over the trend of relief legislation and the failure of the Republican Congress to rally to the defense of the administration, today called upon the Republican leaders to uphold his program.

The President pictured to Senator Watson, the party floor leader, and to Speaker Longworth, the danger of enactment of legislation carrying appropriations that could not be spent for unemployment relief, but which would compel higher taxes.

As the result of the President's attitude, the Republicans in the Senate and House met and decided to stiffen their opposition to what Mr. Hoover termed raids on the treasury made under the guise of aiding employment. In his talk with Senator Watson the President, it is reported, complained not only of the failure of the Republicans of the Senate to hold down excessive appropriations, but of their supine attitude when the administration was attacked in the Senate.

Warns Against Bonus Proposals.

The President's action was the result of the passage by the Senate of the $60,000,000 drought relief bill and the accumulation of proposals which would increase the prospective treasury deficit.

The Republican leaders also were informed, it was said, that unless the Republican opposition was solid, proposals to pay the balance due in adjusted compensation to World War veterans in cash, entailing nearly $3,000,000,000, would be enacted.

The Senate leaders were told that the President, unless the situation becomes more satisfactory, is prepared to issue another statement on the general trend of relief legislation. The statement, it was reported, would be even more positive than his declaration of last Tuesday that Congress was "playing politics at the expense of human misery."

Following the President's complaint, Senator Watson summoned seventeen Republican Senators into a conference, and urged united action by the party to defeat efforts to increase the relief appropriations. He also informed his colleagues, it is said, that the President felt that he had not been supported by his party, in that attacks launched against him in the Senate in the last few days had been met with silence.

The President, it also was reported, not only called upon the Republicans of the House and Senate for cooperation and assistance to oppose "treasury raids," but urged that Colonel Arthur Woods of the President's Emergency Committee on Employment, and John Barton Payne, chairman of the Red Cross, be summoned before Congressional committees to explain that the administration's relief program was adequate, and that additional expenditures would be a waste of money and cause new taxation.

Senators Voice Resentment.

Several Senators participating in the conference resented what they characterized as the President's imputation that he lacked a defense in the Senate. They told Senator Watson that cooperation could not be expected unless the President took the Republicans of the Senate into his confidence.

Senator Watson was asked whether he, as Senate leader, had been informed in advance of the President's recent statement, in which members of Congress seeking greater relief were denounced. Senator Watson replied that his first knowledge of the President's statement was after it had been issued.

Several Senators present declared they did not agree with many things said by Mr. Hoover in his statement,

Continued on Page Three.

Photographic reproduction of the front page of the *New York Times,* December 12, 1930. (*Courtesy of New York Public Library.*)

Marine during and after World War I, and in 1919 had founded the investment banking house of W. A. Harriman & Co., Inc. More recently, he and his brother, E. Roland Harriman, had organized the private banking house of Harriman Brothers & Co.

When Thatcher Brown had finished reading his carefully worded announcement of the impending merger of the Brown and Harriman firms, the reporters began bombarding him and Mr. Harriman with questions. Some of them, as Mr. Brown later revealed in his informal, privately circulated history of the firm, were "naturally . . . quite embarrassing; so we were relieved when we saw the papers next morning, for we had a good press."

They certainly did. The announcement was front page news in the New York *Times* that Friday, and papers everywhere gave the story prominent headlines. For the merger came as a welcome surprise to the financial community, and anything that was good news in such quarters was good news to the general public in those dark December days at the end of the first year of the Great Depression. Stock prices, which had crashed in the panic of October–November 1929, were slumping still lower, despite occasional rallies; more than a thousand banks around the country had failed during the year; farm prices were falling disastrously; industry was curtailing production and closing down factories; and every day thousands more men and women lost their jobs and joined the dismal ranks of the millions already unemployed. The day of the bread lines had come to the world's richest nation, and men who had had good jobs a few months before were peddling apples on street corners. President Hoover had confidently asserted early in May that "we have now passed the worst, and with continued unity of effort we shall rapidly recover," but the economic boom of the late twenties had gone right on shuddering into insolvency. Frederick Lewis Allen, in *Only Yesterday,* tells of a stroller on Broadway who noticed a queue forming outside a theater where Charlie Chaplin was opening in *City Lights* and asked in some concern, "What's that—a bread line or a bank?"

Headlines, reproduced in photostatic negatives from (l. to r.): *The Wall Street Journal,* December 13, 1930, and the December 12th issues of the New York *Evening Journal,* the New York *World,* the New York *Evening Post,* and the New York *Sun.*

JAMES BROWN (1863–1935). This portrait, painted from life by Leopold Seyffert in 1934, hangs in the collection of the New York State Chamber of Commerce, of which Mr. Brown was president from 1932–34. A great-grandson of Alexander Brown of Baltimore, and grandson of the James Brown who established the family business in New York in 1825, Mr. Brown became a partner in Brown Brothers & Co. in 1901, and retired in 1934. He was active head of the firm until his first cousin, Thatcher M. Brown, took over his responsibilities in 1931. His confidential "Diary," covering his activities as a partner from 1917 to 1930, is one of the most valuable documents preserved in the firm's Historical File.

The flood of disastrous financial news in those days was staggering. The *World* ran, on the same page with its story about the Brown-Harriman merger, the following appalling assortment of headlines:

$300,000 DEFICIT LAID TO BROKERS
BANK STOCKS FEEL LOSSES ON MARKET
$4,000,000 FRAUD CHARGED TO TWO
WEST SPRINGFIELD BANK SHUT; TREASURER SUICIDE
BANKER, 73, PLEADS GUILTY
OHIO BANKER KILLS SELF
TENNESSEE BANK CASHIER FOUND DEAD OF BULLET

Things were so bad that—as the front page of the *Times* makes clear—President Hoover was having difficulty rallying even the Republicans in Congress to resist "raids on the Treasury made under the guise of aiding employment," and the Democratic opposition, led by New York's Senator Robert F. Wagner was openly denouncing the President's insistence that it was "as yet too early" to formulate permanent measures to cope with unemployment. The emergency relief measures thus far taken certainly did not justify the hope expressed by Albert Einstein,

newly arrived from Europe, that the United States would "take leadership in the solution of the international economic depression."

Fortunately—and amazingly—there had been no serious outbreaks of violence. The only rioting that hit the front page that day (and the only foreign news) was in Cuba, where the current dictator had suspended constitutional guarantees of free speech, free press, free assembly, and habeas-corpus. But lawlessness and corruption shimmered behind many of the *Times'* domestic headlines. In Washington, Labor Secretary William N. Doak was declaring a War on the Underworld, and the Director of Prohibition Enforcement was promising to go after the big commercial violators instead of harassing flask-toting merrymakers on New Year's Eve. In New York, Samuel Seabury was investigating corruption in the city courts, but it looked as if his investigation might bog down. His special counsel, Isadore Kresel, was a director of the cynically misnamed Bank of the United States, whose collapse was reported in column one. Mr. Kresel might well be too busy explaining his part in the bank's shoddy affairs to spare much time for questioning city magistrates about the sources of their incomes. All in all, it made sense for the *Times* to counterbalance the news of the largest bank failure in American history by setting next to it the report of what one financial journalist called "a merger of financial aristocrats, a combination which unites the best of the old and new."[1]

As all the reporters and journalists emphasized, Brown Brothers & Co. was one of the oldest financial institutions in the United States—"a venerable

1 James Grant Blair, "Custom Bankers," *The World's Work*, September 1931.

banking power," a writer in *The World's Work* called it, "whose history is closely linked with American history." The links with the nation's history will be explored in the pages that follow. Here it is necessary to say only that the firm had developed in the nineteenth-century tradition of international merchant banking, and had long been recognized as one of the nation's most influential private banks.

"Venerable" the Brown company certainly was, with James Brown (about to retire as senior partner) and his cousin Thatcher M. Brown (about to become senior partner of the merged firms) both representing the fourth generation of the Brown family to dominate the firm. Yet seven of its twelve partners were men in their early thirties. Among these, four had been friends of Roland Harriman's at Yale when they were undergraduates. Two had been graduated in 1916, a year ahead of Harriman: Laurence G. Tighe (later treasurer of Yale) and

Charles D. Dickey, III (whose father and grandfather had been partners in Brown Brothers & Co. before him). The other two, Ellery Sedgewick James (a classmate of Harriman's) and Robert Abercrombie Lovett (class of 1918) had been friends of both Averell and Roland Harriman since boyhood. It was these young members of the firm who were largely responsible for effecting the merger.

The Harriman firms, in contrast with Brown Brothers, were relative newcomers to the field, and the press in general was more attentive to their financial resources than to their history. To *The Wall Street Journal,* for example, the significance of the merger was that "To the large resources of the century-old Brown firm is added the tens of millions available to the Harriman interests." And the partners in the newly merged concerns were themselves by no means disposed to play down the importance of the Harriman fortune. In their press releases about the consolidation of their firms, after em-

ELLERY SEDGEWICK JAMES (1895–1932), from a studio portrait by Blank-Stoller, about 1930.

E. ROLAND HARRIMAN (1895–   ), from a photograph by an unidentified news photographer, dated October 16, 1925.

(Culver Service)

(Courtesy of Brown Brothers Harriman & Co., Boston.)

phasizing Brown Brothers & Co.'s long tradition, they inserted a paragraph about the late E. H. Harriman, father of the two young men who had established the Harriman companies. The elder Harriman, they reminded their customers and prospects, had "achieved a spectacular position in American finance and railroading," and through his history-making activities had acquired "a huge personal fortune."

Such emphasis on the Harrimans' inherited wealth was understandable when one remembers that in those days private banks did not publish "statements of condition" as they do now. For in a private bank, owned and operated by partners who have unlimited liability for all obligations of the firm, the outside financial resources of the members of the partnership were naturally of great importance to the firm's credit. And credit was at the heart of the private banker's business, as it was of the nineteenth-century merchant banking tradition in which Brown Brothers & Co. had achieved its international eminence.

But credit depends even more upon character than upon capital. Unless the partners in a private bank are known for their integrity and enterprising good judgment, the combined wealth of a half-dozen men with huge personal fortunes could not long keep the firm in business. When we go shopping for a new car or for two pounds of tomatoes, we need not concern ourselves about the moral character of those who produced the product. We judge cars by their own qualities, not those of the presidents and vice-presidents of the companies that produce them; a thoroughgoing rotter can raise a good tomato. But what a private bank produces—namely credit—rests ultimately upon the scrupulous probity of the partners and those who work with them.

To the financial community, therefore, and to those directly concerned, the brief history of the two Harriman firms was not overshadowed by the glamour of the Harriman fortune. Young as they were, E. H. Harriman's sons and the young men associated with them had already proved themselves. W. A. Harriman & Co., Inc., organized only ten years before (November 13, 1919), was already a leader in the securities and underwriting business. Under the aggressive management of Averell Harri-

man, of G. H. Walker (president of the firm from 1920 until 1930, when he returned to the investment house he had founded in 1900), and of Prescott S. Bush (one of Roland Harriman's Yale classmates and a son-in-law of Mr. Walker), it had grown into an organization with branch offices in several cities, here and abroad. Through its office in Berlin, Ger-

PRESCOTT S. BUSH (1895–   ), vice-president and a director of W. A. Harriman & Co., Inc., and a partner in Harriman Brothers & Co. at the time of the merger with Brown Brothers & Co., is shown here in a photograph taken by George S. Pietzcher at Fresh Meadows in June 1932, during championship matches of the U. S. Golf Association. Mr. Bush was secretary of the U.S.G.A. at the time, and became president in 1935.

(*Brown Brothers Harriman & Co. Historical File*)

many, opened in 1922, it became one of the first American investment houses to assist in rebuilding European industry after the First World War, granting short-term credits to a wide variety of German industries, helping to finance zinc mines in Polish Silesia, and offering in the American market the

KNIGHT WOOLLEY (1895–   ), who had organized the Harrimans' private bank in 1927, was managing partner of Harriman Brothers & Co. at the time when the merger with Brown Brothers & Co. was arranged in the final months of 1930. He is shown here as a Brown Brothers Harriman partner on a business trip to Vienna in the summer of 1933.

(*Courtesy of Miss Julie Brennan*)

securities of a number of European companies. In this country, it backed a number of steamship lines and took an early lead in air transportation, in 1928 heavily financing the Aviation Corporation of America, which later became Pan American Airways. And through the acquisition in 1928 of a controlling interest in American Trustee Share Corporation, which sold more than $60,000,000 of "Diversified Trustee Shares," it pioneered in the development of "Fixed Investment Trusts."

Meanwhile, on St. Patrick's Day, 1927, the Harrimans had set up their partnership bank. Originally called W. A. Harriman & Co. (without the "Inc.") it soon changed its name to Harriman Brothers & Co., to avoid the confusions which the similarity of names inevitably caused. As general manager (and later a partner), the Harrimans got another of Roland Harriman's Yale classmates, Knight Woolley, of the foreign department of the American Exchange National Bank, then in the process of merging into the Irving Trust Co. The bank started with four employees in a single room, and capital supplied by the Harrimans and M. Samuel & Co., Ltd. ("Here's four million. Go ahead and run the bank," Averell Harriman had told Mr. Woolley.) In less than four years Harriman Brothers & Co. had moved twice into larger quarters and had grown into an organization with seventy employees. Mr. Woolley, already an authority on Bankers Acceptances (the first of several editions of his *A B C of Bankers Acceptances* had been published by the American Acceptance Council in 1924), brought several of his former colleagues at the American Exchange National Bank into the new organization, three of them specialists in foreign exchange. By the time of the merger with Brown Brothers & Co., the Harriman banking partnership was doing a very profitable business in acceptances and foreign exchange, had a seat on the New York Stock Exchange, and carried on an extensive brokerage business (though none on margin account).

When the two Harriman firms joined with Brown Brothers, therefore, they brought to it much more than Harriman wealth. "Old-timers in Wall Street," one financial expert reported, had "seldom seen a more potent blend of conservative experience and aggressive practice" than the new partnership offered.

THE FIRST BANKERS ACCEPTANCE CREATED BY THE HARRIMANS' PRIVATE BANKING HOUSE

The document reproduced above, dated October 24, 1927, is the first "bankers acceptance" created by the private banking firm of W. A. Harriman & Co. (later Harriman Brothers & Co.), which merged with Brown Brothers & Co. as of January 1, 1931. Since acceptances are frequently mentioned in this book, a brief explanation of the document may be useful to readers unfamiliar with banking terms.

Bankers acceptances constitute the highest form of commercial credit, and their function is primarily to finance exports and imports by substituting a bank's widely known credit for that of its customer, using the bank's credit-standing instead of its cash to effect the required movement of goods.

For example: the document above enabled one of the Harriman bank's German customers, a metal refining company, to import copper from Chile. The basic document, which looks rather like an ordinary check embellished with a portrait of Washington, is, in fact, a bill of exchange, or "time draft," drawn on the Harriman bank by C. Tennant Sons & Co., a New York exporting firm, calling for payment to itself of $29,689.66 "three months after sight" (that is, three months after the draft was presented to, and accepted by, the bankers—specifically, in this instance, on January 24, 1928).

The draft was drawn not against cash on deposit at the bank, as a check would be, but against a letter of credit (symbol: L/C) which the bank had issued to the Tennant firm at the request of the German refining company (probably Metalgesellshaft A. G. of Frankfort A.M.), to whom the bank had offered credit facilities up to a certain sum (the "line of credit" which the bank felt able to make available to this particular customer).

The letter of credit to the Tennants would have specified that they could draw on the bank for sums up to a total of, say, $100,000 to pay for Chilean copper to be shipped to the German refinery, but for that purpose only, and only

under certain strictly defined conditions. (For an example of an earlier letter of credit, issued by Brown Brothers & Co., see p. 168.) Note that the draft specifies that it is made "On L/C of 10/22/27 ⌗H 1017," and that the "acceptance" stamped across the face of the document specifies that "This acceptance arises out of a transaction involving shipment of copper from Chile to Germany."

When the Tennants presented the draft to the bank, accompanied by all such documents as the letter of credit may have required (including bills of lading, indicating that the copper was on shipboard, and any necessary insurance documents), the bank accepted it. The Tennants then endorsed the draft (as one would endorse a check payable to oneself if one wanted someone else to be able to cash it) and thereupon received from the bankers the face value of the draft, *less discount*—which is to say, with three months interest deducted in advance at the prevailing rate for prime bankers acceptances. This interest rate fluctuates between 1½ and 6%. If the prevailing rate was 6% at the time, Tennant would have received $29,244.32 with which to pay for the copper, presumably by depositing it to the Chilean supplier's account in a New York bank.

The acceptance thus served the New York exporter's interest by assuring him that, upon complying faithfully with the terms of the letter of credit, he would be immediately reimbursed for the copper, even though it would not reach the German purchaser for several weeks. At the same time, the use of the bankers acceptance enabled the German refiners to acquire the copper without having to pay out any money until they provided the bank with funds to pay the accepted draft when it matured, three months after the copper had in fact been purchased and paid for.

Meanwhile, what of the bank? By means of the acceptance it was, in effect, enabled to finance the copper shipment without tying up either the refinery's or its own funds. For as soon as Tennant endorsed the accepted draft,

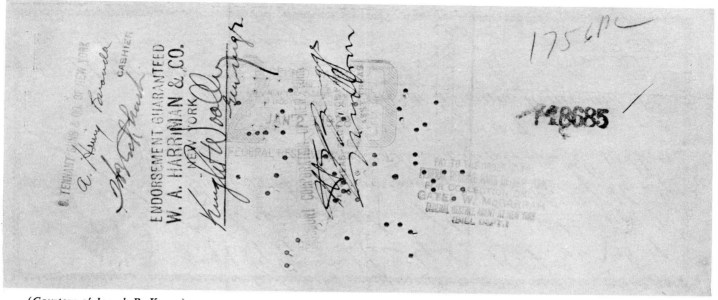

and the bank guaranteed that endorsement (as shown on the back of the draft), the document became "negotiable paper" of the highest quality. The bank promptly sold the accepted draft, at the same rate of discount as was charged to Tennant, to one of the firms which specialize in the purchase and discount of bankers acceptances. In this instance the purchaser was the Discount Corporation of New York, whose endorsement appears below the Harriman guarantee of the Tennant endorsement. Subsequently the bill was purchased in the open market, at a discount proportionate to the time the bill had yet to run, by the Federal Reserve Bank of New York (which regularly invests in such short-term obligations).

When the draft matured the Federal Reserve Bank collected its face value through the New York Clearing House, which debited the Harriman bank's account at the Farmer's Loan and Trust Co. (as per the acceptance stamp across the face of the bill). By that time the German refinery—having received the bills of lading and other documents relating to the copper shipment—would have placed the bank in funds to meet the obligation, and would also have paid the standard accepting commission (computed on the basis of 1½% per annum)—which for this particular three-month transaction would have amounted to about $111.00, the bank's fee for lending its credit and assuming all the credit risks involved.

It is well to remind ourselves that at the time when the new partnership was formed private bankers not only accepted deposits and did a commercial banking business in acceptances, credits, loans, and foreign exchange, but also acted as investment bankers, underwriting and distributing corporate securities. It was not until after passage of the Banking Act of 1933, following the "bank holiday" crisis in the first weeks of Franklin Roosevelt's first term, that commercial banking and investment banking were divorced from one another. By the provision of that act, commercial banks such as the National City Bank and the Chase National Bank were required to divest themselves of their securities-dealing affiliates, and private banking houses were required to choose between the underwriting business and banking. Most of the private bankers at that time chose to give up deposit banking and go into investment banking, but Brown Brothers Harriman—as we shall see in chapter seventeen—elected to remain a bank of deposit. Since 1934, therefore, it has been a private commercial bank, subject to regulation and supervision by the state banking authorities of the three states in which it maintains banking houses—New York, Pennsylvania, and Massachusetts.

In 1931, however, the newly merged firm was one of the "Big Four" houses engaged in investment banking.[2] Indeed, if Brown Brothers & Co. had not

[2] The other three, according to contemporary journals, were J. P. Morgan & Co., Kuhn, Loeb & Co., and Lee Higginson & Co. The Morgan firm, like Brown Brothers Harriman, elected to continue in the banking business after 1933 but ceased to be a private bank when it was incorporated in 1940. The other two firms elected to continue in the securities business, as did Alex. Brown & Sons, J. & W. Seligman, Lazard Freres & Co., and most of the other large private banking houses.

been involved in the securities business, the merger with the Harrimans might never have occurred.

According to Thatcher M. Brown's informal history of the firm, it was principally the losses sustained in the underwriting part of Brown Brothers' business after the 1929 crash that induced the venerable firm to seek new capital. Like all firms in the underwriting business, Brown Brothers was caught with a good many "undigested securities" on its shelves—that is, new issues of the stocks or bonds of various corporations, governments, or municipalities which the firm had underwritten in the expectation of selling them at a profit but which, after the crash, could not be sold to investors without taking considerable losses. Though the market rallied slightly from time to time, "it became clear to us, during the year 1930," Mr. Brown wrote, "that we were doing too large a business for our capital."

The problem was aggravated by the fact that several of "the elder and wealthier partners" of the firm had died or resigned in recent years, and the firm had been unable to accumulate profits sufficient to offset the prearranged withdrawal of their funds. "So," as Mr. Brown candidly put it, "we turned our minds to securing additional capital."

It was Ellery James, as Mr. Brown recollected it, who first suggested talking with the Harrimans, and this fits in neatly with a story—now current in various versions, as all good legends are—that the whole thing began during a card game on the New Haven railroad in the spring of 1930, even before Brown Brothers' need for additional capital had become pressing. It seems that Ellery James, Knight Woolley, and Prescott Bush were en route to a Yale reunion with two other classmates, and had taken a drawing room in a parlor car so they could play cards and converse. At one point, somebody spoke of the large number of bank mergers that had recently taken place, and someone (nobody now is certain who) casually suggested that the Brown and Harriman firms should also merge. That was all; the conversation soon shifted to other topics. But the idea remained in Mr. James' mind, and in the fall he went to see Mr. Woolley one day and reminded him of it. It may well have been after that conversation that Mr. James suggested the possibility of the merger to Thatcher Brown.

Whether or not a chance remark made en route to a Yale reunion had anything to do with the merger, friendships made or reinforced at the college in the years just before the First World War seem, in retrospect, to have made the merger all but inevitable. Roland Harriman's own recollection is that Ellery James talked with him about "working under one roof" even before the stock market crash of 1929.

Ellery James' friendship with Roland Harriman went back to pre-prep school days. They had often visited one another's family homes, and James had been one of the group of friends Harriman took along in 1915 when his mother, Mrs. E. H. Harriman, let him have the family yacht, the *Sultana,* to go out to San Francisco by way of the recently opened Panama Canal.

Mr. James, the son of a well-to-do New York lawyer, began working at Brown Brothers in 1919, after serving in France as a captain in the U. S. Artillery at the front during the Meuse-Argonne offensive and in the Army of Occupation in Germany. He was a partner when his classmates Knight Woolley and Prescott Bush went to work in the mid-twenties with the banking houses established by the Harrimans, and his duplex apartment at 1021 Park Avenue was "the old nest" where Mr. Woolley and Mr. Bush had often stayed when they were in town. So it is not surprising to find that one of the earliest entries in the minute book of the partners in the newly established Harriman Brothers bank, in 1927, records that Mr. Woolley, the general manager, had received through Ellery James, and had accepted, "the offer of a $250,000 participation" along with Brown Brothers & Co. and two other banks in a large acceptance credit in favor of a Berlin metal firm, for the purpose of financing their export shipments. From the earliest days of Harriman Brothers & Co., the young partners in the two firms were friendly competitors.

In a sense, however, the merger had probably been "in the cards" since the day in 1903 when Roland Harriman and Robert Lovett met as eight-year-old boys. As Mr. Harriman tells the story, it was not the sort of meeting that one would expect to have been the basis of a lifelong friendship, but that is what it proved to be.

"The first time I met him," Mr. Harriman said,

in introducing Mr. Lovett at a dinner of the New-comen Society in 1949, "I thought he was a most obnoxious brat." And he went on to tell how it happened:

My father, essentially an out-of-doors man, did all he could to keep physically fit. He even installed a horizontal bar on which to exercise in his business car. I frequently accompanied my father on his business trips —as did all the family—and being the youngest and puniest—I was instructed to make daily use of that bar. My "chin up" record I remember was about one every other day.

At about this juncture, about 1903, on a trip down Texas-way, Judge Robert S. Lovett plus a kid of my own age joined the party at some frontier cow town— probably Houston. While the men were talking business, Bob—for that's who the kid turned out to be— and I were turned loose on the car to amuse ourselves. Of course Bob spotted that bar, and after chinning himself twenty or thirty times . . . ended up in a whirlwind of giant swings. Watching him with awe and envy, I was not aware we had other witnesses to the performance till my father's voice came over my shoulder: "Roland, why can't you do that?"

It may have been on this occasion that E. H. Harriman decided to ask the elder Lovett to serve as general counsel for all the Harriman interests in Texas, a job he undertook in 1904. From then on, at any rate, the elder Harriman and Judge Lovett (as his friends all called him, though he

The snapshot of ROBERT A. LOVETT (1895–   ), with ROLAND HARRIMAN (at left) was taken in 1919 at Santa Barbara, California, by Mrs. Roland Harriman, who had originally been introduced to her husband by Mr. Lovett.

Lovett and Harriman, whose fathers had been close business associates, had been friends since boyhood. The snapshot was taken when Lovett visited the Harrimans soon after returning from France, where he had served during the First World War as a pilot in the Yale Unit of the U. S. Navy Flying Corps, advancing to the rank of Lieutenant Commander and earning the Navy Cross (see p. 192). Harriman, who had served as a lieutenant in the Army Ordinance Department, was in California recuperating from an attack of what the doctors had thought was incurable tuberculosis.

Soon after this photograph was taken, Harriman was working in the office of his brother Averell's Merchant Shipbuilding Co., and had become a director of W. A. Harriman & Co., Inc., and Lovett, having married Adele Quartley Brown, daughter of James Brown of Brown Brothers & Co. (see p. 10), returned to Yale to finish (Phi Beta Kappa) the undergraduate studies interrupted by the war and then go on to Harvard for a year in Law School and a year in the Graduate School of Business Administration. (*Courtesy of Mrs. E. Roland Harriman*)

was not on the bench) were closely associated in business and in friendship. When Harriman died in 1909, Judge Lovett became the administrator of the estate and president of the Union Pacific and the other Harriman railroads. And in spite of the inauspicious first meeting between young Robert Lovett and Roland Harriman, the Judge's son and the two Harriman brothers had become good friends by the time they started out on their own business careers.

That Robert A. Lovett chose to go directly into banking, rather than into railroads and shipping as Averell Harriman and his younger brother did at first, was partly the result of the fact that in 1919 he married Adele Quartley Brown, daughter of James Brown, the senior partner of Brown Brothers & Co. Having started as a clerk in the National Bank of Commerce in 1921, he came to Brown Brothers a few months later, where he was employed at first as a "runner." After an apprenticeship served partly with Brown Shipley & Co. in London, he was granted a power of attorney in January 1925 —at which time Ellery James became a partner. And, in 1926, he was admitted to partnership.

In that year also he was elected a director of the Union Pacific and a member of its executive committee, thus becoming an associate of his boyhood friends. (Both Averell and Roland Harriman were directors of the road, and Averell had served as a vice-president while his younger brother and Mr. Lovett were still in college.) In 1930, therefore, Mr. Lovett was able to bring to the merger negotiations a long and intimate association with the Harrimans and a thorough knowledge of and devotion to the Brown Brothers tradition in banking.

This photograph of ROLAND HARRIMAN (left) and AVERELL HARRIMAN with their father, EDWARD H. HARRIMAN, was taken by an unidentified photographer in San Francisco in 1907— about three years after Roland's first encounter with Robert A. Lovett, (described on pp. 16 and 17). The irregular white line down the left side of the picture results from a crack in the original.

BROWN BROTHERS HARRIMAN & CO.
NEW YORK   PHILADELPHIA   BOSTON

NEW YORK, JANUARY 2ND, 1931.

GENTLEMEN:

WE TAKE PLEASURE IN ADVISING YOU THAT EFFECTIVE JANUARY 1, 1931, THE BUSINESSES OF MESSRS. BROWN BROTHERS & CO., HARRIMAN BROTHERS & CO. AND W. A. HARRIMAN & CO., INC. HAVE BEEN UNITED IN THE CO-PARTNERSHIP FIRM OF BROWN BROTHERS HARRIMAN & CO.

FOR THE AUTHORIZED SIGNATURES OF THE MEMBERS OF THE FIRM OF BROWN BROTHERS HARRIMAN & CO. AND OF THOSE AUTHORIZED TO SIGN FOR US, WE BEG TO REFER YOU TO THE ACCOMPANYING SPECIMEN SIGNATURES.

ALL COMMERCIAL LETTERS OF CREDIT, TRAVELERS' LETTERS OF CREDIT, ACCEPTANCES, BILLS OF EXCHANGE, GUARANTIES, ORDERS FOR PAYMENT OR TRANSFER OF FUNDS AND OTHER AUTHORIZATIONS OR OBLIGATIONS IN THE USUAL COURSE OF THE BUSINESSES OF MESSRS. BROWN BROTHERS & CO. AND MESSRS. HARRIMAN BROTHERS & CO. AS WELL AS OF W. A. HARRIMAN & CO., INC. WILL, FROM JANUARY 1, 1931, BE DRAWN OR ISSUED BY AND IN THE NAME OF BROWN BROTHERS HARRIMAN & CO. AND MUST BEAR AN AUTHORIZED SIGNATURE OF THE FIRM AS ABOVE REFERRED TO.

WE REQUEST YOUR SPECIAL ATTENTION TO THE FACT THAT BROWN BROTHERS HARRIMAN & CO. WILL HONOR OBLIGATIONS DRAWN OR ISSUED OR OTHERWISE ESTABLISHED AND DATED PRIOR TO JANUARY 1, 1931, IN THE NAME AND UNDER AN AUTHORIZED SIGNATURE OF MESSRS. BROWN BROTHERS & CO., OR MESSRS. HARRIMAN BROTHERS & CO. OR W. A. HARRIMAN & CO., INC. THEREFORE, DRAFTS AND/OR OTHER SPECIFIED INSTRUMENTS TO BE DRAWN UNDER CREDITS ESTABLISHED AND DATED PRIOR TO JANUARY 1, 1931, BY MESSRS. BROWN BROTHERS & CO., OR MESSRS. HARRIMAN BROTHERS & CO. OR W. A. HARRIMAN & CO., INC. (UNDER THEIR AUTHORIZED SIGNATURES) SHOULD ACCORDINGLY CONTINUE TO BE DRAWN AND PRESENTED EXACTLY AS INSTRUCTED IN SUCH CREDITS AND IN ACCORDANCE WITH THE TERMS AND EXPIRY DATES THEREOF, AND WILL BE HONORED IN THE USUAL COURSE BY BROWN BROTHERS HARRIMAN & CO.

EXCEPT TO THE EXTENT STATED ABOVE, ALL PREVIOUS SIGNATURE AUTHORITIES ARE HEREBY CANCELLED.

VERY TRULY YOURS,

Brown Brothers Harriman & Co.

CONFIRMED:

Brown Brothers & Co.
Harriman Brothers & Co.
W. A. Harriman & Co. Inc.
W. A. Harriman President

(Original in Brown Brothers Harriman & Co. Historical File)

First page of the original printed circular announcing the merger of the businesses of Brown Brothers & Co. and of the two Harriman firms as Brown Brothers Harriman & Co. See next page for some of the specimen signatures referred to in the second paragraph.

New York

Mr. James Brown *WILL SIGN*

Mr. Thatcher M. Brown *WILL SIGN*

Mr. Prescott S. Bush *WILL SIGN*

Mr. Ralph T. Crane *WILL SIGN*

Mr. Moreau Delano *WILL SIGN*

Mr. John Henry Hammond *WILL SIGN*

Mr. E. R. Harriman *WILL SIGN*

Mr. W. A. Harriman *WILL SIGN*

Mr. Ellery Sedgwick James *WILL SIGN*

Mr. Robert Abercrombie Lovett *WILL SIGN*

Mr. Ray Morris *WILL SIGN*

Mr. Knight Woolley *WILL SIGN*

Philadelphia

Mr. Charles Denston Dickey *WILL SIGN*

Mr. Phillips Blair Lee *WILL SIGN*

Boston

Mr. Louis Curtis Jr. *WILL SIGN*

Mr. Lawrence G. Tighe *WILL SIGN*

Specimen signatures of all the original partners in the consolidated firm of Brown Brothers Harriman & Co. as of January 2, 1931. The three pages of signatures in the original circular announcing the merger included not only those of the partners but also those of all managers and other employees, in New York, Philadelphia, Boston, and Chicago, who were authorized to sign the firm's name, or to sign for the firm *per procuration* (p.p.)—that is, as agents with limited authority.

Similar specimen signature lists, issued throughout the firm's history, make it possible to determine the authorship of all letters signed with the firm's name from the earliest years of Brown Brothers & Co. (*Original in Brown Brothers Harriman & Co. Historical File*)

Two

BACKGROUNDS: CITIES AND MEN

The Brown Brothers tradition in banking evolved out of the experience of a colorful group of related firms, all derived from a linen-importing business established at Baltimore, Maryland, in the final weeks of the eighteenth century. For the Browns—like most of the great private bankers, including the Rothschilds, the Morgans, and the Seligmans—got into banking as a byproduct of earlier success as dry-goods merchants.

Alexander Brown, who opened his "Irish Linen Warehouse" in Baltimore in December 1800, had emigrated from Northern Ireland where he had been a successful auctioneer in Belfast's great Linen Hall market. He settled in Baltimore partly, no doubt, because he had heard of its rapid growth and prosperity from his younger brother, Stewart Brown, in business there as a general merchant since 1797. Thanks to its location at the head of navigation on Chesapeake Bay and the consequent shortness of the expensive overland transportation routes to the interior, Baltimore was an important center for the distribution of heavy goods throughout Maryland and Virginia and for the export of the region's produce.

This shop on Castle Street in Belfast, Ireland, must have been well known to Alexander Brown (1764–1834), who was an auctioneer in Belfast's linen market before emigrating to Baltimore, Maryland, in 1800 and establishing the business of which Brown Brothers & Co. was an offshoot. The shop was just a couple of blocks from the White Linen Hall where the auctions were held, and the Gihons were his cousins.

The undated watercolor, by Frank McKelvey, R.H.A., is based upon an engraved billhead of about 1790, which was reproduced in R. M. Young's *Historical Notices of Old Belfast* (1896).

(Courtesy of the Ulster Museum, Belfast)

The city to which Alexander Brown came in December 1800, is shown in this "East View of Baltimore, Maryland," drawn by G. Beck of Philadelphia in 1801, engraved by T. Cartwright of London, and published in London and Philadelphia by Atkins and Nightingale on January 1, 1802.

The recently incorporated city already had a population of about 27,000 (up 97% since 1790), and its commerce was thriving. Its harbor was studded with ships engaged in the business of exporting wheat and flour to Europe and the West Indies, and importing manufactured goods. Its growing trade with the interior was carried on in canvas-covered Conestoga wagons, drawn by teams of four to eight horses over the old Braddock road and the newer turnpikes that were being constructed as far as the navigable waters of "the West," beyond the mountains.

(Courtesy of New York Public Library)

Brown's knowledge of the linen trade and his aggressive commercial talents soon won him a virtual monopoly of the business in Baltimore. By 1805, when he took his eldest son William into partnership, his activities had expanded to include exporting tobacco, wheat, and other produce and dealing in foreign exchange. By 1808, when his second son George joined the firm, his "Stock Account" ledger recorded capital resources in excess of $119,000. By 1821 Brown had become one of America's first millionaires.

As long as Alexander Brown lived, Baltimore remained the headquarters of the family enterprises, but some years before his death in 1834 the center of American operations had shifted, first to Philadelphia and then to New York. Recently discovered evidence indicates that a branch was started in Philadelphia as early as 1806 when William Brown—newly admitted to partnership with his father—set up as a merchant on South Front Street. Owing, probably, to the curtailment of foreign trade following the 1806 Non-Importation Act, this first attempt to found a Philadelphia house was abandoned, as was another attempt in 1809. Not until 1818 was a Philadelphia branch of the firm durably established by Alexander Brown's third son, John.

(Courtesy of the Historical Society of Pennsylvania)

The aquatint engraving of the "Procession of the Victuallers" reproduced in color above gives some notion of Philadelphia's commercial exuberance about the time when the Browns opened a branch of their business there. The picture, engraved and published by Joseph Yeager in 1821, was made from a drawing by Joseph Louis Krimmel, one of Pennsylvania's most engaging folk artists. "The occasion that gave rise to this SPLENDID PROCESSION," the lengthy caption informs us, was the conveying to market of the meat of some "exhibition Cattle," including five cub bears and two fawns, in addition to more conventional beasts such as oxen, hogs, and sheep.

The procession is shown coming down Chestnut Street and turning left (north) onto Fourth Street, diagonally across from Matthew Carey's bookstore on the corner later occupied by Brown Brothers & Co. from 1887 to 1927.

(Original in Edward W. C. Arnold Collection, Metropolitan Museum of Art. Photograph courtesy of the Museum of the City of New York)

This watercolor drawing, showing South Street, New York, southwestward from Maiden Lane, was made by William J. Bennett in 1828. Bennett made a black and white engraving from the drawing which was published by Henry J. Megarey as one of his *Street Views in the City of New York*.

The scene must have been thoroughly familiar to James Brown, who had opened the first office of Brown Brothers & Co. near Maiden Lane on Pearl Street in 1825 and in the following year moved to an office and warehouse just a short way up from South Street on Pine Street—the opening in the wall of buildings just above the breastbone of the white horse in the picture's foreground. The next street beyond Pine was Wall Street, to which James Brown moved the firm's counting house in 1833.

Shortly after John A. Brown & Co. began business in Philadelphia, it moved from its first office on Market Street to South Front Street, not far from where William's office had been twelve years before. William by this time was in Liverpool as head of the recently established English branch of the house, and for the next six years much of the Browns' business was conducted through the Liverpool and Philadelphia offices.

By 1825, however, it was apparent that New York was destined to be the vital center of America's foreign trade, and in October of that year James Brown, youngest of Alexander's four sons, opened the books of Brown Brothers & Co. at 191 Pearl Street, close to the ship-fringed wharves of South Street.

23

"Ruins of the Merchants' Exchange N. Y. After the De-structive Conflagration of Dec^br 16 & 17, 1835" is one of the earliest lithographs made by N. Currier of Currier & Ives fame. J. H. Bufford, by whom it was "sketched and drawn on stone," may well have made the drawing from the window of Brown Brothers & Co.'s office in the build-ing at 46 Wall Street (later 58), where they had moved from Pine Street a few months before. The fire-gutted build-ing at the extreme left, at 47 (later 59) Wall, directly opposite No. 46, was replaced in 1836–37 by a new bank-ing house which Brown Brothers bought and moved into in 1843.

Soon after Alexander Brown's death in 1834, James Brown sold the dry goods part of his busi-ness and moved into new quarters across from the Merchants Exchange on Wall Street. New York by that time was the unrivaled "Commercial emporium of America." Her merchants were directly or in-directly involved in handling almost a third of the nation's total exports and more than half of its imports, and Brown Brothers & Co. was already one of the principal merchant banking firms supplying the credit and the foreign exchange that made this vast commerce possible.

This anonymous wood engraving, somewhat enlarged in this reproduction, is the best available indication of what the Browns' early offices in Baltimore, Philadelphia, and New York may have looked like to their contemporaries. It was designed to represent the interior of a "typical" merchant's counting house of the 1830s, as an illustration in Edward Hazen's popular book about *Professions and Trades* (New York, 1839).

The merchant, seated at his desk in the foreground, is apparently looking over documents connected with the arrival of merchandise on the ship visible through the doorway at left. In the doorway his chief clerk is checking the items received against invoices or bills of lading. (The heavy cask being shown to him suggests a shipment of tobacco, sugar, or molasses—all commonly shipped in these heavy hogsheads, as they were called.) And in the background other clerks and bookkeepers perch on tall stools at high desks, entering records of the merchant's transactions in huge volumes labelled Cash Book, Warehouse Book, Ledger, and so on.

(Author's Collection)

ALEXANDER BROWN (1764–1834), from a portrait painted circa 1832, probably by Sarah Peale.

The original is in the collection of Alexander Brown Griswold, Baltimore.

(Photograph courtesy Frick Art Reference Library)

The map of the world hanging on the wall in the typical merchant's counting house pictured above, the ship unloading at the wharf outside, and the huge ledgers shelved next to the map were the symbols by which the designer of this crude wood engraving evoked the "idea" of the merchant for his contemporaries.

The validity of the symbols is borne out by Alexander Brown's career. For years the seas were white with the sails of ships—some flying his house flag—bringing linens and other goods he imported from Great Britain and elsewhere and returning with cargoes he exported from half a dozen American ports.

A careful risk-taker in the years of blockade, embargo, and war during which he laid the foundation of his fortune, he was—as his portrait suggests—a decisive man with relentlessly Presbyterian standards of honor. When he died, the New York merchant Philip Hone wrote in his diary that Brown had been one of "the royal merchants of America, as the Medici of old were of Italy." Less floridly, another New York merchant, Joseph A. Scoville, remembered him as "a fine old fellow," a prime example of what was known as "an *Irish* gentleman," who knew "when to go in, how long to stay in, and when to get out. He coined money."

To his partner sons he was, as George said in letters written to William after his death, "the head which thought for us," the "dear Father" to whose judgment they all "gave up" as long as he lived.

25

The earliest known picture of WILLIAM BROWN (1785–1864) is this mezzotint engraving by J. Stephenson, made from a portrait by C. Agar. It was probably made in the early 1840s when Brown was first elected to Parliament as the Anti-Cornlaw League's candidate.

(Courtesy of the Brown, Picton and Hornby Libraries, Liverpool)

There is evidence that Alexander Brown was not "the head which thought for" William Brown in quite the same degree as he was for his other three sons, but details are lacking. Unfortunately (and perhaps significantly) none of Alexander Brown's letter books survive from the 1804–1810 period during which William was admitted to partnership, tried twice (in 1806 and 1809) to set up a house in Philadelphia, resigned from the partnership, went back to Ireland to marry a Gihon cousin in Ballymena, and then, early in 1810, established in Liverpool his own firm, William Brown & Co., entirely distinct from the Baltimore house.

"There is a family tradition," wrote Alexander's grandson John Crosby Brown in his history of the firms, "that William was so much like his father in character, both being endowed with strong wills, both liking to have their own way, and both being somewhat quick of temper, that Alexander Brown thought it wiser not to risk the chance of a serious difference with his son, and preferred on that account to leave him with a free hand in the conduct of the Liverpool business. . . ." In any event, even after 1814 when William's brothers in America became partners in his reorganized Liverpool house, Alexander Brown did not become a partner.

In the light of subsequent events, it is interesting that the new house was styled William & James

The building in which William Brown had his Liverpool counting house in 1818, as sketched by Jay Robinson in February 1965. The building, 7 Union Court, off Castle Street, has been much renovated, the original brick having been faced with smooth plaster.

One of the buildings shown on Chapel Street, left of, and behind, the church in this "View of the Church of St. Nicholas, Liverpool," was William Brown's warehouse and counting house in 1825—the year the engraving by H. Meyer was published in Corry's *History of Lancashire*. In the right foreground is the basin of George's Dock, where the Browns' own ships and others bearing their cargoes could be loaded and unloaded almost within sight of William's office. So convenient was the location that for more than thirty years Brown's headquarters remained at the foot of Chapel Street, successively numbered 3, 4, and 7 (on the south side).

Brown & Co. Earlier histories of the Brown firms have passed over without comment the fact that James, the youngest of the brothers, was the one whose name was linked with William's in the Liverpool enterprise. Perhaps it was already evident that James was by temperament better suited than the other brothers to cooperate with William in developing the international merchant banking activities that the family's linen importing business had got them into.

(*Photograph courtesy Mrs. Moreau D. Brown*)

JOHN A. BROWN (1788–1872), from a portrait painted circa 1818, possibly by Rembrandt Peale. The original is in the collection of Mrs. T. Emory Eysmans, Villanova, Pennsylvania.

(*Courtesy Free Library of Philadelphia*)

First published advertisement of John A. Brown & Co., from the *American Daily Advertiser*, Philadelphia, October 10, 1818. A similar advertisement appeared the same day in the Philadelphia *Union, United States Gazette and True American.*

Technically, however, the banking business now known as Brown Brothers Harriman & Co. was established not by James Brown but by his next older brother, John A. Brown. John was "the most conservative of all the four brothers," according to his nephew John Crosby Brown, "and less fitted by temperament than William and James for the competition and hurry of modern business life." Nevertheless, it was he who went to Philadelphia in 1818 to establish John A. Brown & Co.—the first house founded in the United States by one of Alexander Brown's sons, whose business was later taken over and continued by Brown Brothers & Co., the New York firm established in 1825 by James.

As William Brown's earlier attempts to start a Philadelphia branch of the Baltimore house suggest, the city's advantages as a center for the firm's trad-

ing operations had been clear a decade before. Since then Baltimore's relative importance as a trading city had declined. The successful introduction of steamboats on western rivers after 1811 meant that manufactured goods could now go by ship from Europe, or by coastwise vessels from New York or Philadelphia, to New Orleans and thence by steamboat up the Mississippi and the Ohio more cheaply than by wagon on the overland routes from Baltimore. By 1817 the falling off of Baltimore's western trade had so alarmed that city's merchants, according to the architect Robert Mills, that public works were "nearly at a stand." Meanwhile, Philadelphia's superior shipping facilities had made it second only to New York in the tonnage of vessels in the foreign and coastal trade, and as headquarters of the recently established Bank of the United

Ten years after establishing the firm in Philadelphia, John A. Brown moved into the comfortable residence on the southeast corner of 12th and Chestnut Streets, shown in this watercolor by D. J. Kennedy. According to Scoville's *Old Merchants of New York City,* the house was built by John McCrea, a prominent Philadelphia merchant and shipowner, for his own use. But before he could move in, McCrea failed. The Browns had advanced credit for many of his transactions in 1826 and 1827, including shipments of raw silk from China, purchases of sheet copper from England and cochineal from Mexico, and sales of yellow nankeens in Tampico—all recorded in Brown Brothers' first letter book—and he was heavily indebted to them at the time of his failure. To settle his debts, therefore, he gave up to the Browns the house he had never occupied, and it was John A. Brown's home for many years. It was torn down in 1867 to make way for Bailey's famous jewelry store and other commercial buildings.

States (the second of that name) it was the nation's undisputed financial capital.

Soon after establishing the Philadelphia firm as "Importers of Irish Linens," John took as his partner a dry-goods commission merchant named Johnston McLanahan, whose sister had married George Brown, the brother who remained in Baltimore. Then, in 1820, John's wife died and he returned to Baltimore for almost three years, during which James Brown took charge of the Philadelphia business—especially the foreign exchange and trading operations that were carried on with William & James Brown & Co. in Liverpool. After 1823 John again resumed control in Philadelphia, but by 1837 he had had enough of active business and retired from the firm.

(Brown Brothers Harriman & Co. Historical File)

JAMES BROWN (1791–1877) standing between his older brothers JOHN (left) and GEORGE (1787–1859). The picture reproduced here is a photographic copy, made by F. Gutekunst of Philadelphia, of a since-lost daguerreotype probably made about 1841, when James was 50 years old.

CIRCULAR.

October, 1825.

For some time past we have had it in contemplation to establish a house in New-York, with the view of promoting the interest of Messrs. WILLIAM & JAMES BROWN & Co., *of Liverpool*, and of affording greater facility, and the choice of markets, to our southern friends, who are disposed to give them or us their business; for that purpose, our JAMES BROWN has established himself, at *New-York*, to conduct a Commission Business, under the firm of BROWN, BROTHERS, & Co. The partners in that house, are the same as those composing our respective firms.

ALEXANDER BROWN & SONS, *Baltimore.*

JOHN A. BROWN & Co.,   *Philadelphia.*

New-York, 31st October, 1825.

In announcing our establishment, allow us to offer you our services. Should you send us Cotton or other produce, we will either dispose of it in this market, or re-ship it to our Liverpool house, Messrs. WILLIAM & JAMES BROWN & Co., as you may direct.

If a sale is made here, we charge a Commission of 2½ per cent.; and if we guarantee, the customary charge will be made. Should the property be re-shipped to our friends, Messrs. WM. & JAMES BROWN & Co., no charge will be made for our agency.

We are willing, at all times, to make reasonable advances, on property consigned to us, or our Liverpool house, on receiving Invoice, Bills of Lading, and orders to have Insurance effected, either here or at Liverpool; and to reimburse ourselves for any advances we make, and expenses incurred on shipments to Messrs. WILLIAM & JAMES BROWN & Co., we will draw on them, for which we charge a Commission of 1 per cent., but make no charge for effecting Insurance on property consigned to any of our establishments.

Your obedient servants,

Brown Brothers & Co

REFERENCES.

BENJAMIN STORY, Esq.
JOSEPH FOWLER, JUN., Esq.   } *New-Orleans.*
MESSRS. JOHN HAGAN. & CO.
"   M·LOSKEY & HAGAN, *Mobile.*
"   ADGER & BLACK, *Charleston.*
"   JOHN CUMMING & SON, *Savannah.*
"   F. T. MASTIN, & CO., *Huntsville. Alabama.*

(Brown Brothers Harriman & Co. Historical File)

Circular sent out by Alexander Brown & Sons and John A. Brown & Co. announcing the establishment of Brown Brothers & Co. On November 11, 1825, James Brown wrote to Adger & Black, the Charleston merchants listed among the "References," that though dated October the circulars had just been completed by the printers, "so full of business are they, and in fact workmen of every description." However troublesome the delay had been, James took its cause as "one of the certain marks of the prosperity of the place which the writer has chosen for his future residence."

When James Brown founded Brown Brothers & Co. in New York, he was not yet the dominant figure among the American brothers that he was soon to become. Yet it is interesting that the circular announcing the new firm does not call it "a branch" of the Baltimore house, as the Philadelphia firm had been called, and makes no reference to the family's traditional business as importers of linens. This new house was established to promote "the interest of William & James Brown & Co. *of Liverpool*," and the backbone of its "Commission Business" was to be the sale in New York or reshipment to Liverpool of cotton raised by the Brown firms' "Southern friends." Shifts in the family's business had already made it inevitable that after Alexander Brown's death it would be his youngest son, in New York, who assumed the leadership of its international merchant banking operations.

(Courtesy of the New York Historical Society)

Three

FROM PEARL STREET TO WALL STREET

This detail (slightly reduced in size) from the so-called "Goodrich Plan" of New York shows the part of the city best known to James Brown after he settled here in 1825. The original, "A Map of the City of New York," was engraved on copper by H. Anderson and published in 1827 by A. T. Goodrich, who in the following year brought out a guide book, *The Picture of New-York and Stranger's Guide to the Commercial Metropolis of the United States.*

The slips along the East River shore from Whitehall Slip at the Battery (lower left) to Rutgers Slip (upper right) can serve readers unfamiliar with New York's topography as guides in locating important streets and buildings. About two inches northeast of Whitehall Slip is Old Slip, pointing inland toward Hanover Square. A little beyond is Coffee House Slip at the foot of Wall Street, between which and Fly Market Slip were the wharves at the foot of Pine Street where many Liverpool, Havre and London packets tied up. Peck Slip, about an inch and a half beyond Fly Market Slip, points inland toward City Hall in the triangular park between Broadway (at left) and Chatham Street (Park Row), south of Chambers Street.

New York's busy prosperity, which James Brown noted in reference to the printer's delay in getting out his circular (p. 31), was no illusion. More than three thousand new buildings were in course of construction during 1825, and five hundred new mercantile houses were established in the first few months of the year. There were already twelve banks and ten marine insurance companies in town, yet the 1825 legislature was deluged with applications for charters for twenty-seven more banks and thirty other corporations. From the wharves north of Coffee House Slip and Peck Slip, sixteen packets sailed on regular schedules to Liverpool and four to Le Havre. The duties collected at the Custom House exceeded $15,000,000—considerably more than the total of all duties collected at Philadelphia, Boston, Baltimore, Norfolk, and Savannah.

Brown Brothers early offices were all strategically related to the Liverpool packets' docks. The first was on Pearl Street—"the peculiar and favorite resort of wholesale dry goods merchants," as Goodrich's 1828 guide book tells us—on the west side near Maiden Lane, just three blocks up from Fly Market Slip at the north end of the Liverpool packet docks. Then, in May 1826, Brown Brothers acquired a warehouse at 63 Pine Street, on the south side between Pearl and William Streets, directly up from the packet docks. And in 1835, as already noted on p. 24, came the move to Wall Street, where the firm took offices in No. 46 (later 58), shown on Goodrich's map just above the letters *re* in the word "street," across from the Exchange from whose dome flags telegraphed the first news of all arriving vessels.

On November 4, 1825—just a month after James Brown made the first entry in Brown Brothers & Co.'s day book ledger—the canal boat *Seneca Chief,* with Governor Clinton, distinguished guests, and a barrel of Lake Erie water aboard, arrived at New York, having completed the first passage through the Erie Canal from Buffalo. It was a day of great celebration in New York, with a marine parade recorded in this fine painting by Anthony Imbert.

Imbert was a former French naval officer who had studied painting and drawing while a prisoner in England, and had a good reputation as a marine artist when he came to the United States in 1824 to set up New York's first lithographic press. He did all the lithograph illustrations for Cadwalader Colden's *Memoir* of the Canal celebration, published in 1826 (though dated 1825). In his painting we are looking from the Jersey shore toward lower Manhattan, with Castle Clinton and Battery Park at right, and Governor's Island and the Narrows in the right background.

The merchant, as depicted in an early nineteenth-century typographical ornament reproduced in C. P. Hornung's *Handbook of Early Advertising Art,* New York, 1956.

Some of the city's prosperity in the decade after 1825 was owing to the newly completed Erie Canal, which gave western merchants and farmers easier access to New York's markets. But, as Robert G. Albion showed in his masterly study of *The Rise of New York Port,* the city owed even more to innovations in shipping that were introduced by its merchants.

The chief of these was what Albion calls "the invention of the ocean liner"—the establishment by a group of Quaker merchants of what became known as the Black Ball line. In December 1817 New York and Liverpool papers carried advertisements announcing that "In order to furnish more certain Conveyance for Goods and Passengers, between Liverpool and New York," the owners of the ships *Courrier, Pacific, James Munroe,* and *Amity*

(*Author's Collection*)

One of the early Black Ball liners, the *New York,* is shown in this little-known view of "South St. near Dover St.," drawn circa 1827 by Alexander Jackson Davis, engraved by J. Yeager, and published in 1828 by A. T. Goodrich in his New York guide book. The drawing was made from a point on South Street just north of Peck Slip (see map, p. 32), looking northeast across the wharves at the foot of Dover Street where for many years the Black Ballers tied up. (The Brooklyn Bridge tower now occupies the site.)

The *New York,* a 516 ton ship built for the Black Ball line at Brown & Bell's shipyard, was launched in 1822— "one of the largest, most commodious, and most luxuriously equipped packets" of the time, according to Carl Cutler's *Queens of the Western Ocean.* Ralph Waldo Emerson, who returned on the *New York* from his first trip to Europe in 1833, vividly recorded in his journal how "very long, crooked, rough, & eminently disagreeable" the road from Liverpool to New York could be even in such a splendid ship. There were gales so violent that Emerson's sides were soon sore with rolling in his berth in the "wild distressful noisy nights." For the steerage passengers it was even worse: "Old women & children sitting up all night or lying in wet berths." Even the "poor cow refuses," Emerson noted, "to get up & be milked, & four dogs on board shiver & totter about all day, & bark when we ship a sea."

had undertaken to establish "a regular succession of Vessels, which will *positively sail, full or not full,* from Liverpool on the 1st, and from New York on the 5th of every month, throughout the year." As promised, the *James Munroe* sailed from New York on January 5, 1818, in a heavy snowstorm, even though she had only seven passengers and a light cargo of apples and mail aboard. Hitherto, mails, passengers, and cargo had awaited the vagaries of the so-called "regular traders," the best of which commonly disregarded advertised sailing dates, waiting for full cargoes and good weather. To change the pattern was risky, as the *James Munroe*'s unprofitable first cargo suggests. But Jeremiah Thompson and his Quaker associates were wealthy and determined men, convinced that regular service on commodious ships would eventually command the most lucrative and desirable branches of the shipping business: "fine freight" in small bulk, specie or coined money (constantly crossing the Atlantic to rectify international balances), mails, and cabin passengers.

This view of "New-York" from Governor's Island, drawn by J. H. Dakin and engraved by Barnard & Dick, was published in June 1831, as Plate I in Peabody & Co.'s *Views in the City of New-York,* with text by Theodore S. Fay. It and the other Peabody views on this page and the next are reproduced here the same size as the originals.

(Author's Collection)

The city James Brown knew as a rising young merchant is charmingly depicted in contemporary engravings, especially the so-called Peabody views, published, with rather florid commentary by Theodore S. Fay, in 1831–1832 under the title *Views in the City of New-York and its Environs . . . from Accurate, Characteristic, and Picturesque Drawings, Taken from the Objects Themselves.* Commenting on the view of the city as seen from near Castle Williams on Governor's Island (above), Fay says of the Hudson, in left background, that "Its steamboat navigation is unobstructed, and it presents facilities for commerce of an extraordinary and tempting nature"—linked as it is by the new canal to "the most western portion of the Union." But the picture itself makes clear that the sailing ships clustered along South Street dominated the port.

James Brown certainly was familiar with the scene depicted below, for his first warehouse and office—much like those shown here, no doubt—was just a block up Pearl from the warehouse to the right of the hotel. Down past the last building in the dark-colored row, around the corner and up Wall Street a short way, on the south side, was the Merchants Exchange, begun in 1825, a few months before Brown came to the city, and completed in 1827. He must frequently have visited the Post Office, in the basement of the Exchange, and attended "High 'Change" in the domed Merchants Room before the building was destroyed in the great fire of December 1835 (p. 24)—soon after Brown Brothers had moved into offices diagonally across the street.

This view of "Pearl Street House & Ohio Hotel. (Hanover Square in the distance.)," drawn and engraved by M. Osborne, was another in the Peabody series. The hotel is indicated on the map, p. 32, by a small square on the west side of Pearl Street (two blocks up from the end of Coffee House Slip), between Wall and Pine Streets.

(Edward W. C. Arnold Collection, lent by the Metropolitan Museum of Art. Photograph courtesy of the Museum of the City of New York)

"Merchant's Exchange, Wall St., New-York," drawn by C. Burton and engraved by H. Fossette, was one of the so-called "Bourne Views" of the city, published by George M. Bourne in 1831. It is reproduced the same size as the original.

"View of Wall Street," engraved from a painting by Winslow, was published by J. W. J. Niles for the *Amateur,* October 1831. No. 46 Wall, across from the Merchants Exchange, where Brown Brothers & Co. had its offices from 1835–39, is hidden from sight by the trees left of center.

"Merchants Room, Exchange," No. 12 in the series of Peabody views, was drawn by A. Dick, engraved by J. Archer, printed by J. & G. Neal, and published by Peabody in November 1831.

"City Hotel, Trinity & Grace Churches"
drawn and engraved by A. Dick.

The Peabody views on this page give some idea of scenes James Brown witnessed daily on his way home from work in the late 1820s and early 1830s. In 1828 he moved into a large house he had built half a block west of Broadway on the south side of Leonard Street—the fourth street north of where Chambers Street crosses at the top of City Hall's triangular park (center of map on p. 32).

"Broadway from the Park"
drawn by J. H. Dakin, engraved by Barnard & Dick.

Walking up Pine Street from his warehouse at No. 63, Mr. Brown would have turned north on Broadway just a block above Trinity Church (the second on the site at the head of Wall Street, replaced in 1846 by the present structure). Here he might have taken a coach like the one passing the City Hotel, or one of the new open-sided "Accommodations," introduced in 1827, like the one to the right of St. Paul's chapel in the middle picture.

"Residence of Philip Hone Esq."
drawn by J. H. Dakin, engraved by Barnard & Dick.

Two blocks up Broadway beyond St. Paul's on the block opposite the park between Barclay Street and Park Place (where the Woolworth building now stands), he passed the shop of Peabody & Co., publishers of these views, and next to it the residence of Philip Hone. Hone had retired, when elected Mayor in 1826, from the auction house where—as James Brown's first day book shows—his brother John Hone in the late 'twenties annually sold for Brown Brothers' account goods valued at a million dollars or more.

SAMUEL NICHOLSON (1795?–1857), who became James Brown's partner in 1826, from an unlocated portrait as reproduced in John Crosby Brown's *A Hundred Years of Merchant Banking*, New York, 1909, opposite p. 198. (*Brown Brothers Harriman & Co. Historical File*)

STEWART BROWN (1802–1880), from a portrait by an unidentified American painter, probably done in 1827— the year he joined his cousin James Brown as a partner in Brown Brothers & Co. The original painting was formerly in the possession of W. Harman Brown; its present location is unknown. (*Photograph courtesy of the Frick Art Reference Library*)

191 Pearl Street, where Brown Brothers had its first office, was also the address of Samuel Nicholson, a dry-goods merchant, and it is probable that the Browns or their friends in Ireland and Liverpool had done business with him for some time. At any rate, one of the first letters in James Brown's letter book—to Wm. Gihon & Sons of Ballymena, dated October 22, 1825—says:

Gent[lemen]

We have made an arrangement with Mr. Nicholson to conduct a commission business here under the firm of Sam¹ Nicholson & Co. We are his partners and have an oversight of the business but it will be conducted principally if not entirely by himself. Our exchange business and money negotiations will be conducted by

Your friends
B B & Co.

From the start, therefore, it was clear that James Brown intended to specialize in the banking aspects of the work.

So rapidly did the new business expand that additional help was needed, and in July 1826, James Brown's young cousin Stewart Brown came on from Baltimore to work for Brown Brothers. He had learned the business as a clerk in his Uncle Alexander Brown's firm, and on January 1, 1827, James made him a partner. At first, both Nicholson and Stewart Brown participated only in the New York firm, their compensation being a percentage of the business done there, not a share in the general profits of the associated Brown firms. But in 1836, after the settlement of Alexander Brown's estate, both became general partners in all the houses.

The arrangement with Nicholson turned out very well indeed. For one thing, he was apparently a

New York 1st January 1826

Messrs Wm & Jas Brown & Co.
dear Sirs, Mr Sam Nicholson has made arrangements with us for your Guaranteeing the consignments of any English, Irish or Scotch Goods which may be shipped through you to his house, they will write you herewith which attend to, Yours respectfully Brown Brothers & Co.

Gentln,
Referring to the foregoing letter to our friends Messrs Wm & Jas Brown & Co of Liverpool, through whom you will receive this, we have merely to add, that we will give our best attention to any consignments you may make us, and hope to give satisfaction to those who intrust us with the Sale of their property. our Charges will be for Sale & Guarantee two per Cent, for Storage, Postage & Advertising one half per Cent, and one eighth per Cent for Insurance against Fire. In cases where we deem it the Interest of the owner to sell at Auction, our charge will be only 2½ per Cent. Should our funds meet the remittances guaranteed we will do so for 1 per Cent. Messrs Jno A Brown & Co of Philadelphia & A Brown & Bros Baltimore receive consignments on the same terms, two we keep each other advised of our respective Markets, consignments to either of our establishments can have the advantage of all should the owner so direct our desire will be to dispose of them in that Market

First page of a three-page circular letter, sent to English, Irish, and Scottish merchants early in 1826, announcing Brown Brothers' arrangement with Samuel Nicholson and describing the facilities offered by the Brown firms in Liverpool, New York, Philadelphia, and Baltimore. The dark spots at the top of the sheet are where sealing wax holds the three sheets together. Multiple copies of the handwritten circular were produced by the lithographic process which Anthony Imbert (p. 34) first introduced to New York in 1825—though there had been lithographers in Philadelphia and Boston for several years. (*Original in Brown Brothers Harriman & Co. Historical File*)

man of great charm and affability. Joseph A. Scoville, whose garrulous and entertaining recollections of *The Old Merchants of New York* were pseudonymously published in the early 1860s as by "Walter Barrett, Clerk.," remembered Nicholson as "a fine looking man in his young days," a gay youth who with two other young bachelors kept open house, "entertained in a most liberal manner, and invited every foreigner of any note who touched the shore." As a married man and Brown Brothers partner he may have been less gay, but his hospitable and ingratiating qualities—no doubt especially appealing to the Southern planters and merchants who dealt with the firm—probably contributed to his success in establishing the branch house, or agency, in New Orleans which he ably supervised from 1838 until he retired in 1856—a millionaire, with what Scoville described as "a superb house in the Fifth avenue, near Twenty-first street." If, in the pages that follow, there seems to be an atmosphere of reserve and earnestness surrounding the early Brown Brothers partners, however tempered by domestic affections, it should be pleasant to recollect the Sam Nicholson Scoville describes—"one of the old school beaux [who] was at every City Hotel ball, and a leader of fashion."

Four

DOCUMENTS OF COMMERCE

The printed circular reproduced earlier (on p. 31) was directed primarily to the cotton and tobacco growers of the Southern states, as indicated by the fact that all the "References" listed at the bottom of the page were merchants in South Carolina, Georgia, Alabama, or Louisiana. The circular whose first page is reproduced on p. 40 (opposite) was intended for British manufacturers of cloth and other goods for the American market. The two circulars —taken together with a revised version of the latter which was sent out the following June—show how Brown Brothers in New York and William & James Brown in Liverpool participated in one of the most spectacular developments in America's international trade: the so-called "cotton triangle" by which, as Robert Albion has shown, New York's merchants "dragged the commerce between the southern ports and Europe out of its normal course some two hundred miles to collect a heavy toll upon it."[1]

The handwritten circular begins with a short letter addressed by Brown Brothers & Co. (James Brown) to "Messrs. W^m & Ja^s Brown & Co" (William Brown), dated January 1, 1826. It announces simply that "Mr. Saml Nicholson has made arrangements with us for your Guaranteeing the consignments of any English, Irish or Scotch Goods which may be shipped through you to his house," ending, in the abrupt business prose of the day: "they will write you herewith, which attend to." Following this is a letter signed by "Saml Nicholson & Co" announcing the commissions they will charge for their services and describing the advantages of dealing with a firm that has houses in Philadelphia and Baltimore as well as New York. And the circular concludes with a letter signed by the Liverpool house, of which more later.

By the following June, when this circular was superseded by another somewhat briefer one, the

[1] *The Rise of New York Port*, New York, 1939, Chapter VI.

commissions charged had been slightly altered, but the chief difference was that the "arrangements" with Samuel Nicholson had changed. Nicholson had by that time become a partner of James Brown, and the commission business was now a part of Brown Brothers' own operations, carried on under its own name.

As commission merchants, Brown Brothers (like Samuel Nicholson & Co. in the earlier circular) were "happy to receive & attend to any Consignments our Friends may please to place under our care." Their charge for attending to (and guaranteeing) the sale of such goods was 6%, with additional charges of ½% covering "storage, postage, and advertising" and ⅛% for fire insurance. In cases, however, "where we deem it the Interest of the owners to sell at Auction"—turning the goods over to the Hones or one of the other great auction houses to be disposed of by them—the charge was less (2½% in the first circular, 3% in the second). If the owner of the goods wished Brown Brothers to guarantee the bills of exchange remitted as payment, an additional 1% would be charged, for—as they explained in a letter to Wm. Gihon & Sons, August 23, 1826, advising them of "the first [remittance] the house here have made,"—the 6% commission covered "risk of Sales *only*" not risks on remittances.

The circulars point out that John A. Brown & Co. in Philadelphia and Alexander Brown & Sons in Baltimore received consignments on the same terms, and that, since the three firms kept one another advised of market conditions in all three cities, the owners might direct that their consignments be sold in whichever market was likely to be most profitable.

Thus far, the circulars deal with the part of the business James Brown had turned over to Samuel Nicholson. But from here on they are concerned with the merchant banking operations in which the

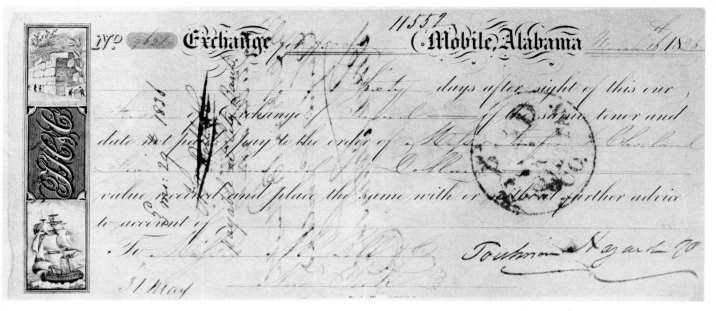

This accepted bill (or "acceptancy," as James Brown would have called it) served much the same purposes in 1836 as the bankers acceptance reproduced on pp. 14–15, which was created by W. A. Harriman & Co. ninety years later. Until the organization of the Federal Reserve System in 1914, the acceptance of bills of exchange was almost unknown to banks, but for a century or more it had been the province of merchant bankers.

Dated March 16, 1836, the bill was drawn by Toulmin Hazard & Co., cotton merchants of Mobile, Alabama, on Abraham Bell & Co., their New York correspondents (well known to Brown Brothers—see pp. 46–48), calling for payment of $5000 to Sanford & Cleveland of Mobile. Bell's acceptance, dated two weeks later (a reminder of the time consumed by the mails), is written across the face of the bill, indicating that it will be payable at the City Bank in New York.

Showing through the thin paper are the endorsements:

"Pay to the order of Messrs. Brown Brothers & Co. [signed] Sanford & Cleveland," and beneath that "Brown Brothers & Co." in James Brown's hand. Presumably, the $5000 was an advance on cotton shipped through Brown Brothers to Wm. & Jas. Brown. Bell having accepted the draft (i.e., guaranteed to pay it), Brown endorsed it and discounted it at his own bank—at that time the bank of the Manhattan Company, whose round stamp, in red ink, indicates that the bill was paid at maturity.

Notice that the engraved words on the bill indicate, with the blanks filled in, that it is to be paid sixty days after sight "of this our *First* of Exchange (*Second* of the same tenor and date not paid)."

With the uncertainty of the mails in those days, it was necessary to send duplicate bills by different ships or routes. In this case, probably one went by ship to New York and the other overland. (*Original in Brown Brothers Harriman & Co. Historical File*)

Browns were increasingly involved. Owners who did not wish to wait for cash returns until the goods were sold were informed that Brown Brothers was "quite prepared on the arrival of the goods to make liberal advances to such of our Friends as may wish us to do so"; or the owners could arrange for such advances through William & James Brown & Co. in Liverpool.

Furthermore, Brown Brothers and the other two American houses attended to "the collection & remittance of money for European houses" for a 1% commission, or—if they guaranteed the bills—for a commission of 2%. The extra commission might be advisable in risky times, but the circulars proudly refer to the fact that the "general knowledge of Business in the U. S." accumulated in twenty-six years by the firms Alexander Brown had inaugurated "has prevented us in the worst of times taking any bad Bills worth notice."

Almost as an afterthought (indeed, it was a P.S. to "Wᵐ & Jaˢ Brown & Co." ['s] letter in the first version), the circulars offer a service which shows how the commission business they advertised was related to the cotton shipments which the printed circular of October 1825 had been concerned with. "Should our Friends [the exporters of English,

Enlarged detail from the bill of exchange on opposite page, engraved by Rawdon, Wright & Co. of New York, banknote engravers. Above the monogram of Toulmin Hazard & Co. the individual bolls on the sprig of cotton plant framing the scene at right are larger than the figures of the slaves, dwarfed by the huge bales they are stacking. Below, a bluff-bowed ship like those that flew the house flag of Alexander Brown and Sons. (*Brown Brothers Harriman & Co. Historical File*)

Irish or Scotch goods] wish the Nett Proceeds of their property sent home in Cotton," Brown Brothers would buy it for them "in New York or such Southern port as will be most the Interest of our Friends."

As a commission merchant, James Brown avoided getting directly involved in cotton speculation, refusing to go into "joint-account" operations with Southern cotton factors who invited him to do so. And when a New Orleans correspondent reported hearing rumors that "Wm & Jas Brown & Co." had speculated on their own account in 4000 bales, James sternly wrote that the firm "never did, and never will speculate in an article so long as they continue to do a commission business." There had been a time, soon after the Philadelphia house was established in 1818, when William had considered investing in an English cotton mill, but a letter from Alexander Brown & Sons, dated October 27, 1819, set him straight with a blunt statement of the family's unanimous disapproval. Either George Brown or James (who was in the Baltimore house at the time) must have written the letter, since it begins by saying it had been written in time for their father to see it before he left town; something in its tone suggests that James was the author. "If we look round here," the letter says, "we find that those persons who have kept steadily to one pursuit are far the richest men, & those who are interested with one & another in different pursuits, no matter how profitable they may be or appear to be at first, are always ruined sooner or later." Furthermore, "In the management of one's business it's not only necessary to be correct but not to be suspected of incorrectness." A cotton shipper who learned that

COMMISSION BUSINESS.

1. *In the Supreme Court of the United States, January Term,* 1840. *William and James Brown and Co., Plaintiffs in Error,* v. *Thomas McGran.* In error to the Circuit Court of the United States for the District of Georgia.

Mr. Justice Story delivered the opinion of the Court :—

This is a writ of error to a judgment of the Circuit Court of the District of Georgia, rendered in an action in which McGran (the defendant in error) was originally plaintiff.

In the spring of 1833, McGran, a merchant in Georgia, shipped 200 bales of cotton, consigned to the plaintiffs in error, a house of trade in Liverpool, England, there doing business, under the firm of William and James Brown & Co., for sale on his account. The shipment was made under an arrangement with the house of Brown, Brothers, & Co., of New York, composed (as seems admitted) either wholly or in part of the partners in the Liverpool house, by which the New York house accepted a draft drawn upon them by McGran for 9,000 dollars, the invoice value of the cotton being only 9,151 dollars 77 cents, and were to reimburse themselves by a draft on the Liverpool house. Accordingly, the New York house on the 12th of March, 1833, addressed a letter to the Liverpool house, in which they state, " We enclose bill of lading for 200 bales of cotton, shipped by McLoskey, Hagan & Co., of Mobile, per ship Mary and Harriet, on account of Mr. Thomas McGran, of Augusta, on which you will please effect insurance. This cotton cost per invoice 9,151 dollars 77 cents. We have accepted Mr. McGran's draft against this cotton for 9,000 dollars—for which we shall draw on you for our reimbursement when it' matures. In handing this draft for acceptance, Mr. McGran says he would not have drawn for so large an advance, were it not that there is a balance at his credit with you, which has accumulated within the past two years—so that if this should not produce enough to meet the advance, it will be covered by what is at his credit." The existence of any such balance was utterly denied at the trial, and the Liverpool house contended that there was a balance the other way.

The cotton only arrived at Liverpool on or about the 9th of April, 1833. The New York house drew on the Liverpool house, for their reimbursement, a bill dated the 7th of May, 1833, for 1,871*l.* 9*s.*, at 60 days sight, being the amount of the advance, and that bill was accepted by the Liverpool house on the 3d of June, 1833, and became payable, and was paid, on the 5th of August following. On the 3d of June, 1833, the very day of the acceptance, the Liverpool house sold the 200 bales of cotton (the market then being on the rise) on a credit, for the nett sum of 2,073*l.* 4*s.* 6*d.* After deducting the charges (which amount to nearly twenty-five per cent.) which became due and payable on the 16th September, 1833, and, according to an account current rendered to McGran by the Liverpool house, on the 29th June, 1833, the whole transactions between the parties, including the sale of this cotton, left a balance of 392*l.* 15*s.* 8*d.*, due to McGran.

At the time when the shipment was made, and the advance arranged therefor, no instructions were given by McGran touching the sale of the cotton. It accordingly went to the consignees as factors for sale, the advances having been as above mentioned, without any other contract than that implied by law as between a principal and a factor making advances, that is to say, that the factor is to make sale of the goods consigned to him according to his own judgment, in the exercise of a sound discretion as to the time and mode of sale, having regard to the usages of trade at the place of sale, and to reimburse himself out of the proceeds for his advances and other balance due him.

After the shipment and advance were so made, namely, on the 20th April, 1833, McGran addressed a letter to the Liverpool house, in which, after acknowledging the receipt of letters of the 4th and 5th of March from them, he added, " if you have any cottons on hand when this reaches you, in which I am interested, I wish you to hold them until you hear from me again."

The Liverpool house, in a reply to this letter, on the 25th of May, 1833, used the following language : " We are in possession of your esteemed favor of 20th ultimo, and your wishes, in respect to the cotton we now hold on your account, are noted accordingly." At this time, by advices received from other correspondents, the Liverpool house were in possession of information that at least as early as the 8th of April, 1833, McGran had failed in business. On the 22d July, 1833, McGran wrote a letter to the Liverpool house, acknowledging the receipt of their letter of

From *Hunt's Merchants' Magazine,* April 1840, pp. 336–37.
(*Brown Brothers Harriman & Co. Historical File*)

William or a member of his family was interested in a cotton mill "might conceive there was a risk if sent to you of being sold to your own establishment lower than it ought. You know how such persons are always disposed to grumble and find fault on losing sales." Let William remember that "a small business well attended to" is conducted "with much more satisfaction & comfort" than a large one, and if there is an excess of capital it can be profitably invested.

The business had grown enormously since then, but the basic philosophy had not changed. Writing on January 11, 1826, to McLoskey Hagan & Co. of Mobile—for whom Brown Brothers handled the cotton raised by General Winfield Scott, among others—James Brown made it plain that he did not want the business to grow "faster than it will naturally come to us through the recommendations of our friends who know our safety in any property entrusted to us."

A writer in *Hunt's Merchants' Magazine* called attention, in October 1839, to "how much of law is contained in an ordinary mercantile transaction." Sometimes the legal issues were so complex they had to be carried to the U. S. Supreme Court. An interesting case was that of William & James Brown & Co. *vs* Thomas McGran, a Georgia merchant, reported at length in *Hunt's* issue for April 1840. Enough of the report is reproduced at left to show the basis of the suit. It concerned cotton shipped for McGran on the *Mary & Harriet* (opposite) by McLoskey Hagan & Co., under a credit granted by Brown Brothers. A Georgia court had awarded damages to McGran on the grounds that the Liverpool house sold his cotton before he instructed them to do so, at too low a price. The U. S. Supreme Court, in a decision written by Justice Joseph Story, reversed the lower court's judgment. McGran had given no specific instructions as to time and mode of sale when he made the consignment, and the Browns were quite within their rights, as "factors," to sell at their discretion. The fact that William Brown learned, soon after the cotton arrived, that McGran was insolvent, no doubt made a prompt sale seem a discreet way of reimbursing the house for an advance much larger than McGran could have gotten from Brown Brothers without misrepresenting his credit with the Liverpool house.

MARY & HARRIOT NEWYORK.

This anonymous watercolor of the *Mary & Harriot,* as the artist misspelled her name, was painted at Altona, Germany, in 1839, and shows her passing the island of Helgoland. McLoskey & Hagan's wharves in Mobile, from which she sailed with Thomas McGran's cotton, are shown on the map reproduced on p. 50. (*Courtesy of the Peabody Museum of Salem*)

THOMAS ADDIS EMMET (1764–1827), the great Irish patriot, brother of Robert Emmet who was hung by the English in 1803, was Brown Brothers & Co.'s first legal counsel. He came to New York in 1804, having been released from prison in Ireland on condition of his perpetual exile. Several entries in James Brown's first day book record payments to Emmet for such things as "advice on filling up Bills of Lading 25.00" and "counsel fee for insurance for Ship Henrietta—$10.00." And a letter by James Brown, dated March 7, 1826, indicates that Emmet drew up the "guarantees" tendered by firms that applied to Brown Brothers for "uncovered credits." The portrait reproduced here was painted by S. F. B. Morse, probably in the early 1820s. (*Courtesy of the New York Historical Society*)

THE TRANSATLANTIC STEAM SHIP "LIVERPOOL"
Lieutenant R. J. FAYRER, R.N. Commander.
On her First Voyage to New York, October 1838

The documents on this and the next two pages related to shipments of British goods made through the Liverpool house (Brown Shipley & Co. after 1839) to Abraham Bell & Co. of New York under Brown Brothers' credits. Bills of lading (like the one at lower right, for goods shipped on the steamship *Liverpool,* shown above on her first voyage to New York in October 1838) were retained by Brown Brothers until Bell settled for the goods by check (below) or "approved bills."

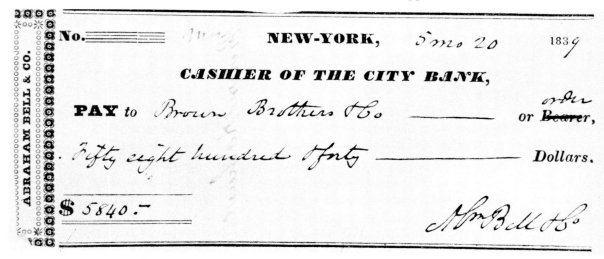

The lithograph, opposite, of the *Liverpool* was made by T. Fairland from a painting by Samuel Walters. An uncomfortable and ill-fated ship, she belonged to the short-lived Transatlantic Steamship Co., of which Abraham Bell was the New York agent. (*Courtesy of the Mariners Museum, Newport News, Va.*)

The reproduction of the check (lower left) and the bill of lading (below) are the same size as the original documents in Brown Brothers Harriman & Co.'s Historical Files. The insurance policy, part of whose first page is shown, considerably reduced, covered goods Bell had in a Brooklyn warehouse. James Brown and Bell were both trustees of the insurance company. (*Brown Brothers Harriman & Co. Historical File*)

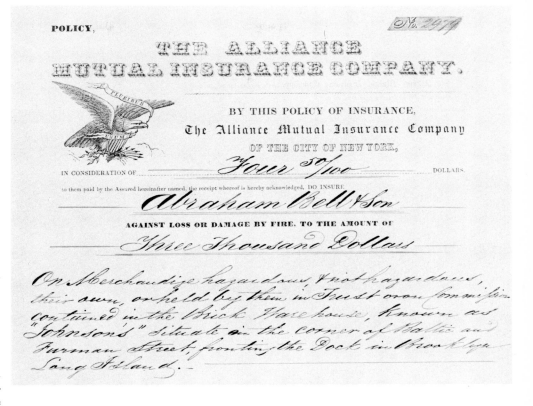

POLICY,

No. 2979

THE ALLIANCE MUTUAL INSURANCE COMPANY.

BY THIS POLICY OF INSURANCE,

The Alliance Mutual Insurance Company

OF THE CITY OF NEW YORK,

IN CONSIDERATION OF _Four 5/100_ DOLLARS.

to them paid by the Assured hereinafter named, the receipt whereof is hereby acknowledged, DO INSURE

Abraham Bell & Son

AGAINST LOSS OR DAMAGE BY FIRE, TO THE AMOUNT OF

Three Thousand Dollars

On Merchandize hazardous, & not hazardous, their own, or held by them in Trust or on Commission contained in the Brick Warehouse, known as "Johnson's" Situate on the corner of Baltic and Furman Street, fronting the Dock in Brooklyn Long Island. —

Shipped, in good order and condition, by BROWN, SHIPLEY & CO. of *Liverpool*, in and upon the good Ship or Vessel called the _Liverpool_ whereof is Master for this present voyage, now lying in the Port of *Liverpool*, and bound for *New York*.

Three Casks one case Mer= chandize

being marked and numbered as per margin; and are to be delivered in the like good order and condition, at the aforesaid Port of *New York*,

(all and every the dangers and accidents of the seas and navigation, of whatsoever nature and kind, excepted) unto

Mess Louis Thier

or to Assigns; he or they paying Freight for the said Goods, at the rate of

14/ Shillings British sterling ℔ Ton of Forty Cubic Feet for Dry Goods,
Shillings British sterling ℔ Ton of Forty Cubic Feet for Hardware,
Shillings British sterling ℔ Ton of Forty Cubic Feet for Coarse Woollens, &c.
Shillings British sterling ℔ Ton of Forty Cubic Feet for Earthenware,
Shillings British sterling ℔ Ton of Forty Cubic Feet for Castings, Chains, &c.
Shillings British sterling ℔ Ton of Forty Cubic Feet for Scythes,
Shillings British sterling ℔ Ton of Forty Cubic Feet for Nails, Slates, &c.
Shillings British sterling ℔ Ton of Twenty Cwt. for Steel, &c., and
Shillings and pence British sterling per Bundle, &c.

With five per Cent. Primage and Average accustomed, payable at the rate of 4 Dollars and 80 Cents ℔ Pound Sterling. In witness whereof, the Master or purser of the said Ship or Vessel hath affirmed to Three Bills of Lading, all of this tenor and date; one of which being accomplished, the rest to stand void.

Dated in *Liverpool*, this _17_ day of _Sept 1859_
Contents unknown.

Captain

B
Bc67 - 3 Casks
8 = 1 Case } m₈ 70 " 1
@ 3/6 £ 12 " 5 " 3
12 " 3
£ 12 " 17 " 6 N

67

Freight payable at New York at $4.80 ʋ pound Sterling

TO BE SENT TO THE PUBLIC STORE ON ARRIVAL

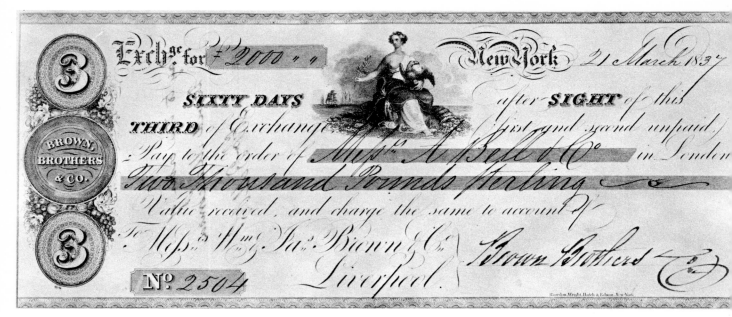

This "Third of Exchange" for £2000 sterling, drawn by Brown Brothers & Co. (Stewart Brown's signature) on Wm. & Jas. Brown & Co. in favor of Abraham Bell & Co. was apparently used by Bell to pay for goods bought of David Malcomson, in Britain, to whom Bell endorsed the draft. The engraving, by Rawdon, Wright, Hatch & Edson of New York, is a fine example of their elaborate bank-note style. (*Brown Brothers Harriman & Co. Historical File*)

This page (reproduced about half the size of the original) was sent by the Liverpool office to Abraham Bell & Co., showing their year-end accounts involving 650 bales of cotton. (*Brown Brothers Harriman & Co. Historical File*)

Transactions like those documented in the last few pages would have been impossible without the participation of the agents and correspondents with whom the Brown firms were in constant communication. The granting of credits and the acceptance of bills of exchange presupposed reliable knowledge about the character and fortunes of the men involved. To a firm in Albany, New York (where the Browns had no agent or correspondent at the time), James Brown wrote on June 15, 1826, that he could not accept their thirty-day sight bill "to be candid, because we have not sufficient knowledge of your house."

Among the firm's Southern correspondents, James Adger, of Adger & Black in Charleston (see list of references on p. 31), was notably successful. Like Alexander Brown the son of a linen weaver in County Antrim, Northern Ireland, he started out in Charleston as a hardware and general commission merchant. According to his son John B. Adger's autobiography (*My Life and Times,* 1899), Adger's connection with the Browns' firms, begun in 1818, was "the real founding of his fortune."

In Savannah, Georgia, the Browns relied on John Cumming, brother-in-law of Alexander Brown's brother, Stewart Brown. But in New Orleans and Mobile—especially Mobile—it was for a long time difficult to find suitable agents. John Hagan, one of New Orleans' wealthiest and most respected merchants, was one of the Browns' earliest correspond-

This unsigned and undated portrait of JAMES ADGER (1777–1858) was probably painted about 1819 or 1820, soon after he became the Browns' correspondent (later agent) in Charleston, South Carolina. The original, in the possession of Mr. Ellison A. Williams of Charleston, a descendant of Adger's, was photographed for this book by Louis Schwartz, through the courtesy of Mrs. S. Henry Edmunds, Director of the Historic Charleston Foundation and a great-great-granddaughter of James Adger.

Adger owned many ships and built the granite wharves known in Charleston as North and South Adger wharves. In 1833 he was one of the founders of the South Carolina Railway (now part of the Southern Railway system). Later he was the principal owner of the Adger Line of steamships running between Charleston and New York—one of which, the *James Adger,* participated in the first, unsuccessful, attempt to lay Cyrus Field's Atlantic cable and later saw service as a warship in the Union Navy, ironically serving among the blockaders of Charleston harbor. (*Collection of Ellison A. Williams*)

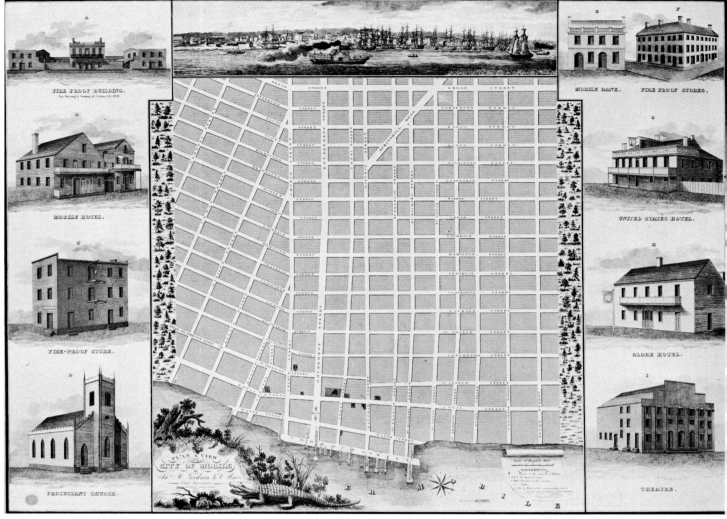

(Courtesy of the Library of Congress)

The "Plan & View of the City of Mobile," reproduced above, was drawn and published in Mobile by James M. Goodwin & C. Haire, city surveyors, from a survey made in 1824. It was engraved by R. Tiller, Jr.

The view at top center shows the city as seen from the left (east) bank of the Mobile River, looking west. In both the view and the plan, north is to the right. The two wharves owned by Philip McLoskey, of McLoskey Hagan & Co.—the Browns' Mobile correspondents in the 1820s and 1830s—are shown on the plan projecting into the river

above the dip in the alligator's tail, directly above the letter *e* in the word "RIVER," just north of the foot of Conti Street (the first one to the right of the wide Government Street). Just a block up Conti, on the n.e. corner of Water Street, is McLoskey's fireproof store (vignette third from top at left). A block further up Conti, on the s.w. corner of Royal Street, is the large fireproof building "For Pressing and Storing of Cotton" (vignette top left) built in 1823 by John Hagan of New Orleans, whose nephew James Hagan represented his interest in McLoskey Hagan & Co.

ents there. In Mobile, the Browns used McLoskey Hagan, in which Hagan's nephew, James, represented his interests.

Brown Brothers' first letter book (1825–1827) makes it clear that the firm relied on its Southern correspondents to "influence . . . consignments to W. & J. B. & Co. by drawing on us for such advances as you may give or endorsing the owners'

drafts on us"—in exchange for which Brown Brothers credited the correspondent with the one percent commission they charged for accepting the drafts. And of course they depended on their correspondents for information about houses "in your place and neighborhood . . . whose business from their correctness and prudence you think it would be desirable to have." In addition to Hagan, Ben-

(*Courtesy of the New York Public Library, Stokes Collection*)

This watercolor of Mobile (from which W. J. Bennett made an aquatint engraving, published by Henry J. Megarey in 1842) was painted by William Todd in 1841. At that time the Browns' Mobile agency was run by George Cleveland, Jr., whose father was probably in the firm of Sanford & Cleveland, endorsers of the bill of exchange reproduced on p. 42. In 1842, the English partners raised questions about Cleveland's popularity, but William Bowen, then a partner in Philadelphia, who had run the Mobile agency for two years prior to Cleveland's appointment, came strongly to his defense as a man generally liked. "No man can be very popular in Mobile," he wrote, "unless he jumps with the views of the class doing business there, a majority of whom are not entitled to any credit. . . . There is no spot where we do business so fruitful in Humbug & no place where more caution is required."

jamin Story and Joseph Fowler were active New Orleans correspondents in the early years, but there was no regular New Orleans agency until 1838, when Samuel Nicholson established one.

The establishment of this agency marked a turning point in Brown Brothers' history. In New York thirteen years earlier, Samuel Nicholson & Co. had handled the firm's first dry-goods transactions; now a new Samuel Nicholson & Co. in New Orleans was to be chiefly engaged in furthering the firm's foreign exchange and credit operations, and Brown Brothers was out of the dry-goods business entirely. Sometime prior to Nicholson's departure from New York—probably in 1837—the firm had sold the dry-goods part of its operations to Amory Leeds & Co.,[2] who—according to the garrulous Scoville—paid "a bonus of $100,000 for the good will" and promptly failed "under such peculiar circumstances that their affairs were overhauled in the law courts."

[2] John Crosby Brown's history (p. 202) gives the date as 1833, but Amory Leeds & Co. first appears in the city directories for 1837–38—at Brown Brothers' old 63 Pine address.

51

Know all Men by these Presents, That *I John A. Brown, of the city of Philadelphia, in the state of Pennsylvania, Merchant,* ——————————————

DO make, constitute, and appoint *James Brown, Samuel Nicholson, and Stewart Brown, of the city and state of New York, Merchants and Copartners trading under the firm of Brown Brothers and Company, jointly and severally,* —— to be *my* true and lawful ATTORNEY**S** for *me* and in *my* name, to receive and enter at the Custom House of the District of *New York* —— any goods, wares, and merchandise imported by *me*. or which may hereafter arrive consigned to *me, on board any and every vessel from any and every port and place at the port of New York; and also on any goods, wares and merchandise imported by me, and by said firm of Brown Brothers &c. into the said port & district of New York, both as Principal and as Surety* to sign *my* name to, seal and deliver for *me* and as *my* act and deed any bond or bonds which may be required by the Collector of the said District for securing the Duties on any such goods, wares, or merchandise; also to sign *my* name to, seal and deliver for *me* and as *my* act and deed any bond or bonds requisite for obtaining the debentures on any goods, wares, or merchandise, when exported for ~~me~~ *me & them;* and generally to transact all business at the aforesaid Custom House, in which *it they* may hereafter be interested or concerned *in relation to all Importations by me & by them,* as fully as *I* could if personally present, and *I* hereby declare, that all bonds signed and executed by *my* said attorney**s** shall be as obligatory on *me* as though signed by *me*, and this *my* power shall remain in full force until revoked by written notice given to said Collector, with power also as attorney or attorneys, under *them* —— for that purpose to make and substitute, hereby ratifying and confirming all that *they* the said attorney**s** or substitute or substitutes shall do therein by virtue hereof. IN WITNESS WHEREOF, *I* have hereunto set *my* hand and seal the *Seventh* day of *January* —— in the year of our Lord one thousand eight hundred and ~~twenty~~ *thirty two*.

Sealed and delivered }
in the presence of }

Alex. Brown

John A Brown

BE IT KNOWN, that on the *Seventh* —— day of *January* one thousand eight hundred and ~~twenty~~ *thirty two* Before me CLEMENT C. BIDDLE, ESQUIRE, *Notary Public for the Commonwealth of Pennsylvania, residing in the City of Philadelphia, duly commissioned and by law authorized to receive proof and acknowledgment of letters of attorney, personally appeared* John A. Brown, of the said city of Philadelphia, Merchant, —— *named in the above Letter of Attorney and* ACKNOWLEDGED *the same to be* his ACT and DEED.

IN TESTIMONY WHEREOF, *I have hereunto set my Hand and affixed my Notarial Seal the day and year aforesaid.*

Clement C. Biddle
Not. Pub.

So heavily was the firm's business concentrated at the port of New York by 1832, that on January 7th of that year it was necessary for John A. Brown in Philadelphia to execute this general Custom House power of attorney authorizing James Brown, Samuel Nicholson, and Stewart Brown "jointly and severally" to sign for him all custom house documents required in connection with "goods, wares, and merchandise" imported by him or which might arrive consigned to him "on board any and every vessel from any and every port and place at the port of New York." (*Brown Brothers Harriman & Co. Historical File*)

This wood engraving of "MR. W. BROWN, M.P. for South Lancashire," appeared in *The Illustrated London News*, July 12, 1851, in connection with an article about him in the magazine's series of "Parliamentary Portraits." The cut was made "from a daguerreotype by Claudet." (*Brown Brothers Harriman & Co. Historical File*)

A NEW SONG.
To the Tune of—" Down, Down, Derry Down !

There's an Irish American settled down here,
Who, like other Yankees, thinks much of a Peer,—
In the front of long Lists, where large sums are set down,—
There ! a-head of them all you'll be sure to find stuck—Billy Brown !
    Brown, Brown, Billy Brown !

Such persons will always be much in request,
Where the length of the Purse is considered the test
Of who should stand first in the ranks of the town,—
And there have his townsmen agreed to admit—Billy Brown.
    Brown, Brown, Billy Brown !

John Bolton ! John Bolton ! you needs must give away,
And the lower you'll fall now the longer you stay,
'Tis vain to look black, and austerely to frown,
You must haul down your colours, and strike to the great—
    Brown, Brown, Billy Brown !

'Tis, by no means enough that his fortune is made,
Or to stand at the top of th' American trade !—
He must, now, with his dust, like a *Gentleman*, down,
And, in turn of Committees the *Chairman* must be,—Billy Brown !
    Brown, Brown, Billy Brown !

But glories like these only appetite give,
And we grow the more hungry, the longer we live ;
So, as Commons, so common, no more will go down,
Why ! a dish from the Lords must be served up to please—Billy Brown !
    Brown, Brown, Billy Brown !

But, where shall I find a Gamekeeper, or Cook,
To catch me a Marquis, or pluck me a Duke ?
Never mind !—a step's gained, if a step towards the Crown !
We must not be too nice, to begin with, exclaims Billy Brown !
    Brown, Brown, Billy Brown !

Thro' a Portland-Stone entrance, the thing may be done,—
For a Lord's Daughter's Husband must be a Lord's Son !
So, I'll send for young Denison forthwith from town,
And I'll make him the Packet-Line Candidate of,—Billy Brown !
    Brown, Brown, Billy Brown !

I'm aware it will cost me no share of Pelf,—
But then I shall have an M. P. to myself—
Who, high *shittiations* would give in town,
M. P. like himself—the Duke's Friend—and then *Sir* William Brown !
    Brown, Brown, Billy Brown !

Joseph Scoville's amiable sketch of Samuel Nicholson in *The Old Merchants of New York City* ends by saying "Mr. Nicholson conscientiously believed that there never had existed so great and so glorious a commercial house as that of Brown Brothers & Co. He was right." And then, in support of this contention, Scoville tells (somewhat inaccurately) how the Bank of England sustained William & James Brown & Co. during the panic of 1837 to avert "a national calamity."

That story takes us to Liverpool, where by 1830 the "Billy Brown" who is lampooned in the political campaign song at left had indeed become a person to reckon with, whether or not he thought it "by no means enough . . . to stand at the top of th' American trade" which Liverpool dominated. It is a sign of his prominence that even though he was not a candidate in the 1830 election many of the campaign squibs and songs attack the candidate he supported (free trade advocate John Denison, son-in-law of the Duke of Portland) by attacking or ridiculing the "Yankee dandy O" with legs "so very awkward and so bandy O," the "Nabob" who—as one disgruntled partisan asserted—"to serve his own purpose and that of America, always gives a preference to Yankee shipping over British vessels."

From p. 49 of *Bethell's Liverpool Squib Book . . . a . . . Collection of the Addresses, Songs, Squibs, and other papers, Issued during the Contested Election, November, 1830,* Liverpool, 1830. (*Courtesy of the Brown, Picton and Hornby Libraries, Liverpool*)

In this 1847 lithograph of Liverpool's merchants, meeting on the Exchange flags, William Brown is the wizened Dickensian figure depicted at full length about an inch in from the right margin in the middle foreground, engaged in conversation with two well-fed colleagues. The lithograph was made from a drawing by Richard Dighton. (*Courtesy of the Brown, Picton and Hornby Libraries, Liverpool*)

William Brown's residence, from 1832 until his death in 1864, was the house known as Richmond Hill, shown here in an 1880 watercolor by E. Beattie. (*Courtesy of the Brown, Picton and Hornby Libraries, Liverpool*)

William Brown was one of the original subscribers to the stock of the Bank of Liverpool—oldest and most powerful of the joint stock banks later consolidated to form the present-day Martins Bank Ltd. Brown was the first chairman of the bank's board of directors, serving from 1831–35. (*Courtesy of Martins Bank Ltd., Liverpool*)

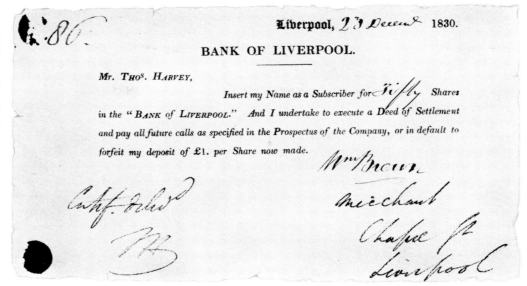

Liverpool, 23 Decem. 1830.

BANK OF LIVERPOOL.

Mr. THOS. HARVEY,

Insert my Name as a Subscriber for *Fifty* Shares in the "BANK of LIVERPOOL." And I undertake to execute a Deed of Settlement and pay all future calls as specified in the Prospectus of the Company, or in default to forfeit my deposit of £1. per Share now made.

Wm Brown
merchant
Chapel St
Liverpool

Brown was also one of the first trustees of the Liverpool Fire and Life Insurance Co. (oldest unit in the present Royal-Globe Insurance Companies, Ltd.) whose advertisement in Gore's 1837 *Directory of Liverpool* is reproduced below, and his firm gave the company its first business. In 1851 the company (then Liverpool and London Fire and Life) opened a New York branch, and William's brother James Brown was elected chairman of the New York board of directors. James Adger of Charleston (see p. 49) was appointed the company's first United States agent. (*Brown Brothers Harriman & Co. Historical File*)

Not that William & James Brown & Co. in 1830 ranked with Rothschild and Baring who, as Lord Byron said in a famous passage in *Don Juan,* held "the balance of the World." Back in 1818 (the year John A. Brown established the Philadelphia house) the Duc de Richelieu, France's chief minister, had named the six great powers in Europe as "Great Britain, France, Russia, Austria, Prussia, and Baring Brothers"—the banking house Francis Baring had established in London in 1763. But even then, the London house that Nathan Rothschild had founded in 1805 and which had financed Napoleon's defeat in 1815 was rapidly moving to supersede the Barings as banker to the nations of the Continent. In the American trade, however, where the Rothschilds did not actively compete until 1835, William & James Brown & Co. was the Barings' chief rival.[1] The Liverpool firm of Cropper Benson & Co., writing to an Edinburgh correspondent, in November 1832, described Brown's firm as "perhaps the most extensive in this country, entirely a commission House, & chiefly in the American Trade," all of whose departments were staffed by "experienced young men, in whose Knowledge & ability and steadiness the House can place perfect reliance."

[1] In 1832 the Barings opened a branch house in Liverpool to compete directly with the Brown firm—"this family of houses" which, as they had observed in a June 1831 letter, "commands an immense business in the U.S." See Ralph W. Hidy, *The House of Baring in American Trade and Finance,* Cambridge, Mass., 1949, pp. 94 and 106.

JOSEPH SHIPLEY (1795–1867), from an undated and unsigned miniature painting probably done in Liverpool shortly before 1826, when Shipley became a junior partner in William & James Brown & Co. Ten years after joining the firm, Shipley was made a full partner in all the Brown firms, and on June 1, 1839, in recognition of his services in the panic of 1837 and the subsequent depression, the name of the Liverpool house was changed to "Brown, Shipley & Co." (*Collection of Mrs. Gordon S. Hargraves, "Rockwood," Wilmington, Del. Courtesy of Mr. Gordon S. Hargraves*)

One of the young men on whose ability and steadiness William Brown had the best reason to rely was Joseph Shipley, Jr., a sensitive and highly intelligent Quaker merchant from Wilmington, Delaware. Shipley had come to Liverpool in 1819 as agent for the Philadelphia firm of John Welsh & Co., and had rapidly become known as an efficient, honorable, and enterprising businessman. So in 1826, when William Brown's delicate health made it essential for him to have a partner who could be trusted to run the business, he selected Shipley.

A letter written to a Philadelphia cousin in November 1834 tells a lot about the kind of man Shipley was. The cousin apparently thought Shipley would make at least $100,000 in a few years. "Such sums & larger ones," Shipley wrote,

are made in a short time by fortunate speculations—where there is the risk of losing as much—or they are made by large capitalists without much risk—but in a *Commission business* such as I am engaged in—which I did not build up but only help to conduct with the aid

"Wyncote," Joseph Shipley's house outside Liverpool, from a watercolor by John McGahey dated August 1840. In 1846, Shipley asked Stewart Brown in New York to send "some of our American *Forest Trees*" to plant on his grounds. The house, which still stands on Liverpool University's sports grounds, was the model for one named "Rockwood" which Shipley later built in Brandywine Hundred, near Wilmington, Delaware, where he lived after retirement and where his collateral descendants still reside. (*Collection of Mrs. Gordon S. Hargraves, "Rockwood," Wilmington, Del. Photograph courtesy of the Henry Francis du Pont Winterthur Museum*)

of my partner's large capital—& running little or no risk of losses—I must be content with small gains. I am quite satisfied to make money moderately in consideration of making it with certainty. . . .

That he made money in comfortable quantities is evidenced by the charming house (above) in which he lived outside Liverpool from about 1840 until he retired from business in 1850 and returned to Wilmington. But even his moderate gains involved graver risks than he foresaw in 1834. In a letter to the same cousin, written May 14, 1837, Shipley tells of "a great and unfortunate change . . . in my affairs and prospects" arising from the panic of 1837, at its height in England and the United States, and Shipley felt that with the failure of so many firms in America and England, it was "not to be supposed that a concern so extensively engaged in this trade as ours can escape great losses." Furthermore, his own increased share in the firm, recently given him by the Browns in recognition of the fact that he now virtually ran the Liverpool house, meant that his share of its losses would be correspondingly increased.

I have past [sic] through two months of unremitting toil, excitement and intense anxiety, but it has been greatly alleviated by the Consciousness that no exclusive blame can rest on me for any one loss or Combination of losses the House may sustain, notwithstanding that so much of the management of the business has devolved on me. —I do not mean to say that blame can be ascribed to any member of the House on either side of the Waters—far from it, but the older partners have been more sanguine, most of them, and greater advocates for an extension of business than I have been. . . . We do not suffer from any Speculation of our own, as we enter into none; we are suffering from the imprudence & misfortunes of others to whom we have given credit, and from protested Bills of Exchange . . . perhaps ten years of similar business uninterrupted by any disaster or check led us to extend our transactions too widely.

WILLIAM EZRA BOWEN (1797–1861), from a portrait painted by S. B. Waugh in 1844. The portrait was painted for the Mercantile Library of Philadelphia, of which Bowen was a founder, and is now in the possession of Bowen's great-great-granddaughters, Caroline Bowen Heyl and Helen Elizabeth Heyl. Bowen, the son of a sea captain who commanded ships owned by the great Philadelphia merchant Stephen Girard, was a successful auctioneer in Philadelphia when, in 1831, he was sent to Manchester, England, as the Browns' special representative. He became a partner in the Liverpool house in 1837, and in 1838 returned to Philadelphia as resident partner after John A. Brown retired from the firm. From 1839 to 1859 (when Bowen retired) the Philadelphia house was known as Browns & Bowen.

(Photograph courtesy of the Historical Society of Pennsylvania)

If the Browns were overextended, it was not surprising. As the London *Banker's Circular* pointed out early in April, "the exchange and loan and credit operations" dominated by the Browns, Barings, and "the three W's" (T. Wilson & Co., George Wildes & Co., and T. Wiggin & Co., all of London) was a "new branch of Traffic"—at least, "new in its extent and ramifications"—and considering how "singularly safe and extremely profitable" the business had been for ten years past, it was astonishing "not that the credit in circulation is so large—but that it should not . . . have amounted to double its present sum."

Many of the firms to whom William & James Brown & Co. had extended credit were manufacturers in Manchester where William Ezra Bowen, a Philadelphia Quaker, had for the past six years had charge of the dry-goods business done by the Browns' American houses. Just before the panic he had become a junior partner in the Liverpool house, and his firsthand knowledge of Manchester's banks and businessmen proved very useful during the months when William Brown and Shipley were struggling to save the firm from failure.

Late in May Shipley went to London to confer with Denison & Co. (properly, Denison Heywood Kennard & Co.), the London agents of Brown's Liverpool banker, John P. Heywood of Arthur Heywood Sons & Co. With him he took a statement of the firm's assets and liabilities (reproduced opposite) in hopes that by pledging securities with Denison he could arrange for the house to be carried by its private bankers until the packets brought sufficient remittances from the American houses.

Assets 27 May 1837 —   Statement A.

£123300 U States Bank Bonds at 94½   £ 116.516

Frs 1100.000 dr.   on Paris   88.000
G. 100.000   "   "   Amsterdam

300 U States Bank Shares   at £24   12.000
Specie at St James   4.537 —
Cotton Sold not paid for   20.000
d.   on hand to be Sold immediately   40.000
Securities pledged to Mess Denison & Co p Statement   230.900
14500 Bales of Cotton advised of as coming and
     insured to be expected in a fortnight   90.000
Our Houses advise that they expect to remit us in
     all May to be received for June payments   200.000
To be reasonably expected from others p Statement   170.000
                                                      £ 971.953

Protested Bills or bills running on Insolvent
     Houses not remitted to Denisons   200.000
                              Total £ 1.171.953

Balance favour Denison & Co including
     June acceptances   } 901.000
Bills running on Insolvent Houses
     not paid to Denison & Co }   31.000   932.000
                              Surplus £ 239.953

The above is taking £377000 protested Bills
     at their full amount but assuming them to
     be worth 10/ in the £ deduct   188.000
                              June Surplus £ 51.953

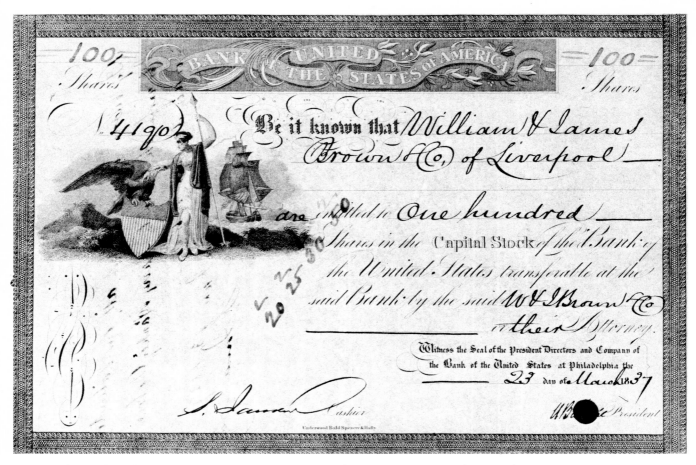

The hundred shares of stock represented by this certificate were a part of the 500 shares listed as the third item in Joseph Shipley's statement of William & James Brown & Co.'s assets (p. 59). This Bank of the United States was the one organized by Nicholas Biddle in 1836, under a Pennsylvania charter, to take over the business of the second congressionally chartered Bank of the United States—the "monster" that Andrew Jackson had destroyed. Endorsements on the back of the certificate indicate that these 100 shares were transferred June 13, 1837 "to Harry Hankey Dobree of London Merchant in trust"—no doubt as security for a guarantee to William & James Brown & Co. (*Original in Brown Brothers Harriman & Co. Historical File*)

But on the 29th of May the packet *Roscoe* arrived in Liverpool with "advises" that made it clear that only the Bank of England itself could save the firm. William Brown at once addressed a letter to Shipley at the London Coffee House, Ludgate Hill: "Nothing can be worse than the news. It is quite certain we cannot sustain ourselves." The only consolation he had was that "for thirty-seven years that I have been in business no one of us was ever accused of a dishonorable act, and that neither our banking or immediate friends are likely to suffer by us."

But that, after all, was cold comfort, for—as he said in another letter—about two-thirds of all William & James Brown & Co.'s engagements arose out of the export of British manufactures, and—as the London *Chronicle* later observed—merchants in Manchester, Sheffield, Birmingham, Leeds, and all the great manufacturing towns, "and, as a matter of course, every man and woman employed, were more or less involved in the fate of this establishment."

On June 1, Shipley submitted a long letter "to the Governor and Bank of England" saying that the news received by the *Roscoe* indicated that remittances from the United States would be "delayed and cut off to such an extent as to forbid the hope of our being sustained unless through your assistance." The letter, accompanied by the statements of the firm's assets, liabilities, and expectations which Shipley had brought with him from Liverpool, frankly appealed for help on the grounds of the "disastrous consequences" that would follow the firm's stoppage, "which we painfully apprehend would be more felt than that of any other house in England."

There were anxious hours of waiting while the fate of the firm was decided—as, Joshua Bates of Barings said, all the Bank's policies were—by "a few individuals in the Bank parlour as little remarkable for their wisdom as for their liberality."[2] But on June 2, Shipley was able to write that "when the board adjourned last night" they authorized the Governor to make advances which would meet the

[2] Quoted in Bray Hammond, *Banks and Politics in America*, Princeton, 1957, p. 458.

Liverpool house's obligations for at least a week, and that both the Governor and Deputy Governor had "expressed an earnest wish to see us carried through."

Bowen reported to Shipley, in a letter from Manchester on June 5, that William Brown was "much agitated" by Shipley's report that there was a probability the firm could carry on. "He had so fully made up his mind, that he had written a circular which I have copied ready to put on the [lithographic] stone announcing our stoppage." Bowen was convinced that, so far as William Brown's own interests were concerned, "he would have been quite as well satisfied to stop, but if by any means injury to others is to be prevented, he will do everything to lessen the evil."

Not until June 15 was Shipley finally able to report from London that *"all is right* with us here, the Bank of Eng'd having undertaken to carry us through the year." And later that day: "It must be a gratifying thing to you and to your brothers that this passed the Board unanimously."

One of the most touching mementos preserved among Joseph Shipley's papers is the brief note at right. On June 1st (a Thursday), after submitting his letter to "the Governor and Bank of England" applying for assistance, Shipley sat down to write William Brown. "Of course, unless the Bank takes us up, nothing can be done, and this, I suppose, will be decided in the course of a few hours." He had gone to the Bank with Mr. Kennard, but "Before we got to the Bank the Governor and Deputy Governor had left, but would be back at one o'clock, but it is now four o'clock and they have not returned." Later, he added, "It is now half past six o'clock and we have no reply from the Bank, the Board being still in deliberation." One can imagine, under the circumstances, how he must have felt when finally this note was handed to him.

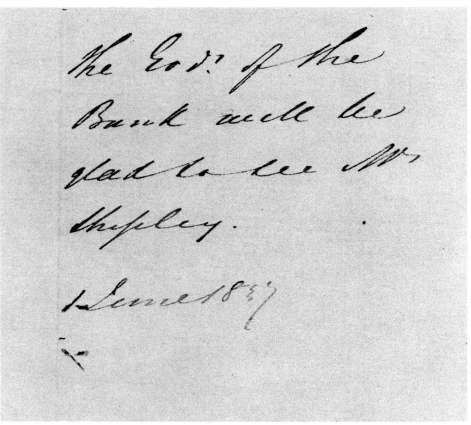

(*Original in Brown Brothers Harriman & Co. Historical File*)

From other correspondence in the Historical File, we learn that Shipley's part in saving the house was warmly acknowledged by his partners and associates, and that arrangements were made to avert the losses he had feared his recently increased interest in the house would entail. Heywood and Kennard of Denison & Co. stanchly supported him throughout. While Shipley was waiting for the Bank's final decision, Kennard wrote him that from his conversations "with the Govr" he was convinced the Bank would carry the Brown firm through on any security "that would justify them to their proprietors & the Public—in case of the worst." And he concluded the letter: "The anxiety & suspense is almost too much for *me* . . . —what must it be to *you*. May God support & direct you sincerely prays yours truly, J. Kennard."

In his own less emotional way, William Brown also gave Shipley full support. On the day the Bank finally announced its decision, but of course before he knew of it, Brown wrote, "Whatever you may have done in London will be satisfactory to me as done for the best." And the following day he wrote that Shipley's *"all is right* with us" letter, just received by "Post Chaise" express, was "particularly gratifying," adding:

I do not know how to express what I feel at the way in which Denison, Kennard & Heywood have acted.

To the Governor, Deputy Governor, Mr. Palmer and the directors of the Bank, I feel as I ought, not only for the aid they have given which I think they will never regret, but from the manner in which you represent to me you were received by them. Mr. Peabody has been a sincere friend.[3]

Brown then went on for several paragraphs about various protested bills and other business matters, but near the close of the letter added, in his curiously compressed and negative way: "It is not among the least of my gratifications Mr. Peabody reporting you in good spirits."

Most welcome of all may have been the letter Shipley received from James Brown, dated New York, September 6, 1837, announcing that arrangements whereby the senior partners relieved him of the losses he had feared were "entirely satisfactory" to John A. Brown and himself, since

We all feel here your great exertions & perseverance saved the house. Your other Juniors no doubt did all in their power and were not less zealous, but I think at one time W^m had given up in despair. . . . We have all had a most anxious and perplexing season. No wealth would compensate. We must now move with more caution and more safety.

Yours truly
JAMES BROWN

[3] George Peabody, the American dry-goods merchant who was soon to become one of England's most powerful bankers and who had just settled permanently in London, was staying at Richmond Hill at the time Brown was writing. He had been extremely helpful in getting signatures on the list of guarantees the Bank required as security for its advances.

Early nineteenth century typographical ornament reproduced in C. P. Hornung, *Handbook of Early Advertising Art,* New York, 1956.

Six

SHIPS AND STEAMBOATS

From Philadelphia *American Daily Advertiser,*
October 10, 1818.

As the next to last stanza of the campaign song on p. 53 suggests, William Brown and his partners were deeply interested in the packet business. While James Brown was managing the Philadelphia house in 1822 he was involved with Thomas P. Cope & Sons in establishing the first line of Philadelphia-Liverpool packets—the so-called Cope Line—of which William & James Brown & Co. were the Liverpool agents; and later in New York he arranged to have William & James Brown & Co. become the Liverpool agents of the Swallowtail Line.[1] In Joseph Shipley's surviving correspondence there are many letters from George Trimble, one of the founders of the Red Star line of packets, who regarded Shipley as "the best man in the trade (not now in the Lines)."

Baltimore had had hopes of establishing its own line to Liverpool before the Cope Line was announced, but—as Carl Cutler says—the announcement of the Cope Line put an end to Baltimore's hopes. The mere establishment of a Philadelphia line probably would not have deterred Baltimore's merchants, Cutler says. "What really mattered was the fact that Alexander Brown & Sons . . . had thrown their weight to the Cope line. They owned the *Alexander,* the largest of the new ships under

[1] See Carl C. Cutler, *Queens of the Western Ocean,* Annapolis, [1961], pp. 153–54 and 162–63.

construction for the line, and it was understood that they would act as the Baltimore agents for the concern."

The Browns had long operated three or more of their own vessels as "spring and fall ships" in the Baltimore-Liverpool trade, and Baltimore's merchants had counted on them to start regular service. A letter of Alexander Brown & Sons to William & James Brown & Co., dated April 12, 1822, reports that Baltimore's dry-goods merchants are very anxious "about having a line of packets . . . , alleging their goods arriving so late is in part the cause why New York and Philadelphia are carrying away all the trade." But it was "out of the question" to run regular packets as there was "nothing to be had here that suits to go to Liverpool" on regular voyages. The best the Browns could do was agree to make their spring and fall ships "be punctual to a day in their departure from Liverpool" in return for the merchants' promise "to order their goods earlier." The letter concludes: "We must be prepared to fill up with salt and crates and be prompt in sailing as agreed on." As to the arrangement with the Philadelphia line, a letter of May 2 assures the Liverpool house that "The overture came from Copes with the understanding they were ready to run the line to you, or we should never have given it consideration."

(Original in Maryland Historical Society. Photograph courtesy of Alexander Crosby Brown)

The Browns' ship *Alexander,* 461 tons, was built for service as a Philadelphia-Liverpool packet in the Cope Line. She is shown here in a detail from a large lithographic poster entitled "Duplicate Signals at the Marine Telegraph for 1852." The drawing of the *Alexander* occupied the position of honor at the top center of the poster, between the words "at" and "the" in the title. The red- and white-striped flag at her foremast, with the white letter *B* on the lower red stripe, was the Browns' house flag. The *Alexander*'s first master was Capt. Stephen Baldwin, a former master of the *Tobacco Plant,* another Brown ship. One of the earliest entries in Brown Brothers & Co.'s first day book records the payment of an insurance premium on the *Alexander,* and as late as December 31, 1842 James Brown still had a ⅙ interest in the ship, then in Baltimore, "ready to sail to Charleston."

Reproduced opposite is a page from John A. Brown & Co.'s consignment ledger listing the cases of linens and bales of kerseys, linseys, and paddings shipped on the *Alexander* from Liverpool on August 17, 1826, and (as the slanted notation at bottom right indicates) entered at the Philadelphia custom house September 16, 1826. *(Original in Historical File at Brown Brothers Harriman & Co., Philadelphia)*

Ship Alexander Baldwin Liverpool 17 August 1826.

				257. 337.7.
₤P	51	1	Case Linens	£ 44..4..8
	52	1	" "	45..5..11
	53	1	" "	45..8..2
	54	1	" "	39..11..1
	55	1	" "	40..16..7
	56	1	" "	45..8..6
	57	1	" "	43..16..2
	58	1	" "	36..17..11
	59	1	" "	37..3..1
	60	1	" "	45..0..3
	61	1	" "	36..14..0
	62	1	" "	33..15..7
	63	1	" "	33..17..3
	64	1	" "	42..13..10

8 mos $303.33 due 17 July 1827
10 " 303 " " 17 June 1827
12 " " 303 " " 17 Augt 1827
$ 909.33.

Reanstitution $616.50 @ 257 $616.50
B " 766 " " 7 191.50
" " 304 @ 337.7 101.33
$ 909.33.

Deduct Bounty — £ 570..13..0
72..16..3

Charges — £ 497..16..9
17..1..1

£ 504..17..10
50..9..9

10% — £ 555..7..7

Dolls 2466 @ 257 — $616.50

B	56	1	Bale Kerseys	£ 31..19..6	62..3..0
	57	1	" Linseys		
	58	1	" Kerseys	36..10..3	
	59	1	" Do	41..18..0	
	60	1	" Paddings	40..0..0	

Dolls 766 @ 257 — $191.50
304 @ 337.7 — 101.33
$292.83

Charges — £ 150..7..9 62..3..0
6..8..11
£ 156..16..8 15..13..8 6..4..4
10% —
£ 172..10..4 68..7..4

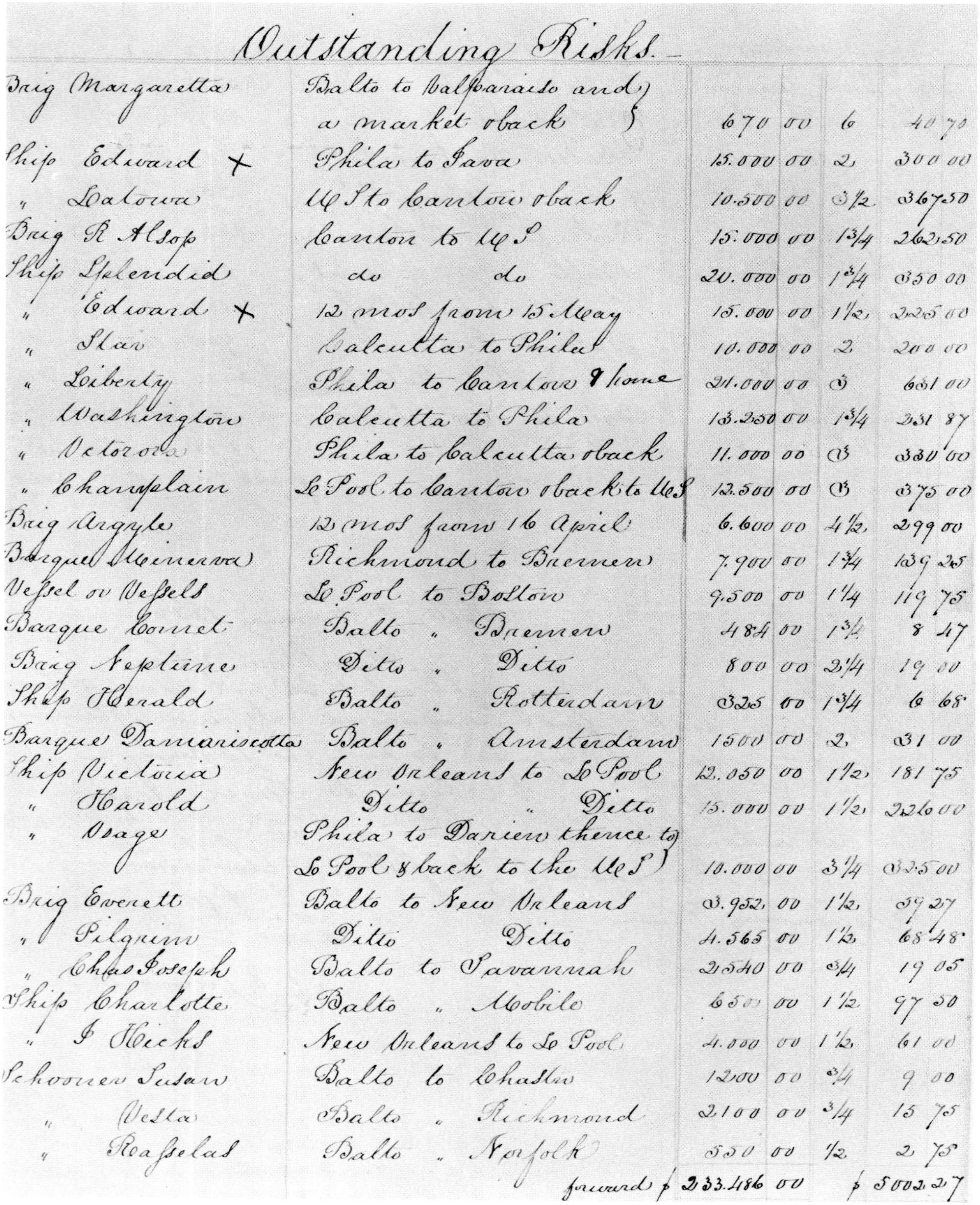

Outstanding Risks.

Vessel	Route	Value	Rate	Premium
Brig Margaretta	Balto to Valparaiso and a market & back	670 00	6	40 70
Ship Edward ✕	Phila to Java	15,000 00	2	300 00
" Latona	U S to Canton & back	10,500 00	3½	367 50
Brig R Alsop	Canton to U S	15,000 00	1¾	262 50
Ship Splendid	do do	20,000 00	1¾	350 00
" Edward ✕	12 mos from 15 May	15,000 00	1½	225 00
" Star	Calcutta to Phila	10,000 00	2	200 00
" Liberty	Phila to Canton & home	21,000 00	3	631 00
" Washington	Calcutta to Phila	13,250 00	1¾	231 87
" Octorara	Phila to Calcutta & back	11,000 00	3	330 00
" Champlain	L Pool to Canton & back to U S	12,500 00	3	375 00
Brig Argyle	12 mos from 16 April	6,600 00	4½	299 00
Barque Minerva	Richmond to Bremen	7,900 00	1¾	139 25
Vessel or Vessels	L Pool to Boston	9,500 00	1¼	119 75
Barque Comet	Balto " Bremen	484 00	1¾	8 47
Brig Neptune	Ditto " Ditto	800 00	2¼	19 00
Ship Herald	Balto " Rotterdam	325 00	1¾	6 68
Barque Damariscotta	Balto " Amsterdam	1500 00	2	31 00
Ship Victoria	New Orleans to L Pool	12,050 00	1½	181 75
" Harold	Ditto " Ditto	15,000 00	1½	225 00
" Osage	Phila to Darien thence to L Pool & back to the U S	10,000 00	3¼	325 00
Brig Everett	Balto to New Orleans	3,952 00	1½	59 27
" Pilgrim	Ditto Ditto	4,565 00	1½	68 48
" Chas Joseph	Balto to Savannah	2540 00	¾	19 05
Ship Charlotte	Balto " Mobile	650 00	1½	97 50
" I Hicks	New Orleans to L Pool	4,000 00	1½	61 00
Schooner Susan	Balto to Chaston	1200 00	¾	9 00
" Vesta	Balto " Richmond	2100 00	¾	15 75
" Rasselas	Balto " Norfolk	550 00	½	2 75
	forward $	233,486 00		$ 5003 27

A two-page record of "Outstanding Risks," signed by "Alex^r Brown & Sons," Baltimore, January 7, 1836, lists the ships in which the Browns were interested at that time, the ports from and to which they were sailing, the value of the Browns' interest in the vessels, their share of the total value, and the insurance premiums: "Balto to Valparaiso and a market & back," "Phila to Canton & home," "New Orleans to L Pool," "L Pool to Boston," "Phila to Darien thence to L Pool & back to the U S"—these and a number of coastal voyages indicate the scope of the firm's shipping interests. A note at the foot of p. 2, signed by John A. Brown & Co., indicates that the ship *Edward* (marked with an *X* where it appears twice on p. 1) "ought only to be put down once it is the same risk—first being insured out, and afterwards taken the round voyage." (*Brown Brothers Harriman & Co. Historical File*)

Chapel S.
27. April 1843.

Gent.

We are requested by the Master of the American Ship "Rose" to inform you that Your Ship "Duke of Lancaster" came in Contact with the "Rose" last evening in the River, when the latter Vessel was riding at her Anchors, and has Caused her Serious damage — and we have hereby to Notify you that the Master of the Rose holds you responsible for the Said damage. —

We are Gent.

Respectfully Yours

Brown Shipley & Co.

Mess.° John Gladstone & Co.
Union Court.

The risks were great—even after vessels safely reached port, as witness this letter of April 27, 1843, addressed by Brown Shipley & Co. to John Gladstone & Co., of Liverpool, informing them that the Browns' ship *Rose,* while riding at anchor in the river Mersey, had been run into and damaged by Gladstone's *Duke of York.* John Gladstone, incidentally, was the father of W. E. Gladstone who became Prime Minister of England.

Ships like the *Victoria, Harold,* and *I* [*saac*] *Hicks* (see p. 66), when going to New Orleans for cotton to be carried to Liverpool, had to be towed across the bar at the mouth of the Mississippi, then through one of the passes in the delta, and up the river a hundred miles to the city's wharves. The painting reproduced here, showing the steam tugboat *Panther* towing the cotton ships *Sea King, Themis,* and *Columbia,* across the bar, was painted about 1850 by J. G. Evans and Edward Arnold. (*Courtesy of the Louisiana State Museum, New Orleans*)

The *Alexander* was only one of many sailing ships owned by the Browns. The first, the *Armata,* was built in New York in 1811–1812, "a square stern'd ship with a billet head," as William Brown described her in a letter of April 2, 1812, of 413 tons, about 108 feet long, with two decks and three masts. Another, the *William Brown* (built in 1824), became famous in 1827 when she crossed from New Orleans to Liverpool in 26 days—the fastest crossing up to that time.

As for steamboats, the firm's earliest interest seems to have been in one of those Western river boats which contributed to Baltimore's decline as a port (see p. 28). Soon after Brown Brothers was established in New York, they were asked by Reynolds Byrne & Co., New Orleans cotton merchants, to act as agents in connection with the building of a Mississippi steamboat of which they were to be part-owners along with Wilkins & Linton, another cotton firm, and Captain H. Reed, who was to superintend construction. On May 19, 1826, Brown Brothers wrote Reynolds Byrne & Co. that "Captn. Reed has made up his mind to build the Steam Boat here Live oak is so plenty he can build a boat of it nearly as low as with Common Oak elsewhere. It will give us pleasure to give him any advice or assistance in our power." On June 7, they wrote that they would furnish Capt. Reed "the means as wanted for the payments a portion of which is to be paid when the frame is up which will be the case in 2 or 3 weeks." Apparently the frame was up by June 23, for on that day they informed Reynolds Byrne that they had paid Capt. Reed $722.22, "being your 1st payment on a/ct of the Steam Boat building under his superintendence."

By November 14 Captain Reed was "getting the masts in"—temporary masts to carry sails for the long voyage to New Orleans—and hoped to be ready to sail by the 18th, but not until December 1 did she finally get off, arriving at New Orleans on Christmas Day.

Brown Brothers' November 25 letter, enclosing Reynolds Byrne's "account current," with a statement of what was still owed on the *Walk-in-the-Water*, contained the following:

The Boat you will perceive costs something more than Captn. Reed calculated on which is generally the case but we think you will find her the best Boat on the Waters of the Mississippi & it will give us much pleasure if she proves a very profitable one. Captn. Reed has effected the Insurance in two of our best Offices & left the policy with us, we hope however there will be no occasion for having recourse to them.

There was no occasion so long as Reynolds Byrne operated the boat on the Natchez run, but in May 1828 they auctioned her—the advertisements describing her as "the most beautiful specimen of naval architecture ever seen on the Mississippi." On December 8, 1835, she burned at Natchez Landing with about 1400 bales of cotton on board. The New Orleans *Bee* of December 11 reported with horrifying calm: "The boat is an entire loss. One negro was burnt to death; he was chained at the time the fire originated."

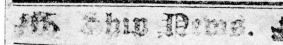

PORT OF NEW-ORLEANS.

Cleared to-day.

Ship Hibernia, Robinson, Baltimore,
J W Zacharie.
Brig Castillo, Frink Havana, G E Russell.
Ship R ma , Dickenson, Havre, T Nicolet & co.
Brig Ursula, Lincoln, Havana,
Lincoln & Green.
Schr Florida, Kilogg, Charleston, J P Payson.
Brig Nun, Davis, New-York, John P. Payson.
Schr. Actor Johnson, New York,
Lincoln & Green.

Arrived this morning.

Steamboat Walk-in-the-water. Reed, Natchez —cargo 417 bales cotton to Wilkins & Linton; 300 to Gilbert, Martineau & co; 150 to A Fisk & co; 86 to Reynolds, Byrne & co; 92 to L Millaudon; 7 to owner on board, total 1052 bales— 9 passengers.

Entered this morning.

Brig Dido, Gorham, from Boston—cargo, 302 empty h ds 44 tons paving stones, 1 bx mdz to R D Shepherd & co.

Arrived yesterday.

Steamboat Packet, Jewell, from Bayou Sarah.

The first steamboat with which the Browns were directly concerned was the *Walk-in-the-Water*, a Mississippi river-boat (not to be confused with the first Great Lakes steamer of the same name). She was built in New York in 1826 for Reynolds Byrne & Co. and Wilkins & Linton, New Orleans, two of the cotton merchants mentioned in the "Ship News" item reproduced above from the *Louisiana Courier* of January 30, 1827, recording what was probably her first return trip from Natchez. Brown Brothers & Co. handled the arrangements for her construction. (*Photograph and newspaper research courtesy of Leonard V. Huber and Miss Mary A. Waits of New Orleans*)

This portrait of GEORGE BROWN, lithographed by E Sachser & Co. from a daguerreotype by Pollock, was published in *A History and Description of the Baltimore and Ohio Rail Road,* by a Citizen of Baltimore, Baltimore, 1853—a volume which was "respectfully dedicated to George Brown, One of the Originators" of the road and to four surviving members of the committee which applied for the original charter. (*Courtesy of the New York Society Library*)

George Brown, of the Baltimore house, saw to the building of the first steamboat owned and operated by the Browns. This was the 791 ton *Natchez,* built at Baltimore the year after the panic of 1837. Her first registry, dated July 3, 1838, shows George Brown as sole owner, but by September 24, when she went into service with the New York-Natchez Steam Packet Co., organized by James Brown as another link in the "cotton triangle," James was part-owner as well as manager of the line, with John Laidlaw & Co. acting as New York agents. The captain of the *Natchez* was William B. Story, no doubt a relative of Benjamin Story, that "most excellent safe and prudent man" (as George Brown called him in a March 1838 letter to James) who was the Browns' New Orleans correspondent.

Carl Cutler records that although the Steam Packet project appeared to be logical and promising, the *Natchez* encountered a series of delays and accidents in the Mississippi, once going aground and "remaining hard and fast on a mud bank for several weeks," which, with the inevitable costly repairs "soon disillusioned the stockholders."[2] Perhaps George Brown was disillusioned, for by November 21, 1842, when the *Natchez* was sunk in a collision, he had got rid of his interest. But James Brown was still operating her, he and John R. Stanhope of Newport, R.I., being the registered owners. James, as we shall see, was not easily dis-

[2] *Queens of the Western Ocean,* pp. 226–27.

This Baltimore street scene, from a hitherto unpublished daguerreotype taken about 1840 by Henry Fitz, Jr., shows the city as it looked when George Brown resigned at the end of 1839 from the partnership then dominated by William Brown in Liverpool and James Brown in New York. Fitz, formerly a locksmith in Cincinnati, had become a well-known maker of telescopes and lenses before going to Europe in 1839 to study Daguerre's new method of making "sun pictures." In 1840 he set up a daguerreotype studio in Baltimore. The original plate of this street scene is badly scratched and scarred, as is evident in this photograph, made for this book by the Smithsonian Institution's photographic laboratory. (*Courtesy of S. Dillon Ripley and the Smithsonian Institution*)

This ornamental title page is all that seems to have survived of a portfolio lithographed and published by Endicott & Swett in Baltimore in 1831. The locomotive shown with its tender is the *Tom Thumb*—the railroad's first, and the first ever built in the United States. It was built by Peter Cooper of New York, who had invested in Baltimore land and was anxious for the success of the railroad which Alexander and George Brown and their associates hoped would revive the city's western trade. First operated in the fall of 1829, on a stretch of track in Baltimore's suburbs, the *Tom Thumb* was not a success until the spring of 1830, when Cooper finally persuaded the road's directors that steam engines would prove more useful than the horses they had from the beginning intended to use.

(Photograph courtesy of the Harry Shaw Newman Gallery, New York)

couraged by the difficulties of steam navigation.

George Brown had had better luck with steam transportation by land. He and his father had actively promoted the first important American railroad—the Baltimore & Ohio. On February 12, 1827, twenty-five of Baltimore's leading citizens met at George Brown's house to consider "the best means" of recovering "that portion of the western trade that has lately been diverted . . . by the introduction of steam navigation." There were at that time only two railroads in the world, both in England, but the bold decision of the meeting was to build a railroad to the Ohio River, over the Allegheny Mountains. George Brown was treasurer of the company formed to carry out the project, and he and his father both took an active part in staffing and managing the road in its early years. Yet, on July 12, 1834, after Alexander Brown's death, George resigned from his job as treasurer of the road (as also from the presidency of the Mechanics Bank), and wrote rather discouragingly to William, who had invested in the Liverpool & Manchester and the London & Birmingham railroads, among others: "I observe you still take a good deal of interest in Railroads. It is to be hoped they will pay better with you than here."

This enlarged detail of the engraving reproduced opposite shows, at left, part of the banking house on the southeast corner of Wall and Hanover Streets which James Brown bought for Brown Brothers & Co. in 1843, thus establishing the firm on the corner it still occupies one hundred and twenty-five years later. At the time of the purchase the building was numbered 47 and 49 Wall Street, but when the street was renumbered in 1845 it became 59 and 61.

By the terms of the contract (preserved in Brown Brothers Harriman & Co. Historical File), James Brown paid one Maurice Power $130,000 for the property and building. $73,000 of this was "satisfied" by his assuming a mortgage on the premises made by Power to George D. Post in 1841, and $5,000 more by James Brown's giving Power a deed for a brick dwelling house on 7th Street, east of First Avenue.

Seven

"A ROGUE, A BAREFACED ROGUE"

By 1840 both John A. Brown and George Brown were out of the firm, having sold their shares to William and James in 1837 and 1839, respectively, and James Brown in New York was at the head of American operations. In 1843 he moved Brown Brothers & Co. into the banking house he had just bought on the southeast corner of Wall and Hanover Streets, across Hanover from the Merchants Exchange.

The building had an interesting history. Deeds preserved in the firm's Historical File show that in 1836—after the 1835 fire destroyed the dwelling house on the site then owned by Joel Post, a well-to-do druggist—the property was bought by Thomas E. Davis, a real estate speculator of the period whose New Brighton Association (which owned most of the northern part of Staten Island) was to go down in the crash of 1837. Davis in turn sold the property to J. L. & S. Joseph & Co., New York agents of the Rothschilds, who in the fall of 1836

began erecting what was to be the finest private banking house in the city.

Brown Brothers at that time was across Wall Street at No. 46 (later 58), and James and Stewart Brown doubtless watched with interest the new building rising opposite. When they came to work on March 14, 1837, they must have been shocked at what they saw. For, at quarter past one the night before, as Philip Hone carefully noted in his diary, "the large unfinished granite building belonging to the Messrs. Josephs came down with a crash like that of an earthquake."

It was a premonitorily symbolic crash, for three days later, on March 17 the firm of J. L. & S. Joseph & Co. itself crashed—"the first thunderclap," as Horace Greeley's *New Yorker* said two months later, "of the mighty storm" that culminated in the panic of 1837. On March 27 the Josephs sold the wrecked property back to Davis, who rebuilt the banking house and, in December 1838,

The earliest known picture made of the banking house at 59 Wall Street after James Brown bought it in 1843 is at the left in this engraving of the Merchants Exchange. The engraving was made by F. B. Nichols from a drawing by Wade, probably done in 1847. It was published (same size as here) in the best mid-century guide book to New York—E. Porter Belden's *New-York: Past, Present, and Future*, New York, 1849 —which is advertised on the sign being carried by the man at lower right.

The Merchants Exchange, replacing the one destroyed in the great fire of 1835 (see p. 24), had been completed in 1842 from designs by Isaiah Rogers. It still stands as the lower floors of the First National City Bank's building, across Hanover Street from Brown Brothers Harriman & Co.

(*Author's Collection*)

JAMES MUNCASTER BROWN (1820–1890), shown here (seated at right) in an 1870 family photograph taken at his summer home in Manchester, Vermont, joined the firm in 1847. A half-brother of Stewart Brown, he had married in 1845 Julia Post (seated next him), daughter of Waldron B. Post (seated at left) whose family had owned the 59 Wall Street corner and still owned "Posts Buildings" on Hanover Street (just behind the banking house), where Brown Brothers had had its offices from 1839 until they moved into their own building.

James Brown brought James M. into the firm after A. J. Kieckhoefer—Brown Brothers' confidential clerk for fifteen years or more—resigned to take a higher paying job at Prime Ward & Co. (who failed a few months later). James M. was "a thorough man of business, smart & intelligent," James Brown wrote in a letter to Thomas B. Curtis, the firm's Boston agent, "& I think after a little practice will suit us better than Mr. K as it is my purpose if my Brother W^m. consents to bring him as a Junior partner." Though James M. had been a partner in other houses for several years, he had had his early training at Alexander Brown & Sons. So James Brown was able to assure Curtis that "as we brought James M. up from the stump we know all about him & his habits which are unexceptionable."

sold it to Joseph D. Beers, president of the North American Trust & Banking Co. Maurice Power—from whom James Brown purchased the property—acquired it in December 1841 after Beers' bank failed.

Brown Brothers' main-floor offices on the Hanover Street corner were reached by the steps at far left in the picture on p. 72, and various departments of the business were housed on the upper floors of No. 59. Beneath, a few steps down from the sidewalk, were offices leased to the Fireman's Insurance Co., whose sign is visible in the engraving. The chief tenant in the 61 Wall Street part of the building in 1849 was the City Fire Insurance Co. (of which Abraham Bell was a director—see p. 46), the upper floors being rented as offices to various

In Philadelphia as in New York, the Merchants Exchange was the focus of much of the firm's business, and Browns & Bowen's office was just a little more than a block away from the curved colonnade of the handsome Exchange building, shown here in a calotype taken in 1849 by W. & F. Langenheim. Built in 1832–34 from designs by William Strickland, the Exchange still stands as one of the finest examples of Greek Revival architecture in the city. Beyond the Exchange on Third Street, at the right edge of the picture, is another still-extant Greek Revival building, designed by Samuel Blodgett and erected in 1794–98 for the first Bank of the United States. Stephen Girard acquired it for his private bank after 1811. Up Third Street at the next corner is Chestnut Street, where Browns & Bowen had its office at No. 209, on the north side between Strawberry Alley and Second Street.

(*Courtesy of George Eastman House*)

lawyers and brokers including Henry Dwight, Jr., an exchange dealer whose indebtedness to Brown Brothers in 1855 led, as we shall see (p. 118), to the firm's becoming deeply involved in the 1856–1857 reorganization of the Chicago, Alton & St. Louis Railroad. (By one of the fascinating coincidences of Brown Brothers Harriman history, this road was again reorganized by E. H. Harriman forty years later in a controversial transaction highly profitable to both the railroad and Mr. Harriman.)

Across Hanover from Brown Brothers' new building, in the ground-floor corner office of the Merchants Exchange (p. 72), was the Atlantic Insurance Company (properly Atlantic Mutual after 1842), whose headquarters nowadays is at 45 Wall Street. James Brown was one of the largest early stockholders of the company, and from 1886 to the present time a Brown Brothers or Brown Brothers Harriman partner has always been a trustee. But by no means all the firm's near neighbors in the eighteen forties and fifties proved to be so reliable.

Just back of the new banking house in 1849, in one of the buildings owned by the Post family (see caption on p. 74, opposite), were the New York offices of Nicholas Biddle's now defunct Bank of the United States (Pennsylvania), still winding up its shabby affairs after finally closing its doors in 1841,

following Biddle's resignation in 1839. On January 29, 1841, William E. Bowen in Philadelphia had written Joseph Shipley in Liverpool about "the strange doings" resulting from Biddle's speculations in cotton and about the suit against the Bank (during which John A. Brown personally provided bail for the Bank's directors). The Bank, he said, by its "reckless loans to unprincipled & wild speculators," had been "a curse to the steady & honest Merchant and Tradesman who can only regret its disastrous end on account of the loss & suffering it may bring on many a widow & orphan. . . . If Mr. Biddle could live a century longer & devote all his talents & energies to good he could not repair the evil he has occasioned. Yet he walks & smiles in the busy haunts of trade. . . ." Bowen "much regretted" that John A. Brown had had anything to do with trying to save the Bank.

But there were "strange doings" in New York banks too. James Brown had written William, on April 14, 1838, about the doings of John Delafield, cashier and vice-president of the Phoenix Bank, "a *rogue,* a barefaced rogue" who involved the bank in practices it would disgust William to learn were engaged in "by chartered corporations favoured to protect the public interest & morals & not to destroy it."

75

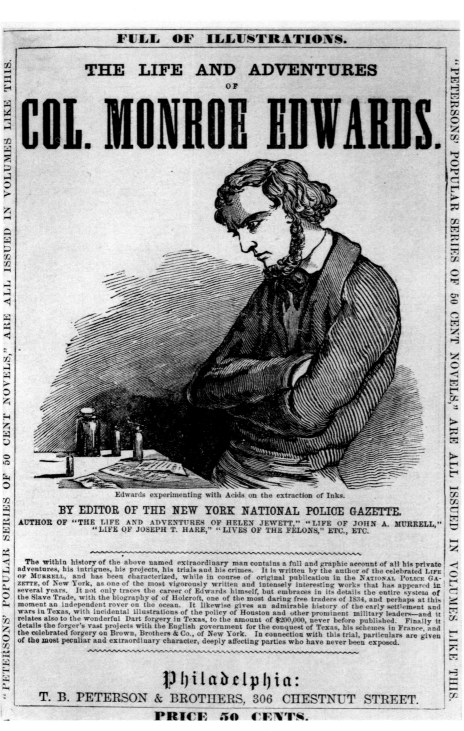

FULL OF ILLUSTRATIONS.

THE LIFE AND ADVENTURES
OF
COL. MONROE EDWARDS.

Edwards experimenting with Acids on the extraction of Inks.

BY EDITOR OF THE NEW YORK NATIONAL POLICE GAZETTE.

AUTHOR OF "THE LIFE AND ADVENTURES OF HELEN JEWETT," "LIFE OF JOHN A. MURRELL," "LIFE OF JOSEPH T. HARE," "LIVES OF THE FELONS," ETC., ETC.

The within history of the above named extraordinary man contains a full and graphic account of all his private adventures, his intrigues, his projects, his trials and his crimes. It is written by the author of the celebrated LIFE OF MURRELL, and has been characterized, while in course of original publication in the NATIONAL POLICE GAZETTE, of New York, as one of the most vigorously written and intensely interesting works that has appeared in several years. It not only traces the career of Edwards himself, but embraces in its details the entire system of the Slave Trade, with the biography of of Holcroft, one of the most daring free traders of 1834, and perhaps at this moment an independent rover on the ocean. It likewise gives an admirable history of the early settlement and wars in Texas, with incidental illustrations of the policy of Houston and other prominent military leaders—and it relates also to the wonderful Dart forgery in Texas, to the amount of $200,000, never before published. Finally it details the forger's vast projects with the English government for the conquest of Texas, his schemes in France, and the celebrated forgery on Brown, Brothers & Co., of New York. In connection with this trial, particulars are given of the most peculiar and extraordinary character, deeply affecting parties who have never been exposed.

Philadelphia:
T. B. PETERSON & BROTHERS, 306 CHESTNUT STREET.
PRICE 50 CENTS.

Low as commercial and financial morality was in the early 'forties, it is little wonder that Brown Brothers & Co. itself got cheated by a "barefaced rogue," as recorded in the best-selling paperback of 1848 that is sampled on these pages. The author was George Wilkes, co-founder of the *Police Gazette* in 1845 and its editor for ten years. In 1856 he was co-founder of another important magazine, *Porter's Spirit of the Times,* in which the distinctively American humorous tradition that flowered in Mark Twain's writing was developed and exploited. But there was little humor in his life of Monroe Edwards, as the long paragraph on its title page makes clear.

A copy of this 1848 best-seller was presented in 1863 to "Messrs. Brown Bros with Compliments of F. C. Wagner," Captain and Provost Marshal of the 7th District, New York. As the blurb on the pink paper cover indicates, Edwards' "celebrated forgery on Brown, Brothers & Co." and his subsequent trial climaxed a long and larcenous career.

Tempting as it is to quote liberally from Wilkes' narrative of Edwards' early exploits in New Orleans, Texas, and Brazil, his slave-trading ventures and his fantastic "anti-slavery" schemes in England and France, we must content ourselves with recording that the young man was "too handsome and too fond of pleasure" for his own good, and early "adopted the maxim that the world owed every good fellow a good living, and . . . that it mattered very little how a good fellow got it, provided he could keep himself clear of the interference of the law."

The picture on the cover shows Edwards learning the forger's arts while in Natchez in 1834, from a counterfeiter with whose paramour—"a dashing courtezan"— Edwards was carrying on an intrigue. In August, 1841, armed with those arts, he forged a letter to Brown Brothers from Maunsell White & Co., cotton factors in New Orleans, introducing "Mr. John P. Caldwell . . . a solvent and very wealthy gentleman" who would like an advance of "25 or 30 thousand dollars" on 1011 bales of cotton then in Maunsell White's hands. "Caldwell," of course, soon thereafter got in touch with Brown Brothers.

Writing from Alexandria, Virginia, on August 25, 1841, Edwards (alias Caldwell) explained to Brown Brothers that he would come in person to New York were it not for the dangerous illness of his brother. "Thus circumstanced," he hoped Brown Brothers would advance him $25,000 on the cotton in Maunsell White's hands, remitting the advance to him at Alexandria in bills of exchange on Richmond, if possible (since he wanted to use the funds there to purchase more slaves for his plantation), or on Baltimore or Washington. Replying on August 28th, Brown Brothers enclosed seventeen checks and certificates of deposit on brokers and banks in Richmond, Norfolk, Baltimore and other cities totalling $25,119.52. They regretted being able to get so few Virginia funds but said they had "cleared the market both for these as well as for Baltimore funds," and they concluded by saying they felt "much indebted to Maunsell White & Co. for the pleasure of your correspondence" (a line which drew the only laughter at the trial when the letter was read in court). One of the checks was on Johnson & Lee, Baltimore bankers, and the illustration at right purports to show Edwards (Caldwell) cashing it.

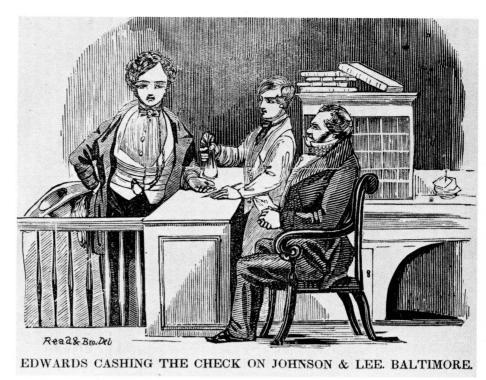

Read & Bro. Del.

EDWARDS CASHING THE CHECK ON JOHNSON & LEE. BALTIMORE.

(*This wood engraving and the title page, opposite, are reproduced from a copy of the book in the Brown Brothers Harriman & Co. Historical File*)

Johnson & Lee's white marble banking house shows at right in this 1845 daguerreotype by Henry V. Marshall, showing Calvert Street north from below Baltimore Street to the Battle Monument. Here Edwards had little difficulty. "Mr. Johnson hesitated at first about the identity of John P. Caldwell . . . but, on his clerk, a lad of seventeen named Hanson, telling Mr. J. that the $494.45 was the exact balance of account existing between them and the New York house by which the draft was drawn," he counted out the sum in gold. The boy put it in "a *shot-bag* . . . stamped with the sign of the firm 'J. & Lee'" which later figured importantly as evidence at Edwards' trial.

At the Bank of Baltimore, however, Edwards had more difficulty. The cashier refused to cash the $10,000 check drawn by the City Bank of New York until Edwards could prove that he was the John P. Caldwell in whose favor it was drawn. Blandly remarking that he had transactions with Brown Brothers & Co. of New York, Edwards then asked "if they had not agents or a branch in Baltimore?" Indeed they had (Alex. Brown & Sons having assumed the agency in Baltimore after George Brown's retirement from the firm), and if Mr. Caldwell could but induce Mr. George Brown "to call back with him,

(*Courtesy of the Peale Museum, Baltimore. Gift of J. B. Marshall*)

and say it was all right," the cashier would cheerfully pay the money. "Nothing daunted," Edwards went and introduced himself to George Brown, who "willingly recognized in the gentlemanly stranger, the Mr. John P. Caldwell of whom his connections in New York had written," and "without hesitation took his hat in hand to return with him to the bank"—where the duly impressed cashier handed over the $10,000.

It was not until September 17th that Brown Brothers received a (genuine) letter from Maunsell White & Co., disabusing them of the notion that any J. P. Caldwell cotton was in their hands. It took about a month for the police and Brown Brothers' special agents to catch up with the forger, and on June 6, 1842, he went on trial. George Brown and A. J. Kieckhoefer (James Brown's confidential clerk) both testified at the trial, which opened with an address to the jury by George F. Allen, James Brown's son-in-law (see pp. 98–99). Edwards was convicted and sent to Sing Sing prison where he died in 1846.

Wilkes' book about Col. Edwards, the forger (pp. 76–77) puts part of the blame for his downfall on his early associates in New Orleans—"adventurers . . . perverted from all gravity of principle, by lives of license, disappointment, peril and misfortune." And there is ample evidence in Brown Brothers' correspondence with its New Orleans agency as late as the 'fifties that it was difficult to keep clear of outfits such as Sheehan & Sons, "notorious pawnbrokers, or as the police call them *fences: receivers* of stolen goods & gamblers," or Gregor & Wilson whose Mr. Gregor was "in the habit of making lotteries on board steamboats, by casting dice, to get rid of watches, rings, & jewelry sent down to

him." And in 1858 one of the agency's own men (a relative of one of the partners) was caught embezzling the firm's funds to pay his gambling debts.

The moral climate in Boston was different. Here Thomas B. Curtis carried on the firm's agency with charm and distinction, doing business with merchants such as C. H. Minot ("a gentleman in all senses, fully posted in the Calcutta trade"), and refusing (in 1853) to be a trustee of the newly organized New York Central Railroad's bond issue, "not liking the business itself and not *knowing* the parties to be safe"—even though "the men who were about this business" told him Brown Brothers "had been quite friendly to *them,* or *it.*" Even in Curtis's

When Thomas B. Curtis became Brown Brothers' agent his job was complicated by the fact that the credit business in Boston was largely in the hands of the Barings, whose Boston agent was Thomas W. Ward. Ward was one of Curtis's intimate friends and a fellow member of the Friday Club, a group of the city's eminent merchants and professional men pictured in this 1855 photograph. Curtis is seated at far right, with Ward next to him. Others in the group were the lawyer Charles P. Curtis, Thomas B.'s brother (at far left); Thomas Motley, father of J. Lothrop Motley, the historian (second from left); Nathan Hale, editor of the *Daily Adver-tiser* and father of Edward Everett Hale (third from left); Lemuel Shaw, Chief Justice of the Massachusetts Supreme Court and father-in-law of Herman Melville (seated behind the table at center); and Nathan Appleton, merchant and father-in-law of Henry Wadsworth Longfellow (seated right of the table). (*Courtesy of Louis Curtis*)

E No 497   Stephen P. Blake

Captain D. K. Small, Master of the barque "Vernon", (or his successor upon notice being given to Brown Shipley & Co. by the agent of the vessel in the port where the change is made duly certified by the American or British Consul) at any port in the world,

is hereby authorized to value on Brown Shipley & Co. Liverpool payable in London at usance,

for account of Messrs H. Harris & Co. of Boston,

for any sum or sums not exceeding in all six hundred pounds sterling

the same to be used for repairs of vessel if necessary

The Bills must be drawn within   twelve   months from this date.

And Brown Shipley & Co. hereby agree with the drawers endorsers and bona fide holders of Bills drawn in compliance with the terms of this Credit that the same shall be duly honored on presentation at their counting house

For £600.

The user of this Credit will please to sign the drafts as drawn under Credit No 497. dated 6 Oct. 1859.

Brown Shipley & Co.
By Attorney,
Thos. B. Curtis

Thomas B. Curtis, who signed the letter of credit reproduced above, was Brown Brothers' first agent in Boston. The agency was opened December 31, 1844, to secure a larger share of the business of granting credits to firms engaged in trade with the East Indies—a trade largely controlled by merchants in Boston and its vicinity. In his reports to Brown Brothers, Curtis always distinguished between credits granted "for use in Europe," "for use in South America," and "for use Beyond the Capes" (meaning, of course, the Cape of Good Hope and Cape Horn). More than half the total were for use "Beyond the Capes."

The form of these credits in the 1850s was like the one pictured here—the earliest letter of credit preserved in the firm's Historical File. This one probably survived because Curtis found, after filling out the printed form in ink, that changes (indicated by the pencilled additions) were necessary and therefore drew up a fresh copy for his client. It was a twelve month credit for use "Beyond the Capes," or "at any port in the world," authorizing the master of the barque *Vernon* to draw on Brown Shipley & Co. for sums not exceeding £600 sterling—"to be used for repairs of vessel if necessary" as the pencilled addition specifies. (*Original document presented to the Historical File by Louis Curtis, grandson of Thomas B. and resident partner in Boston from 1922–62*)

This 1858 clipping from the Boston *Post,* referring to Brown Brothers' liberal policy with credits during the depression of 1857, was enclosed by Thomas B. Curtis in his letter to Brown Brothers dated May 20, 1858. Curtis says he does not know who wrote the piece, but thinks it "kindly meant, and I believe it expresses what many people know & feel—Several persons . . . have said that Barings never allow of no delay, & compelled great sacrifices thereby."

Brown, Brothers & Co.—Now that the financial storm is pretty nearly blown over, it is due to notice how successfully and quietly, as far as outward appearances show, these respectable and worthy bankers have pursued the even tenor of their way. They have not appeared to suffer much from the inability of those who were indebted for credit on London granted to them, but, on the contrary, if it was understood that a delay of payment of what was due would be of service to the parties, it was generally granted; and, in most instances, it proved of the utmost importance to many importers, saving them from failure and ruin. We can speak more particularly of our own merchants, whose business with Brown, Brothers & Co. passes through the hands of their efficient attorney, THOMAS B. CURTIS, Esq.

(*Photograph given to Brown Brothers Harriman & Co. Historical File in 1965 by Mrs. Arthur Burkhard*)

CHARLES D. DICKEY (1818–1897), whose grandmother was sister of Mrs. Alexander Brown of Baltimore, was born in New York in the year John A. Brown established the firm in Philadelphia. In 1835, when he was seventeen, he went to work at Brown Brothers as a clerk and by 1841 was cashier of the firm. In that year, at Samuel Nicholson's urgent request, he went to New Orleans as general manager of Nicholson's agency there, and a couple of years later was agent in Savannah. In 1847 he went to Mobile and set up the firm of Dickey & Morrell, which succeeded to the agency formerly held by George Cleveland (see p. 51). While still in Mobile he was admitted to partnership in Brown Brothers & Co., in October, 1859.

agency, however, the cashier was caught juggling accounts "after twelve years of unbounded trust" on a salary Curtis had thought would "conduce to keep him honest."

In general, however, Curtis was an excellent judge of men, and in spite of the Barings' long association with many of the wealthiest and most influential Boston merchants, Curtis soon gained a strong foothold. By granting credits to young and enterprising men, whose intelligence and honesty he felt he could trust, he successfully established Brown Brothers' connections with New England firms that would take the lead in years to come.

Of the Southern agencies, the one in Mobile gave least trouble in the 'fifties, thanks largely to Charles D. Dickey, who took over from George Cleveland there in 1847. A number of Dickey's letters from Mobile have survived, which reinforce the impression given by John Crosby Brown's description of him as "a man of unusual business ability" and "the most even-tempered man that I have ever known." A letter dated February 9, 1853, gives his reaction to some harsh things said about a business decision of his in one of Brown Shipley & Co.'s letters about a credit he had granted—remarks which Stewart Brown in New York thought might offend him. Writing to Stewart, he says:

I have received too many proofs of the Confidence reposed in me to allow for an instant the least misconstruction of their remarks, called forth as they are by circumstances of so startling a character. My aim is to act so as to merit a continuance of that confidence, which can be best attained by having *no secrets* in my business, and by never entering into any transaction of which I could doubt your full approval. This *has* been, and will continue to be my endeavor so long as I continue your agent. . . .

Another letter, written December 20, 1859, sums up his observations during a four-day visit to the New Orleans agency soon after he became a partner in the New York and Liverpool houses. His remarks about Andrew B. Morrell, then in charge of the agency, reveal his talents as an observer of men: "Very well disposed, & inclined to open everything fully to me," but with "such a very peculiar & mysterious manner of communicating his ideas" that his explanations were sometimes "far from lucid." He was "thoroughly posted about every Drawer of Sterling, and if there is any thing irregular about any man he finds it out and treasures it all up"—a quality which on the whole seemed to Dickey desirable for an agent in New Orleans "where there is a great deal of rascality constantly occurring in business." Of his zeal and integrity there could *"be no question,"* Dickey wrote, but his manners were "rather gruff & coarse" and his habits of life "too unsocial to make him a favorite in business" or in Society—"except among a few old bachelor cronies." Nevertheless, "one thing he can do *well,* and which is *very important,* is to say 'no' positively to a Bill that is decidedly objectionable, and he allows I am quite sure, no personal friendships to operate when they ought not to."

N E W   Y O R K

The picture of "New York" reproduced above is the third state of an aquatint engraving made from a painting done in 1852 by J. W. Hill. It was engraved by Himely, with changes by C. Mottram, printed in England by McQueen, and published in New York by F. & G. W. Smith in 1855.

(Courtesy of the Mariners Museum, Newport News, Va.)

Eight

AT HOME IN MID-CENTURY MANHATTAN

The description of Manhattan island at the beginning of Belden's 1849 guide book to New York (see p. 73) points out that only the southern portion —"about one fifth of the whole area"—was built up at mid-century, the rest being "mostly under tillage." The upper four-fifths of the island had been laid out with "noble streets that traverse nearly the whole length of the city without a deviation to the right hand or to the left," but in the southern part there were "a few narrow and crooked streets that have existed from the days of Pieter Wolfertsen Van Couwenhoven" which had "occasioned much scandal as to the irregularity of New-York."

It was, however, among those narrow, crooked streets that the city's capital was chiefly concentrated, "invested in works of internal improvement, as well as traversing the whole world, transporting our own products to foreign countries, and bringing to our shores the merchandise and commodities essential to our convenience and happiness."

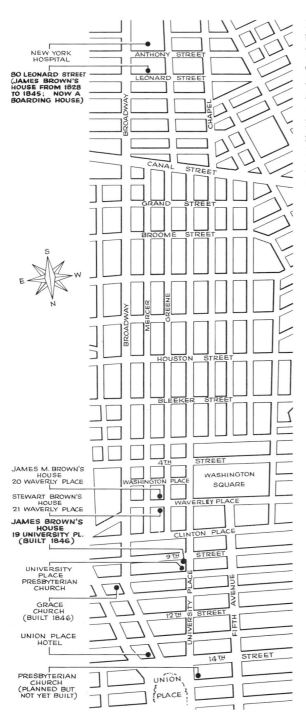

Map drawn for this book by Sigman-Ward, based upon one in Belden's *New-York: Past, Present, and Future* (1849) showing locations of residences of James Brown and his partners in picture at right.

This bird's-eye view of "New York," looking south from a point above Union Square (then called Union Place), was drawn and lithographed by C. Bachmann and published by John Bachmann in 1849. Most of the fine buildings around Union Square that are colored reddish- or pinkish-brown were only planned or projected in 1849, the city directories showing vacant lots and houses "now building" on these sites as late as 1851. The area between 14th Street and Washington Square, however, looked much as it is shown here.

Belden's guide book called the vicinity of Union Square and Washington Square "the most fashionable portion of the city" and it was here—in the setting described by Henry James in his novel *Washington Square*—that James Brown and his junior partners Stewart and James M. all had their residences at mid-century. Until 1845 James Brown had remained in the Leonard Street house he built in 1828 (indicated at top of chart at left above), but the "encroachments of trade" rapidly changed the neighborhood, and on April 2, 1846, the *New York Commercial Advertiser* reported that James Lenox, William H. Aspinwall, and James Brown were among those who had moved "north of

Bleecker Street," the latter two to University Place. By 1850 Brown's nearest neighbors included De Witt Clinton's widow and the son of Brown Brothers' first legal counsel, Thomas Addis Emmett (p. 45).

Meanwhile Stewart Brown and James M. Brown had moved into houses across the street from one another on Waverley Place, as next-door neighbors of James M.'s father-in-law, Waldron B. Post (p. 74), and George D. Post, who had held the $73,000 mortgage on the banking house at the corner of Wall and Hanover when James Brown bought the property (pp. 73–4).

83

It was, of course, at the banking house on Wall Street that the Brown Brothers partners spent most of their time in the early 'fifties, though James Brown did make a point of telling Thomas B. Curtis, in a letter dated December 26, 1853, that Brown Brothers "would be closed . . . on all occasions on Hollydays," since he felt that "business men & clerks have not as much recreation as they ought to have."

The lithograph of the "Exchange" reproduced here (part of which is used in larger scale on the title page) was drawn on stone by C. Autenrieth from a watercolor by J. Bornet, and was published as one of a series of twenty "Views of New York" by Hoff & Bloede in 1850. The Brown Brothers staff at No. 59 Wall (left edge of print) included, besides the partners, a head clerk, cashier, bill-clerk, bookkeeper, assistant bookkeeper, and general clerk, plus two "boys" and a porter.

If James Brown walked east to the foot of 12th Street at the East River (out of sight to the left of the area included in the Bachmann view on pp. 82–83), he came to the Novelty Iron Works, of which he was the principal owner, and in which two of his sons-in-law were officers. George F. Allen, who married Brown's daughter Grace the year after he took part in the conviction of Monroe Edwards (p. 77), was now an executive at the iron works his brother Horatio Allen had established. Howard Potter, who married Brown's daughter Louisa in 1849, went to work in the Novelty's offices soon thereafter, becoming secretary of the company in the late 'fifties.

The iron works took its name from the first coal-burning river steamer, the *Novelty*, whose boiler and engines had been built here in 1836. In the early 'fifties more than a thousand men were working for $1.50 per day in its eighteen shops, turning out, along with other work, the largest and most powerful marine engines yet built. These engines were for the *Atlantic* and the *Arctic*, two ships built for another enterprise of which James Brown was the principal owner—America's first transatlantic steamship line, known as the Collins Line. One of those ships—as we shall see in the next chapter—brought bitter tragedy into the lives of James Brown and his son-in-law George Allen.

James Brown's son John Crosby Brown, in some unpublished "Reminiscences," said of the University Place house (shown here in an unsigned and undated watercolor that illustrates the manuscript): "The exterior was plain and rather ugly, but the proportions of the principal rooms inside were excellent. . . . This house was altogether more spacious, and on the inside more elegant than the one in Leonard Street. As one entered the front door, the housekeeper's room was on the left, on the right a room for the children's dining-room, another for the servants' dining-room, and in the rear the kitchen. Behind the housekeeper's room on the left, were the sleeping quarters for the old colored cook and her husband, the butler—John and Mary Johnson." The family attended the Presbyterian church (at left on the corner of University Place and 10th Street) of which James Brown was a founder and for many years an Elder.

(*Brown Brothers Harriman & Co. Historical File*)

"A short flight of stairs led from the entrance hall to a small library . . . , gothic in design, with bookcases to the ceiling. On the right of the staircase on the south side [to the right in picture below] were two drawing-rooms, very handsome for those days, and especially well proportioned." The front drawing-room, or parlor, the "Reminiscences" tell us, "was decorated and furnished in French design by [Leon] Marcotte [a New York architect], and was considered at that time one of his best pieces of work. It was at his suggestion . . . that the old glass chandeliers were taken from the Leonard Street house and used in these rooms." It was in this front room that James Brown and his second wife, Eliza Coe Brown, were sitting when Mathew Brady, the great photographer of the Civil War, came to the house (probably in the late 'fifties, when he also took the photograph on p. 87) to take the picture reproduced here.

(*Brown Brothers Harriman & Co. Historical File*)

(*Brown Brothers Harriman & Co. Historical File*)

Sometime in the 'forties James Brown also built a country house, which he named Clifton, across the Hudson on Weehawken Heights, three miles north of then lovely Hoboken whose "Elysian Fields" were the objective of many picnickers from the city. This undated and un-attributed photograph of the house was probably taken in the 'fifties. To quote John Crosby Brown's reminiscences again: "Owing to my father's business relations with the South, our home in the country in the summer, especially in the months of July and September, was to a certain extent a rendezvous for his southern friends, and it gradually became the custom that he and my mother and the rest of the family should be at home on Wednesday afternoons after three o'clock. Supper was served about seven, and on those days my father's Southern friends and business con-nections, with their families, who happened to be in the City, would drive out from New York to spend the after-noon at Clifton. . . . Sometimes there would be ten or fifteen people present, and they came without special in-vitation, bringing their children and their friends. . . . Among them I remember distinctly . . . the members of the Adger family from Charleston."

Sometime in 1856 Mathew Brady introduced what he called "Imperial Photographs"—paper prints of large size (almost 16 × 19 inches), enlarged from wet plate negatives and "tinted" or painted by artists he hired to work in his studio. They were what a contemporary newspaper called "the ne plus ultra of art," and Brady's wealthy clients were apparently attracted, rather than repelled, by their cost which went as high as seven hundred dollars each.

JAMES BROWN had his "Imperial" portrait taken (probably in 1857 or 1858), though he was by no means one of "the lions of the town" who reportedly flocked to Brady's studio. As Joseph Scoville said in the early 'sixties, the firm of Brown Brothers was "rarely heard of" even though it was involved in "mammoth" operations. "The main partners, James and Stewart, are the most modest and unassuming of our citizens. There is no show or parade with them. James never rides except in a one-horse coupe. Stewart never rides except in an omnibus. He walks quick—one hand behind in the small of his back, and carries a little cane."

In addition to his two homes, James Brown (or the firm) owned a good deal of real estate in the city and else-where. Some of the properties were acquired when loans or credits, for which they had been put up as collateral, were not repaid. Among these, apparently, was a Louisiana sugar plantation which was managed in the early 'fifties by Brown Brothers' New Orleans agency. In the records of disbursements and receipts at "James Brown's St. James Plantation" for 1853 there is a May 25th entry recording payment of $4.50 to the cashier of the barque *Gipsy* for the freight charges on 1 cask, 4 barrels, and 4 half-barrels of sugar "shipped to N. Y. Worlds Fair." That fair, the first in the New World, was held at the Crystal Palace, facing Sixth Avenue on the present site of Bryant Park between 41st and 42nd Streets. Brown's partner Samuel Nicholson, who managed the New Orleans agency, was one of the directors of the Crystal Palace, shown here in an 1853 engraving by Capewell & Kimmel.

(*Author's Collection*)

This "View in Wall Street from Corner of Broad" was drawn and engraved for *The Ladies Wreath* in 1850 (artist and engraver unknown). Crude as it is, this view conveys more vividly than most contemporary prints a sense of the everyday world of which the Brown Brothers partners and their clerks and bookkeepers were a part. Together with the hitherto unpublished sketches on this and the two following pages, made between 1849 and 1851 by the Swedish architect H. G. Cantzler, it helps us believe in the actuality of mid-century life in a "commercial metropolis" where—as a writer in *Putnam's* said—nothing seemed to hinder growth and expansion, not even "the mean and unsuitable docks and markets, the filthy streets, the farce of a half-fledged and inefficient police, and the miserably bad government, generally, of an unprincipled common-council."

The one-horse vehicle left of center, approaching the viewer, is a coupe such as the one James Brown is said to have ridden in (p. 86). The telegraph wires, which first appeared on the streets in 1845, ran along Wall Street to a pole on Brown Brothers' corner, just beyond the Merchants Exchange, and then down Hanover to No. 5 (in Posts Buildings) where the three principal telegraph companies had their offices. Note that one of the trees that hid from view Brown Brothers' earlier Wall Street offices in 1831 (see p. 37) still survives.

This sketch of the predecessors of Con-Ed's "Dig we must" crews, forever unpaving the streets of Manhattan, is from the recently discovered sketchbook of H. G. Cantzler, a Swedish architect who visited the United States in 1849–1851. Cantzler labelled the sketch "Broadway from ⚹50, May 8, 51. Cantzler labelled the sketch the west side of the street a few doors south of Exchange Alley, about half-way between Bowling Green and Trinity Church. Four years later the houses Cantzler saw (one of which has a "To Let" sign by its door) had all been torn down and replaced by the commercial buildings shown in the print reproduced opposite.

Cantzler's sketches were acquired by the New York Public Library's Prints Division in 1964, from one of his descendants in Sweden, but have not hitherto been published. The one labelled "Wall Street 4th Novbr 1849" shows the same oyster stand pictured at the right-hand edge of the engraving reproduced opposite. The stand, which stood for many years on the southwest corner of Wall and Broad Streets, was first set up about 1830 by a negro named Thomas Downing, who came to be known as "Prince Saddleback" among the merchants, bankers, brokers, lawyers and politicians who made his establishment "a sort of social exchange," according to Benson Lossing's *History of New York City* (1884).

The view (below) of the west side of Broadway between Morris Street and Exchange Alley was lithographed by F. Heppenheimer and published in 1855 by W. Stephenson & Co. The third building from the right edge (the store and warehouse of a lace importing firm) occupies the site of the house with the "To Let" sign in Cantzler's sketch (opposite). All but a few of the residences that still stood only four years before have been replaced by five-story commercial structures, and the remaining houses have all been converted to commercial purposes.

(The Edward W. C. Arnold Collection, lent by the Metropolitan Museum of Art. Photograph courtesy of the Museum of the City of New York)

On March 15, 1851 Cantzler sketched this auction at Peck Slip, foot of Ferry Street at South Street. (The slip has been filled in since the map on p. 32 was made.) The auctioneer is urging the assembled crowd to bid on "A beautiful Pair of Pants, only $1.—," possibly one of a damaged lot recently brought in by one of the ships in the background. Apparently Cantzler was more interested in the scene than the gentleman at the left, who is saying "Mr. Cantzler why don't you come now."

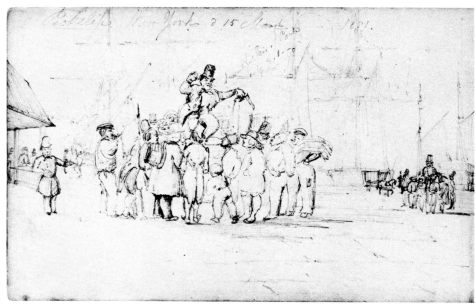

(Courtesy of the New York Public Library, Prints Division)

"New York East River February 1851," another of Cantzler's sketches on South Street, records the polyglot flavor of the waterfront.

(Courtesy of the New York Public Library, Prints Division)

In Cantzler's undated sketch of a Broadway-Battery stage the driver is shouting "Go a'head!" The man at his left is singing "O! Susanna don't you cry for me," and the newsboy on the rear step shouting "Express 2¢ Niagara arrival" is selling copies of the New York *Daily Express* containing the news just received from Liverpool by the Black Star packet *Niagara*.

(Courtesy of the New York Public Library, Prints Division)

Nine

MR. COLLINS' STEAM SCHEME

A letter of January 8, 1848, from James Brown to his brother George, begins: "The contract with the Government for conveying the mail between New York & Liverpool had to be executed before Congress met or abandoned and being fully convinced other parties were willing to take it on more favorable terms, to control the business arising from [it] to themselves & friends on the other side we joined Mr. Collins in the contract. . . ."

Collins, the able operator of the fast and luxurious Dramatic Line of sailing packets (of which the Browns' Liverpool house had been agents since it started in 1837), had been trying since 1841 to interest the Browns in his "Steam Scheme," as Stewart Brown called it, a steamship line to compete with the British Cunarders, in regular service between Liverpool and Boston since 1840. William Brown (one of the largest original Cunard stockholders) would have none of it; "on no question," Joseph Shipley told Stewart Brown in September 1844 was William "so fixed and determined," and Shipley agreed. In March 1846, however, Stewart wrote that "Our friend Collins requests me to say, if writing to friend Shipley, that he need not be surprised to hear of the establishment of a line. . . . —I think he *will* make *this* go. His plan is to get a large patronage from our government."

By January 1848 Collins had a $385,000 annual mail subsidy from Congress, and Brown Brothers & Co. had put $300,000 in the New York and Liverpool United States Mail Steamship Co. (the Collins Line). James, the company's president, assured his brother that the line promised "ample" remuneration, "certainly" 25% per annum, perhaps 50%, and that George would "never regret it" if he too subscribed.

(*Courtesy of the Mariners Museum, Newport News, Va.*)

EDWARD KNIGHT COLLINS (1802–1878), from an unsigned portrait probably painted in the 1850s. Brown Brothers & Co. and William & James Brown & Co. worked closely with Collins in developing the Dramatic Line of sailing packets from 1837 to 1853 and the so-called Collins Line of steamships from 1848 to 1858. In 1844, Stewart Brown wrote Joseph Shipley that Collins was "a person who looks to his own interest before anything else." He was "certainly a strange being" who had "a low unrefined mind with an overbearing disposition." Yet he was "very cordial" with Brown Brothers, "having the Steam Scheme again in his head," and Stewart Brown concluded by saying: "I have so much confidence in his ability prudence & perseverance that I think if he undertakes it—i.e. if he can obtain the means to undertake it—he will be very apt to succeed."

The first Collins liner was the *Atlantic,* which sailed from New York for Liverpool on April 27, 1850. On her return trip she broke Cunard's record; on her second voyage broke all records, both directions. Another Collins liner, the *Pacific,* made history in 1852 by first crossing the ocean in less than ten days. A Collins steamer, thought to be the *Atlantic,* is shown in this hitherto unreproduced painting, unsigned and undated, now owned by J. Crosby Brown, Jr., of Chestnut Hill, Pennsylvania. (*Photograph courtesy of the Mariners Museum, Newport News, Va.*)

The Collins liners sailed from a Hudson River pier at the foot of Canal Street, shown here in an illustration from Jacob Abbott's *Rollo on the Atlantic* (Boston, 1853)—one of the inordinately popular "Rollo" books which edified generations of American youth. (*Courtesy of the Mariners Museum, Newport News, Va.*)

The stateroom illustrated in *Rollo on the Atlantic* was "beautifully finished and furnished" with two curtained berths (at right) and a washstand where the pitcher, soap dish and brush tray were set in sockets cut in the marble slab so they would not slide about in rough weather. Alexander Crosby Brown used both these Rollo illustrations in the version of the book he edited for *The American Neptune,* April 1966. (*Courtesy of the Mariners Museum, Newport News, Va.*)

"You must not take . . . any ship yet built as any pattern of what we hope to do & will do," James told George in that January 8th letter. And the Collins liners did indeed break with tradition. Designed by George Steers (who later designed the yacht *America*), they were not only the fastest and most powerful ships afloat, but also—with the exception of Britain's unsuccessful *Great Western* —the largest (exceeding the Cunarders by more than 500 tons). They had straight stems, or bows, instead of the traditional curved stems and bowsprits, and carried much less auxiliary sail than other steamers. They were the first ships whose cabins were steam-heated, the first to have complete barber shops aboard, the first to have bell cords by each berth which, when pulled, registered on an "annunciator" the number of the berth to which the steward had been summoned.

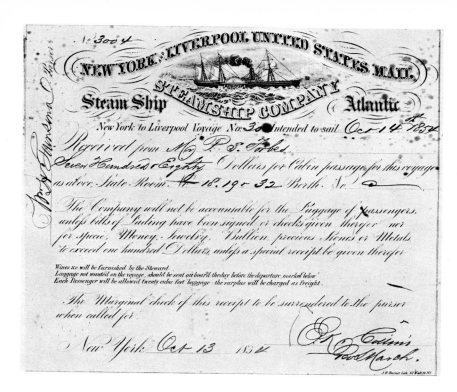

Receipt issued to Paul S. Forbes, a partner in Russell & Co., for payment for three staterooms on the *Atlantic*'s thirtieth New York to Liverpool crossing, "intended to sail" October 14, 1854. (Forbes also paid for two berths in "Second Cabin," presumably for servants who accompanied the family.) The elaborate receipt was lithographed by J. H. Burnet, the stationer who occupied the basement of the 61 Wall Street half of Brown Brothers & Co.'s building. (*Courtesy of the Harvard Business School archives, Baker Library, Harvard University*)

When the *Atlantic* was in Liverpool in July 1851, William Brown gave a dinner on board in honor of the foreign dignitaries connected with the "Crystal Palace" exhibition in London—the first World's Fair. They had come down to Liverpool as his guests to inspect the city's docks and warehouses. He is shown standing at left in this wood engraving from the *Illustrated London News,* July 26, 1851, no doubt proposing one of his many toasts to "Peaceful Commerce," "The World's Commercial Fleet," and so on.

Brown Shipley & Co., as agents of the Collins Line, had charge of provisioning the ships in Liverpool, and their private letters to Brown Brothers indicate that the English partners spent a great deal of time attending to complaints about the vegetables, fruit, and wines. ("We have always put aboard a *good* wine, but your passengers do not seem to appreciate it, so we will in future give them cheaper 'tonic' as you suggest.") Captain Nye of the *Pacific* ("without exception the most disagreeable man we ever met") gave them special trouble. In May 1855, he behaved in a "disagreeable & offensive manner" when Brown Shipley stopped dealing with a greengrocer named Taylor, married to one of Nye's stewardesses, who was caught using measures with false bottoms. Yet for all Brown Shipley's efforts there were complaints. The passengers arriving in New York on the *Arctic* in early September 1852 sent a remonstrance to Collins, complaining that the food was "no better than could be found in a Common tavern." Stewart Brown personally investigated and reported (in a letter to Browns & Bowen): "The tea was complained of—the writer tried it last night and found it not as good as he likes but still not so *dreadful bad*. The butter was complained of, this is the fault of the providers on the other side. Some side dishes, Irish Stews &c were not cooked well. . . . The champagne was represented to be bad, this is furnished on the other side." (*Courtesy of the New York Society Library*)

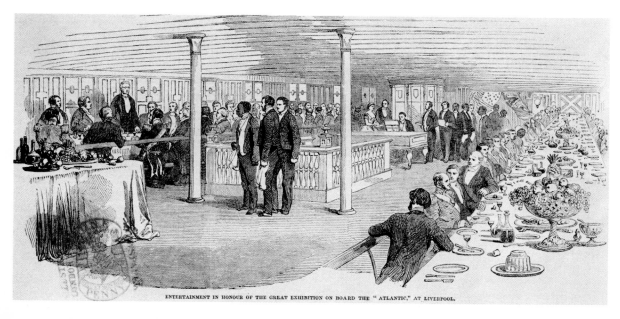

ENTERTAINMENT IN HONOUR OF THE GREAT EXHIBITION ON BOARD THE " ATLANTIC," AT LIVERPOOL.

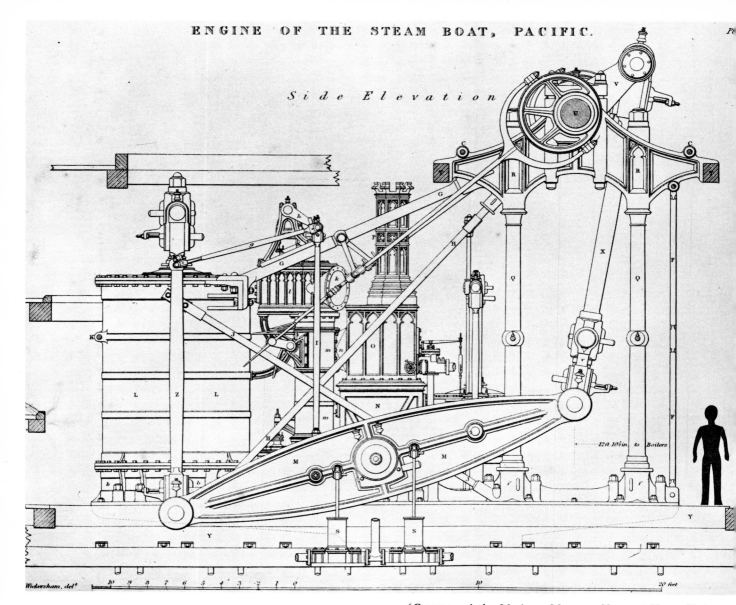

Side Elevation

Wickersham, del.^t

The engines for two of the four original Collins liners, the *Atlantic* and the *Arctic,* were built at the Novelty Iron Works (p. 84), of which—as one of James Brown's sons wrote several years later—"father owns almost the whole of the stock." The Novelty works had built smaller engines for many steamboats, including the first ocean steamship built in New York—the *Washington*—in 1846. In his January 8, 1848, letter to George Brown, James Brown had specified the *Washington* as an example of the sort of vessel the Collins Line would *not* build. "Mr. Collins pronounced that model a failure for the purpose for which she was built as soon as he saw her on the stocks She wants floor, buoyancy to carry her machinery." The machinery, he adds proudly, "is excellent & does its part to entire satisfaction, but it has no chance on such a model."

No picture of one of the engines built for Collins liners by the Novelty works is known to exist, but they were similar to the one shown above, built for the *Pacific* at the Allaire works in New York, who also built the *Baltic*'s engines. Some idea of the size of these engines, with their arched and crenellated Gothic castings, is given by the little figure representing an engineer, drawn to scale by the maritime historian Alexander Crosby Brown on our photo-

graph of the original plate, engraved by Wickersham for Tredgold's *Steam Navigation* (1850).

Though George Steers, at Collins' insistence, provided flat "floors" to support the huge engines in the Collins liners, the vessels were driven so hard, in the successful attempt to win and hold the "Blue Ribbon" for speed on the Atlantic crossing, that the hulls and the engines themselves were constantly in need of expensive repairs. Rumors to that effect were rife at the time and are confirmed in Brown Brothers' unpublished correspondence with Brown Shipley. On March 27, 1855, Brown Shipley wrote that "for weeks past, if not for months, we have been told in one quarter & another that the 'Pacific' imminently required laying up, & notwithstanding Captain Nye's repeated assurances . . . that she was 'in perfect order, never better' we have now the confirmation of the rumors from yourselves." And on January 17, 1857, in a letter addressed to James Brown, they reported that the *Baltic*'s expansion joints gave way, two days out of Liverpool in bad weather. "This accident was not known to the passengers & we shall try to keep it quiet here. Captain Comstock reports that he shall get all put right by Tuesday in ample time to start to his time on Wednesday."

James Brown's long letter of January 8, 1848, to George, telling of Brown Brothers' decision to invest in the Collins Line, makes clear how dependent the line would be on congressional support, and how much the mail subsidy was tied up with the idea of developing a steam navy:

This line has an advantage in the fact of $385ᵐ [$385,000] per annum over any *American competition* that can be got up and rely on it we shall have a preference when ready over British Boats. . . . In case of war this kind of Tonnage is valuable as the Govt will require it. . . . The Secretary of the Navy [John Y. Mason] assures us there would be no difficulty in getting more time to complete our contract in getting the ships ready as we are building larger than the contract called for, which the Government preferred; . . . . If necessary we shall try to get an extension of time from Congress, but there is not the least fear of their annulling the contract if [we are] not ready to perform it in full they are too anxious to provide this kind of Navy to be ready for them at a moment's warning.

Collins, according to Brown, had "taken every pains to come at the expenses" of the ships and machinery, and was "entirely satisfied they will fall short rather than exceed the estimates," but the vessels actually cost vastly more than the $1,200,000 capital originally subscribed. (Each of the captains who commanded the Collins liners was required to be a stockholder.) The best estimate of the actual cost, according to an unpublished Columbia University thesis by John G. Dow, is $2,800,000. A loan from the government provided part of this, but more than $624,000 worth of bonds were bought by James Brown and the principal stockholders to provide necessary funds.[1] By January 10, 1852, Collins and the Browns had to address a memorial to the Senate and the House of Representatives praying for "additional facilities" in transporting the mails. The cost of each voyage was over $65,000 whereas only an average of $48,000 was recovered in receipts. "Unless we are met

[1] See statement of condition of the line as of January 1855, supplied to Representative Chandler of Pennsylvania by John A. Brown—*Congressional Globe,* 33rd Congress, 2nd Session, p. 778.

by Congress in a national spirit, responsive to that by which we ourselves have been actuated," they could not, they said, continue. And to prove that their own motives were truly national, not personal, they offered to "withdraw from the enterprise," if the government wished and transfer the ships and the mail contract to "any person named by the government."

James Brown's conviction that his boats would "have a preference when ready over British Boats" was based partly on his confidence in the ships themselves and partly on the fact that some at least of the Cunarders had to stop at Halifax. "The line that goes via Halifax will take few passengers from this country unless the others are full," he told his brother. His prediction was sound. In the first eleven months of 1852, the Collins liners carried almost twice as many passengers as the Cunarders (though the Cunarders carried more than three times as much mail). But the Cunarders were making money and the Collins liners were not. Joseph Shipley—then living in retirement at Rockwood, outside Wilmington, afflicted with gout—patiently drafted a long letter to a member of Congress explaining why:

Experience has shown [he wrote on February 21, 1852] that the company was right in projecting Steamers of such great size & power but what was at that time wanting was the experience of the much greater relative cost of ships and machinery of this magnitude, combining for the first time the necessary strength & qualities for formidable war frigates. Hence in a spirit of enterprise and with a National zeal for the credit of the Country in Ocean Steaming, then monopolised by British capital & skill, the proprietors carried out their plans under what has proved a very inadequate appropriation from our Government.

Shipley assured the congressman that he was not and never had been himself "directly interested" in the company, but that—having been a partner in the line's Liverpool agency—he knew that the company's statements as to its heavy losses were true, and that there was "no concealment or aim at jobbery in the affair."

Copy — Private

My dear Sir

I take the liberty to deduct from the $500. the following sent from my Store to *Certain parties* important to our cause at W[ashington] City whilst I was there. viz

2 Doz Wild Cherry Brandy	$24.
1 . Extra Sparkling Moselle	18
2500 Segars — $20. + $56. —	76.
Brandies & Scotch. Ale	35.75
	153.75
I endn balance of	346.25
	500.

please return my check by Brunot & believe me — my dear Sir

Most truly Yours
Jacob Snider Jr

Phila July 24/52

Wm E Bowen Esqr,

(*Brown Brothers Harriman & Co. Historical File*)

In order to get favorable action from Congress on the petition for an increased subsidy, Collins and the Browns found that they had to play the political game as it was currently being played. There were bitter debates in the House and Senate, opposition to the increase coming chiefly from Southern and Western Democrats who were jealous of New York. In February, therefore, Collins pulled off one of his most spectacular lobbying feats. He took the *Baltic*—which then held the Atlantic speed record—up the winding channel of the Potomac to Alexandria and invited President Fillmore, the members of the Cabinet, and all the Senators and congressmen (a total of 2000 people) to dinner on board. But there was less spectacular—and probably even more effective—lobbying to be done. By June the Ways and Means Committee had acted favorably on the petition, but on June 12th William E. Bowen wrote from Philadelphia that a local Representative thought it would require "every vote we can procure" to carry the measure through the House, calling as it did for an increase from $385,000 to $858,000 annually, retroactive to January first.

On July 24th, after the measure passed, Bowen sent to James Brown a copy (reproduced here) of a bill he had received from Jacob Snider, Jr., a Philadelphia merchant with whom he and John A. Brown occasionally had dealings. The bill was for $153.75 worth of Cherry Brandy, Sparkling Moselle, Brandies, Scotch ale, and "2500 Segars" sent from Snider's store "to *certain parties* important to our cause at W[ashington] City whilst I was there." Since Bowen had recently loaned Snider $500, Snider deducts the $153.75 from that amount, leaving a $346.25 balance due. Bowen planned to debit Brown Brothers & Co. for the amount Snider had deducted.

John A. Brown (then summering, as usual, in Newport) had written Bowen on the 19th: "I presume Snyder [sic] ought to be congratulated when all is settled—Some three or four weeks ago he called on me to say that $1500—I think this was the sum, would relieve him from all his embarrassments and wanted to borrow this sum upon some kind of security which he considered himself not very available. I said to him then if he had any thing that was like security I would loan it to him—He made no allusion at that time to the steamers, nor did I suppose he had any influence in Washington or *I* might have alluded to *them*." If Bowen still thought Snider "rendered *most* important services," John A. suggested he confer with "my Br. James" on the subject and "do what is right." So Bowen wrote James Brown that if Snider "had not taken hold as he did at the time, the [Collins] Relief Bill would not have passed. It was at his instance that West [Captain James West of the *Atlantic,* one of the line's ablest and most affable commanders] went to Washington & he can tell you what Snider's services were." West's report was apparently favorable, for James Brown soon wrote Bowen that it would be "quite satisfactory" for him to debit Brown Brothers for Snider's $153.75 charges.

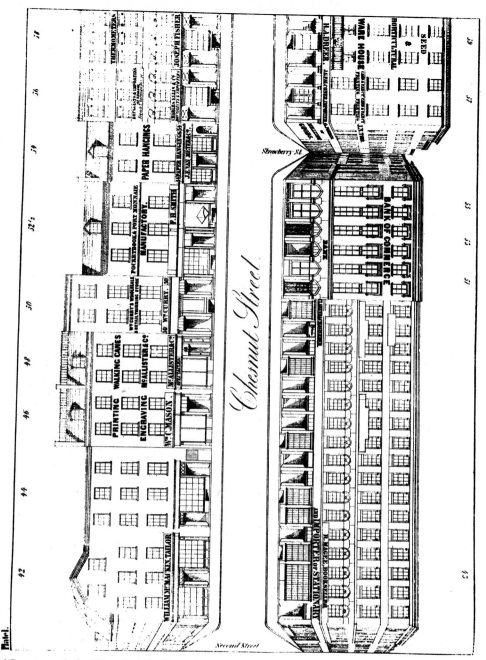

(Courtesy of the Historical Society of Pennsylvania, Philadelphia, Penna.)

Even after the increased subsidy was finally passed by Congress, Bowen was busy at the Browns & Bowen office on Chestnut Street, keeping track of congressional sentiment. (The office is shown here in a lithographed plate from Rae's *Philadelphia Pictorial Directory and Panoramic Advertiser* (1851). Browns & Bowen's sign—probably illegible in this reduced reproduction of the plate—is under the ground floor windows of No. 55—later 209—Chestnut, the large building on the right whose upper floors were occupied by the Bank of Commerce. For almost forty years, starting in 1848, Brown Brothers & Co.'s Philadelphia offices occupied these quarters.)

"Now the battle is fought and *won*," Bowen wrote Brown Brothers on July 15th, "it is well you should know

who are your enemies & who friends." And five months later he reported to James Brown that one Ambrose W. Thompson had been invited to "unite in a movement" in Washington designed to see that the increased subsidy would be cancelled in 1854, and that there was also a scheme "to levy more 'black mail' from the line." James Brown's reply, dated December 14, 1852, was characteristic and a pleasure to quote: "Our minds are made up to go on with our Contract irrespective of any threats of Black mail; if we are ultimately to lose by it, we would rather make the less and be done with it when our time is up. . . . If Mr. Thompson and others choose to unite in a movement against the Collins Line they must do so as we will make no payments to prevent it."

On Wednesday, September 27, 1854, the Collins liner *Arctic,* largest and most splendid of the company's ships, sank off Cape Race, Newfoundland. Walter Lord (author of *A Night to Remember,* about the sinking of the British liner *Titanic* in 1912) has called the sinking of the *Arctic* "This country's greatest ocean tragedy," and Alexander Crosby Brown's account of it in *Women and Children Last* (New York, 1961) is a restrained but deeply moving narrative which is a classic of our maritime history. As the caption of N. Currier's lithograph records, "On her homeward voyage from Liverpool during a dense fog, she came in collision with the French iron propeller 'Vesta,' and was so badly injured that in about 5 hours she sank stem foremost, by which terrible calamity nearly 300 persons are supposed to have perished." The lithograph was made

"From a sketch by James Smith of Jackson, Miss., a passenger on board the 'Arctic' "—and shows (rather murkily in the right foreground) Smith himself on a raft wearing a high hat.

Sixty-one of the 153 officers and crewmen aboard survived, but only twenty-four of the 182 passengers—not one woman or child included. Among those lost were E. K. Collins' wife, only daughter, and youngest son, and six members of James Brown's immediate family: his son William Benedict Brown (who had recently become a partner in Brown Brothers), William's wife Clara Moulton Brown, their infant daughter Grace; his favorite daughter "Millie"; his daughter Grace (Mrs. George F. Allen) and her infant son Herbert. (*Courtesy of the Mariners Museum, Newport News, Va.*)

In Greenwood Cemetery, over in Brooklyn, James Brown erected a monument to the memory of the six members of his family who perished with the *Arctic.* Resting on a solid granite base, four columns support a Gothic canopy above a carved marble representation of the sinking ship (shown above in a photograph by C. Bradford Mitchell). The monument, which still attracts visitors to the city's most beautiful cemetery, was designed by Edward Tuckerman Potter, a brother of James Brown's son-in-law and partner Howard Potter. (*Courtesy of Alexander Crosby Brown*)

Sole survivor of the Brown group on the *Arctic* wa GEORGE F. ALLEN (1815–1863), opposite, whose wif (James Brown's second daughter Grace Davison Brown and infant son were beside him on the quarterdeck—a was Millie Brown—when the mortally wounded *Arcti* commenced her final plunge. Allen, an officer of th Novelty Iron Works which built the *Arctic*'s engines, wa one of those who, with Captain James C. Luce, miraculousl escaped from the sucking vortex of the sinking vessel an found refuge on one of the ship's paddle boxes whicl bounded up from the depths (killing Captain Luce's so as it fell back into the sea). "Why am I here, wh am I here! Why was I saved when all the rest were lost? he cried out bitterly when, after being rescued, he reache James Brown's house in New York. The photograph re produced here from a Brown family album was taken in th late 'fifties, about the time that his friend George Temple ton Strong wrote of him in his diary: "Poor soul, what life of bitter memories his must be! . . . . I thought could see that the black shadow of the past came sweepin over him every now and then." (*Brown Brothers Harrimar & Co. Historical File*)

WILLIAM BENEDICT BROWN (1825–1854), second son of James Brown by his first wife Louisa Benedict Brown, was admitted to partnership in Brown Brothers & Co. on January 1, 1853, after working for some time with Thomas B. Curtis in the Boston office. He was apparently destined to become head of the firm, since his elder brother James Alexander Brown had been accidentally killed, shortly after his marriage to Maria Louisa Howland in 1847, by a toy Fourth-of-July gun he had given his wife's young brother. But William and his French wife Clara Moulton Brown, their infant child and the child's nurse all perished with the *Arctic*. The photograph was made from an original daguerreotype in possession of Madame Emily Moulton Verger. (*Courtesy of Alexander Crosby Brown and the Mariners Museum, Newport News, Va.*)

MARIA MILLER BROWN (1833–1854), known as Millie, was James Brown's favorite daughter. The *Arctic*'s fatal voyage had started on her twenty-first birthday. A New York stockbroker named William W. Gilbert was very attentive to her on the voyage and there were rumors they were to be engaged. Gilbert saved himself in one of the two lifeboats that reached Newfoundland. Millie, last seen on the quarterdeck, went down with the ship. Her portrait, undated and unsigned, has been handed down through the Brown family and is now in the possession of Alexander Crosby Brown of Newport News, Virginia. (*Courtesy of Alexander Crosby Brown*)

ALEXANDER GRANT, one of the *Arctic*'s firemen, was picked up by the same ship (the *Cambria*) that rescued George Allen and Captain Luce. A "Bluenose" from the Gut of Canso, Nova Scotia, he had been shipwrecked twice before, and in 1857 survived a fourth sea disaster when the steamer *Central America* foundered off Cape Hatteras. This picture of him accompanied an article about "The Man Who Couldn't Be Drowned" in *Harper's Weekly,* October 17, 1857. (*Author's Collection*)

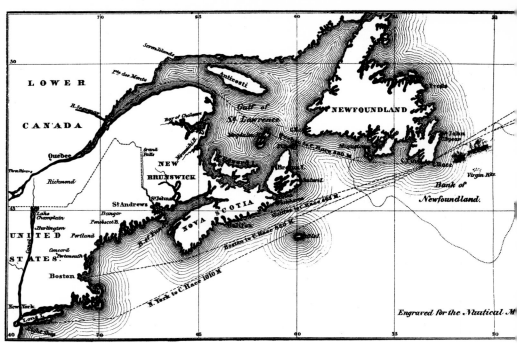

This engraved chart was published in *The Nautical Magazine*, November 1854, illustrating an article on "The Loss of the *Arctic.*" The two vessels shown east of Cape Race represented the *Arctic* and the *Vesta* colliding. (*Courtesy of the Mariners Museum, Newport News, Va.*)

The personal tragedies endured by James Brown and E. K. Collins were heavy. Strong's diary records that Brown was "so crushed and shattered" that he was "hardly expected to live." And the loss of so many lives in the finest Collins ship might well, one would suppose, have been a serious blow to the line itself. But the line kept on and even survived a second disaster when the *Pacific* left Liverpool in January 1856 and was never heard from again, presumably having hit an iceberg.

Ironically, Brown Brothers' Boston agent, Thomas B. Curtis, soon after the *Arctic* was lost, had advocated a more southerly route for the Atlantic crossings than the one shown on the chart (above right), partly to avoid icebergs. On February 5, 1855, he sent the newspaper clipping reproduced above to Brown Brothers with a letter urging that "Mr. Collins should advertise *that the Collins line would adopt*" Matthew Maury's proposed southerly routes.

But what doomed the Collins Line was the withdrawal of its congressional subsidy. In 1858, after the line's new *Adriatic* had made one round trip, James Brown and Collins finally gave up, as reported in the article reproduced at right.

The article part of which is reproduced below appeared in *Hunt's Merchants' Magazine*, May 1858. James M. Brown (not J. N. Brown as in the article) was the Brown Brothers partner present at the sale. Clarkson N. Potter—an older brother of Howard Potter—was the firm's legal counsel. (*Brown Brothers Harriman & Co. Historical File*)

RAILROAD, CANAL, AND STEAMBOAT STATISTICS.

SALE OF THE COLLINS LINE OF OCEAN MAIL STEAMERS.

The steamers Adriatic, Atlantic, and Baltic, of the Collins Line, were sold on Thursday, the 1st of April, 1858, at their wharf at the foot of Canal-street, New York. The U. S. District Attorney gave notice before the auction commenced, that the General Government had a lien upon the steamers to the amount of $115,500. A notice was read from the Board of Supervisors that the city had a claim of $39,000, for the taxes of 1856-7, upon the company, and that the Atlantic was held for the amount. Capt. Briggs announced that the hands attached to the steamers had also a claim of $3,000 against the company. A counter proclamation was made on behalf of the line, that all the claims of the United States Government had been duly satisfied, and that the tax claim of the city was unauthorized. A further announcement was then made, that Messrs. Clarkson, N. Potter, and J. N. Brown had a liability of the company of $500,000, dated May 1, 1855, drawing interest from Nov. 1, 1857, also a mortgage dated Nov. 30, 1857, to secure the claim. The three steamers were purchased by Dudley B. Fuller, Esq., (as agent for other parties,) for $50,000. The terms were 20 per cent on the spot, and the remainder on the next day.

What is to be the final disposition of these steamers has not yet been announced, but it appears to be probable, if not certain, that they cannot be kept in successful operation between New York and Liverpool without government subsidy. The amount which our government expends in maintaining American ocean mail steamers is much less than is paid by either Great Britain or France.

On p. 629 of this number of our Magazine we have given a statement of the amount which Great Britain pays annually to her lines of steamers for conveying the mails to her colonies and to foreign countries. The aggregate sum is about five-and-a-half millions of dollars a year. The Cunard line receives a much more generous subsidy than the Collins line hitherto enjoyed.

Ten

ATLANTIC SHUTTLING

Letter from James Brown, dated July 31, 1860, to Joseph Shipley at Rockwood, outside Wilmington, Delaware. Shipley's notation (upper left corner) indicates it was received and answered on August first. James and his wife, with their twenty year old son Clarence, are going abroad to attend the opening of the free library William Brown had built for the citizens of Liverpool, and James asks if there is anything he can do for Shipley while there. It was a good time to go, James said, since "some of the Great Men of the Nation" would be there.

(Brown Brothers Harriman & Co. Historical File)

What may have "a little surprised" Joseph Shipley in this letter was probably not the news that Mr. and Mrs. James Brown and their youngest son were going to the opening of "The Library Brother W^m. has built" but that they were sailing on the ex-Collins liner *Adriatic*.

The great ship had been idle ever since James Brown's agent bid her in at the sale on April Fools' Day, 1858, but James had recently chartered her to the North Atlantic Steamship Company, which ran her to Southampton and Havre. She was, after all, as their advertisements said, "unexcelled by any steamship in the world for comfort, safety, and speed."

When the James Browns visited Liverpool in 1860 they
must surely have become familiar with the part of the city
shown in William G. Herdman's 1858 watercolor, reproduced above. The picture shows the east side of Strand
Street, either side of the Custom House (the large building
shown near the center of the map on p. 104), and was
painted looking southward from a point near the foot of
Redcross Street and the northeast corner of Canning Dock.
Just left of the colonnaded Custom House is the warehouse
where William & James Brown & Co. had their offices for
a few years before moving in 1824 to the foot of Chapel
Street, opposite St. Nicholas Church (p. 27) near George's
Dock basin (at left of map on p. 104). (*Courtesy of
Brown, Picton and Hornby Libraries, Liverpool*)

James Brown's son John Crosby Brown, two
years older than Clarence, was already in Liverpool when his parents arrived to attend the opening
of the William Brown Library. Following graduation
from Columbia College in 1859 and a year of travel
in Egypt and Syria he was visiting his Uncle William, and had just abandoned his hopes of going
into the ministry and decided to go into business
with his father, whose two eldest sons had been
killed and whose next oldest, George Hunter Brown,
was in precarious health. Once he had decided, his
father advised him that the place to begin was in
the Liverpool office. "You can get a better training
here than at home," James Brown told him, "as
you must begin at the bottom and take your chances
with every one else." Brown Shipley & Co. had
recently moved into new quarters in the Richmond
Buildings (shown on opposite page).

No. 34 Strand Street still stood in 1965 when Jay Robinson
made this sketch of it, though the building to the left of it
and the Custom House were destroyed during German air
raids in the Second World War. (*Brown Brothers Harriman & Co. Historical File*)

The Richmond Buildings, shown here in a 1965 photograph by Robson & Baxter, Ltd., were built by William Brown in the late 1850s from designs by James A. Picton, the architect who was chairman of Liverpool's Library and Museum Committee at the time William Brown gave the city the building to house its collections. Located at 26 Chapel Street, on the north side two blocks up from the old warehouse and counting house at the foot of the street, it was opposite the group of buildings, including the Exchange and the Town Hall, which were at the center of Liverpool's commercial life (see the number 5 near the left margin of the map on p. 104). Brown Shipley & Co. occupied the principal offices (to the right of the entrance), leasing space elsewhere in the building to various merchants. The firm maintained offices here from 1860 until 1888 when it transferred all its operations to the London office, established in 1863 (see p. 112).

(*Courtesy of "History of Martins Bank" Committee, Martins Bank, Ltd., Liverpool*)

The tympanum above the entrance to Brown Shipley's offices in Richmond Buildings was elaborately carved with William Brown's coat of arms, surmounted by "the red hand of Ulster," and flanked by the flags of the United States and Great Britain, symbolizing the firm's and the family's Anglo-American ties. The leaves and branches forming the wreath around the coat of arms and providing a background for the flags are those of the oak on the British side and of the cotton plant on the American side. (*Courtesy of "History of Martins Bank" Committee, Martins Bank, Ltd., Liverpool*)

"At the time I entered the office," John Crosby Brown later remembered,[1] "Liverpool was at the height of its commercial prosperity, and was the principal cotton market not only for England but for the Continent. . . . In our Liverpool office a very large clerical force was needed to look after cotton and other produce consigned to Brown, Shipley & Company for sale, and to expedite the shipment of manufactured goods from Birmingham, Manchester, Sheffield and other adjacent towns, consigned to us for export to the United States."

The expenses of operating the office in the early 'sixties, as listed in the "Charges Account for 1864," included such items as: Alterations, Painting, Coals, Gas &c—£457; subscriptions to Lloyds, the Exchange News Room, and the Underwriters Rooms for the partners and managers, totalling £21; subscriptions to various papers including the *Shipping Gazette,* the *Manchester Guardian,* the London *Times, Bradshaw's Railway Manual,* and the *Boston Courier,* totalling more than £20; "Luncheons & Teas"—£71; "Subscriptions & Donations to Charities"—£69; "Wages, Porterage &c"—£1830; "Hoops, Bagging, Twine, Sack ties, Cooperage, Guaging Petroleum &c"—£196; and stationery—£259.

[1] *A Hundred Years of Merchant Banking,* New York, 1909, pp. 139ff.

103

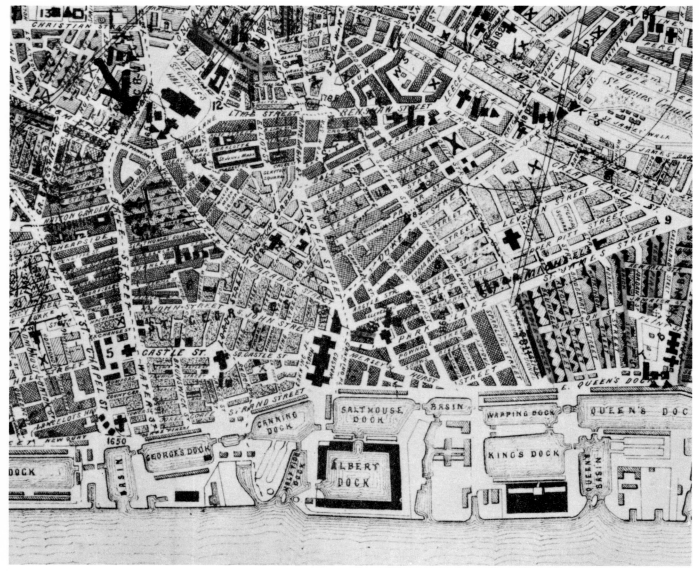

The location of the new library presented to the city by William Brown, and of the various offices his firm occupied over the years, can be seen on this slightly enlarged detail from a map of "Liverpool Ecclesiastical and Social" prepared in 1858 by the Reverend Abraham Hume and first exhibited by him before the National Association for the Promotion of Social Science in October of that year. Canon Hume was an earnest advocate of public education and was deeply interested in the relationships between poverty and morality and health. His map, lithographed by Chaloner & Lawson of Liverpool and published by Whittaker & Co., London, showed "the Locality of Pauperism, Cholera & Violent Deaths" as well as "Church Accommodations" for the Poor and for the Rich (one church or chapel for every 350 rich people, one for every 3000 of the poor).

Canon Hume was one of the Secretaries of the events connected with the opening of the William Brown Library, and he included a copy of his map in a handsome leather-bound album of "Documents Connected with the Opening . . . , 18th October, 1860," which he "collected and arranged for James Brown, New York." On that copy he had marked the route of the huge procession which marched from the Town Hall (the dark cross right of the number 5 at left center) by a circuitous route to the library on Shaw's Brow (upper left, designated by an arrow left of St. George's Hall). Brown Shipley & Co.'s new offices in the Richmond Buildings were across Chapel Street from the square containing the Town Hall and Exchange, in the darkened block opposite the letters *apel* in the street's name. The old warehouse and counting house, occupied by the firm from 1824 to 1858, was at the foot of Chapel, just above the Church of St. Nicholas on the south (right) side. The Custom House, erected in 1826 on the filled-in site of the Old Dock, is represented by the large black figure, formed of two crosses extending from a central block, at the center of the map. William Brown's first Liverpool office, back in 1810, had been at No. 30 Old Dock, and for four years prior to moving to Chapel Street in 1824 William & James Brown & Co. had been at 34 Strand Street, just left of the Custom House (see p. 102). (*Courtesy of the Brown, Picton and Hornby Libraries, Liverpool*)

William Brown had laid the cornerstone of the library on April 15, 1857, at a ceremony recorded by an unknown photographer in the picture reproduced above. The original, now in the library's collection, was formerly owned by Henry A. Bright, a Liverpool merchant and shipowner who also contributed to various literary magazines and was a friend of Nathaniel Hawthorne, the great American novelist who was United States consul in Liverpool at the time the library's cornerstone was laid. Hawthorne is the man standing just left of William Brown, on the second step above the one Brown stands on alone.

On the margin of the original photograph, Bright identified several of the figures. The blurred figure in front of the post at extreme left is Richard Monckton Milnes, "whom I like," Hawthorne recorded in his *English Notebooks*, "and who always reminds me of Longfellow." Next to him, just right of the post, is James Holme, Deputy Mayor. The short man in the plumed hat next to Holme is Lt. Gen. Sir Harry G. W. Smith, in command of the district. Between Sir Harry and Hawthorne is Lord Stanley, son of the 14th Earl of Derby (three times Prime Minister), whose "mincing, slightly affected or made up manner" at first led Hawthorne to suppose he was "a salesman in a dry-goods establishment"—until Milnes introduced him and Haw-

thorne realized he occupied "the foremost position among the young men of England." The three front-row figures to the right of William Brown are the Bishop of Chester ("a little shrimp of a man," Hawthorne noted, "not at all filling up one's idea of a bishop"), the Reverend Dr. Raffles (the city's leading non-conformist clergyman), and at lower right Mr. James A. Picton, chairman of the Library and Museum Committee (after whom the library's reference department is now named).

Hawthorne described the day's ceremonies at length in his notebooks. The procession, he said, "could not have been a very striking object," since it was "merely a trail of ordinary-looking individuals, in great coats, and with precautionary umbrellas"—except for the Bishop "in his flat cap and black silk gown" and Sir Harry "in full uniform, with a star and a half-a-dozen medals on his breast." As for William Brown, he was "the plainest, and simplest man of all; an exceedingly unpretending old gentleman in black, small, withered, white haired, pale, quiet, and respectable." Hawthorne "rather wondered why he chose to be the centre of all this ceremony, for he did not seem either particularly to enjoy it, or to be at all incommoded by it, as a more nervous and susceptible man might."

On October 17, 1860, the day before the library was officially opened, the three-day celebration began with a meeting at Liverpool's Royal Amphitheatre, "intended chiefly for the working classes." Lord Brougham was the principal speaker, but "MR. DANIEL GUILE, a working man"—otherwise unidentified in the newspapers of the time—was permitted to address the meeting following presentation to Mr. Brown of a gilt clock "in the Louis Quatorze style" and a "massive silver salver" on behalf of the city's working men. Daniel Guile, shown in the photograph at right, reminded his listeners that "There was a time . . . when what we now call workmen . . . were looked upon as mere machines, as beasts of burden. Knowledge to them was a hidden thing . . . ; and in later times we were looked upon as a class who knew only to eat, drink, sleep, and work." But there had been spirits who rose out of this "intellectual gloom" to show "that in the masses there was mind"—men like Stephenson, Watt, Brunel, "and last, though not least, our worthy friend Mr. Brown himself." These men showed that "the mind that exists in the masses only needs cultivation and encouragement to make us what God intended we should be—great, glorious, and free." So, he told his "working friends," if their leisure hours, "instead of being spent in the taproom—('hear, hear,' and applause)—the singing room, and the dancing room," were given to study and the persevering acquisition of the knowledge "which now is placed within our reach," they would be "the envy of surrounding nations and the pride of the world."

(*Brown Brothers Harriman & Co. Historical File*)

(*Brown Brothers Harriman & Co. Historical File*)

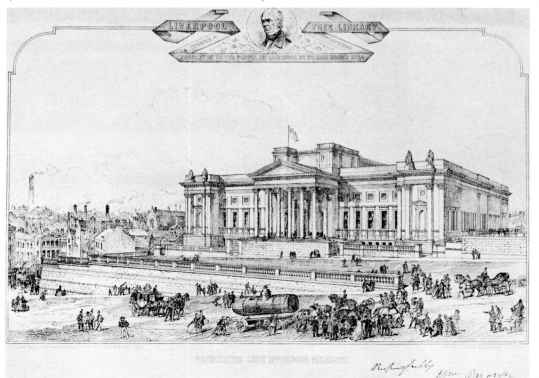

This lithograph of the library building was distributed with the Liverpool *Mercury* two days after the opening. The building, designed by John Weightman, the city surveyor, had a portico "after the Temple of Jupiter Stator in Rome," and was built to house both the Free Library and a museum of natural history based upon the collection of Lord Stanley's grandfather, the 13th Earl of Derby. William Brown paid for the building itself (£40,000, or about $184,000), but—as the *Mercury* pointed out—the city had to spend about £100,000 additional for the land and the terrace required by the unfortunate site, the "hanging level" on Shaw's Brow.

The steam boiler being drayed up Shaw's Brow in the foreground reminds us that the lithograph was made by Maclure, Macdonald & Macgregor, "Lith^{rs} to the Queen by Steam Power" in Liverpool, London, Manchester, and Glasgow.

This photograph of WILLIAM BROWN, paired with that of Daniel Guile on the facing page, was included in the album of "Documents" Canon Hume collected and arranged for James Brown (see p. 104). In acknowledging Guile's speech and the gift from the working men, he reminded them that "We shall always find in well chosen books something . . . which enables us, with advantage to ourselves, our families, and our country, to take a higher position in the social scale," and dwelt at some length on the theme that "Libraries are competitors for customers with improperly conducted public houses."

More of his personality emerges from Hawthorne's notebook entry about the ceremonies in 1857. Following the laying of the cornerstone there had been a banquet in St. George's Hall. William Brown himself had taken Hawthorne up into the gallery before the banquet started, where they had "a fine view of the noble hall, with tables laid, in readiness." Brown had often met Hawthorne before. Back in January 1855, when U. S. Ambassador James Buchanan (later President) was visiting the Browns, Hawthorne had been one of the notables invited to a dinner given at Richmond Hill. "The whole table and dessert-service was of silver," Hawthorne had recorded, but the party had been "rather dull, as almost all Liverpool dinners are."

The banquet at St. George's Hall was not much better. Hawthorne sat between James Picton and a Captain Campbell, "both companionable men," but the speeches and toasts were variously "commonplace," "heavy and frowsy," and "undistinguished," though "less hemmy and haw-y than English oratory ordinarily is." The banquet itself was "only a cold collation, though sufficiently splendid in its way," and Hawthorne was "really tired to death" before his turn to speak came at the end of the program. He could not hear what Monckton Milnes said in introducing him, but there was "a vast deal of clamor" in response

(Brown Brothers Harriman & Co. Historical File)

before he could begin. On the whole his speech went off well, he thought; "certainly it was better cheered than any other, especially one passage, where I made a colossus of poor little Mr. Brown." What he said, according to the papers next day, was in reference to Brown's successful efforts, in 1856, to mediate between the Prime Minister, Lord Palmerston, and United States Minister George M. Dallas after President Pierce dismissed Her Majesty's Minister to the United States. "You have had a proof, and that not long ago," Hawthorne said, "that it was good for both countries that our guest was here, that he grasped as it were England in his right hand and America with his left. (Cheers.) Otherwise the unanimity of the countries might have been sundered, and we should have been in a state of enmity. ('Hear, hear,' and cheers.)"

Brown Brothers Harriman & Co. Historical File)

His gift of the library earned official honors for William Brown (Queen Victoria made him a Baronet in December 1862), but he did not live long to enjoy them. By the time this unattributed photograph was pasted into a scrapbook kept by John Crosby Brown and his wife on their wedding trip (Dec. 1864–Sept. 1865), Sir William had been dead for almost a year. His obituaries had duly recorded his accomplishments and benefactions, but their tone was, on the whole, equivocal—indicating (as the author of one in the March 26, 1864, issue of the Liverpool *Porcupine* said) "that however truly Sir William Brown was a benefactor of this town, he did not know the secret of winning men's hearts or even avoiding their hatred."

(Brown Brothers Harriman & Co. Historical File)

Among those at the head table at the 1860 banquet in St. George's Hall, following the official opening of the library, was FRANCIS A. HAMILTON (1814–1907), who had been a partner in the Browns' Liverpool house since 1845. (The photograph reproduced here is undated, but was probably made in the 1880s.) He had been an apprentice in the office from 1832 to 1837, and from 1839 to 1845 had served as the Browns' agent in Savannah, Georgia. After William Brown became a member of Parliament in 1847, the active management of Brown Shipley & Co. was almost entirely in the hands of Joseph Shipley and Hamilton. After Shipley's retirement in 1850 Mark Collet (see opposite page) joined the partnership and he and Hamilton ran the office. When John Crosby Brown went to work there in 1860, "Mr. Hamilton had charge of the sale of cotton and other produce, while Mr. Collet looked more especially after the credits and financial business, and Mr. Stewart Henry Brown [son of Stewart Brown of New York] attended to the general correspondence and clerical force. From his long experience in Savannah and Liverpool, Mr. Hamilton had become an expert judge of cotton, and it was common report that more disputes between buyer and seller about the quality of cotton had been referred to Mr. Hamilton for settlement than to any other man in Liverpool." And twenty years later, at a time when John Crosby Brown was involved in very trying negotiations with the English partners, he said of Hamilton, in a personal letter to his brother-in-law Howard Potter on June 3, 1881: "a truer, juster & more generous man, in the soundest sense of the latter word, I have never known."

Both Hamilton and Collet seem to have been less venturesome than their seniors, William and James Brown. Brown Shipley & Co's "private" letters to Brown Brothers & Co. in New York in the 'fifties and 'sixties, most of which are written in Hamilton's or Collet's hand, reflect the extremely cautious integrity of the two men and their unqualified disapproval of business men who were "too enterprising." The failure in 1859 of Fraser, Trenholm & Co., New Orleans cotton factors, struck Hamilton, for instance, as "only another evidence how sure trouble is to overtake Houses who unduly push their business." And in 1860, writing of another New Orleans house (headed by a man whose daughter had recently married one of William Brown's grandsons), Hamilton acknowledged that the father and son who composed the firm were well off, and that he and Collet had perhaps placed too limited credits at their disposal "from an old apprehension that the father was apt to be wild & speculative, & also that it was not easy to account very satisfactorily for the rapid acquisition of such ample wealth." And when Brown Brothers in April 1860 declined to grant a credit of $120,000 to the Boston firm of Sampson & Tappan, to enable them "to control the California Quicksilver mines," Hamilton and Collet approved, even though the proposition seemed to involve temptingly handsome commissions, because of Brown Brothers' impression that the house was " 'scheming' & venturesome."

MARK WILKS COLLET (1816–1905) was the first partner in the Brown firms to become Governor of the Bank of England, a position to which he was elected in 1887, about the time this undated photograph was made. When he became a partner in 1851, following Shipley's retirement, he had already had considerable experience both as a merchant and a banker. He had been a clerk in the Liverpool house of Thomas Wilson & Co (one of the "three W's" mentioned on p. 58), had been a submanager of the Bank of Liverpool (1842–48), and had been a partner for three years in a firm engaged in the West Indies trade. The son of an English merchant who died when Collet was young, he grew up in Archangel, Russia, where his mother, of Dutch descent, had been born. When Collet returned to London about 1830, he knew Russian better than English, and in later years he also learned to speak French fluently. Of a legalistic turn of mind ("He has done well as a Banker," Howard Potter once said, "but he would have been even more eminent as a Special pleader in Chancery!"), Collet's business letters were, as John Crosby Brown observed, "apt to be unnecessarily long." It is somehow indicative of his meticulous conservatism that although he remained an active partner into the twentieth century he "always wrote with a quill pen which he made and mended himself."

(*Brown Brothers Harriman & Co. Historical File*)

Early in October 1857, things looked very bleak to the American partners. Joseph Shipley, who had just heard from John A. Brown how serious his brother James thought the situation was, sent off a letter to his old friend William Brown, designed to reassure him that if it were again necessary to apply to the Bank of England for assistance, the Bank would surely remember "the successful result and beneficial effects" of the aid they gave in 1837. But Shipley's report of conditions here was not encouraging. "Unreasoning panic prevails," he wrote; "the Currency is in a great measure annihilated and neither produce nor merchandise nor stocks nor Real Estate can be made available to pay debts—hence Banks & wealthy solvent merchants are prostrated, and the usual facilities of trade & for getting produce to market are suspended."

Then, on October 14th, the New York banks suspended specie payment, producing the scene recorded in the wood engraving below, reproduced from J. S. Gibbons' *The Banks of New York . . . and the Panic of 1857* (New York, 1858). The picture shows the crowd gathered in the street in front of Brown Brothers' building (just beyond the Merchants Exchange at right) to hear W. A. Booth, President of the American Exchange Bank, announce the suspension from the steps of his bank's building at 50 Wall. (Note that the tree shown on p. 88 in front of Brown Brothers' old office at No. 58, formerly 46, still survives.)

But despite the difficulties, Hamilton was able to write Shipley on November 23rd that "(everything is progressing favorably & at no time did the House stand higher than at present." They had "escaped losses by protested Bills wonderfully" and "never were so free of Bills on the Anglo-American Houses." Indeed, they had been able to give a guarantee for £15,000 to George Peabody's "embarrassed" firm, thus returning the favor Peabody did for them in 1837 (see p. 62). But Hamilton doubted that Peabody would avail himself of it "as his pride I fancy makes him desire to get on without our aid." (Several days later Collet reported that George Peabody & Co. "affected not to have taken assistance" from the Bank of England, but the Bank's receipt to Brown Shipley for its guarantee indicated that the "agreed advances" had been made. By December 5th Junius Morgan, the managing partner, had accepted an additional £5000 guarantee from Brown Shipley.)

(*Author's Collection*)

Wall Street on Suspension Day. Oct. 14 1857.

The nature (and profitableness) of the exchange business which formed so large a part of Brown Brothers' and Brown Shipley's private merchant banking activities is made quite clear in the prospectus put out in 1862 by a newly organized corporation known as The British & American Exchange Banking Corporation, Ltd. The copy of the prospectus reproduced on this and the next page was enclosed by Hamilton in Brown Shipley's "private" letter to Brown Brothers dated January 10, 1863. Judging from "the well known energy & ability" of some of the directors listed on the first page, Brown Shipley feared they would "find in this opposition more to contend against than we have yet encountered. The general principal [sic] of all such concerns, is to do a large business on small commissions, looking more to the extent of their transactions, on the Insurance principle, than to contracted & prudent operations on larger charges."

Speaking for the firm, Hamilton pointed out that the new company would have "great advantages, by having Branches in London, as well as Liverpool," and that its connection with the Oriental Bank Corporation (listed on p. 1 among the new company's bankers and represented on the board of directors by its chairman, Harry George Gordon) would give it "a good deal of power" in the foreign credit business in the Far East. Furthermore, Brown Shipley had heard that the new corporation would soon select an agent in New York.

Brown Shipley was obviously concerned, and their letter suggests two ways in which the Brown firms could "forestall the Company in some measure." One was to advertise in American and British newspapers "that we are prepared to undertake every description [of] Banking & Commission Business." The other, "to charge on both sides [of the Atlantic] as moderate commissions as possible on deposits, collection of dividends, transmission of Funds, & all other business involving little or no risk," and to grant "marginal credits for cash in hand or for approved security available, charging a quarter %, if we could get it, in the former case, or if not, taking the interest for our compensation, & in the latter [charging] possibly not over ½%, when the security was undoubted." Many banks willingly did business on such terms, Hamilton pointed out, and "the constant intercourse between nations by steamers & telegrams is reducing all commissions throughout the world." If the Brown firms adhered to "stringent rates" the business would go "past us." In the light of these remarks, the last paragraph on the first page of the prospectus and the first at the top of page two take on added interest.

THE

BRITISH & AMERICAN
EXCHANGE BANKING CORPORATION,
LIMITED.

ESTABLISHED UNDER THE COMPANIES' ACT, 1862, WITH LIMITED LIABILITY.

CAPITAL ONE MILLION STERLING.

In 20,000 SHARES OF £50 EACH.   FIRST ISSUE 10,000 SHARES.

It is not intended to call up more than £25 per Share.

(With power to the Shareholders to increase the Capital.)

Deposit £1 per Share on Application, and £1 per Share on Allotment.

DIRECTORS.

ARCHIBALD BOYD, Esq., Director of the Union Bank of London - - - - LONDON.
WILLIAM JAMES FERNIE, Esq., of the Firm of FERNIE BROTHERS & Co., - - LIVERPOOL.
JOHN GILCHRIST, Esq., of the Firm of GILCHRIST, WATT & Co., of Sydney, Director of the Union Bank of London - - - - - - - - LONDON.
ROBERT GILLESPIE, JUN., Esq., of the Firm of GILLESPIES, MOFFATT, & Co. - LONDON.
HARRY GEORGE GORDON, Esq., Chairman of the Oriental Bank Corporation - - LONDON.
HAROLD LITTLEDALE, Esq., of the Firm of T. & H. LITTLEDALE & Co. - - LIVERPOOL.
WILLIAM M. NEILL, Esq., of the Firm of NEILL BROTHERS & Co. - - - MANCHESTER.
THOMAS REES, Esq., of the Firm of R. & T. WOODWARD & Co. - - - LIVERPOOL.
WILLIAM RENNIE, Esq., of the Firm of CAVAN, LUBBOCK, & Co. - - - LONDON.
SAMUEL STITT, Esq., of the Firm of STITT BROTHERS & Co. - - - LIVERPOOL.

BANKERS.

LONDON:	- -	THE UNION BANK OF LONDON.
LIVERPOOL	- -	THE BANK OF ENGLAND.
MANCHESTER	-	THE BANK OF ENGLAND.
INDIA & CHINA	-	THE ORIENTAL BANK CORPORATION.

SOLICITORS.

LONDON:	- -	MESSRS. COTTERILL & SONS.
LIVERPOOL: -	-	MESSRS. FLETCHER & HULL,

BROKERS.

LONDON: - - SHEPPARDS, PELLY, & ALLCARD, 28, Threadneedle Street.
J. & J. WHITEHEAD - - - 8, Moorgate Street.
LIVERPOOL: - HORSFALL & ADDISON.

TEMPORARY OFFICES.

6, NEWMAN'S COURT, CORNHILL, LONDON.
MIDDLETON BUILDINGS, RUMFORD STREET, LIVERPOOL.

THE British and American Exchange Banking Corporation, Limited, is formed for the purpose chiefly of dealing in Exchanges, a business which, excepting with British possessions, has hitherto been mainly in the hands of private firms; and it is well known that with many countries such Banking facilities have not been afforded to merchants and others as the vastly extended commerce of the present day demands. This is particularly the case in the trade between England and America, and it is proposed that this Corporation shall commence its operations by the establishment of an agency in New York.

The profitable nature of Exchange business is well known, especially that with the American States, and although the profit is at present greater than can be calculated upon in ordinary years, there is generally a much larger margin than is usually found remunerative by bankers. The purchase and sale on commission of securities in New York and London, the dealings in which amount annually to many millions sterling, and the remittances of interest and dividends will afford other sources of profit.

The practice now become very general of attaching Bills of Lading to Bills of Exchange as collateral security, renders exchange operations more than usually safe, whilst the shipment of gold involves scarcely any risk whatever.

The shipments of produce and specie from New York alone for the past year have amounted to nearly forty millions sterling, and the average of several years has not been much less. There is thus, a very extended field for the operations of the Corporation, and the facilities which it will afford, both in this country and America, must tend to promote, and still further to extend the commercial and monetary transactions between the two countries.

The same remarks are applicable to other places in which the establishment of Agencies is contemplated.

A large business is also anticipated betwixt America and the ports in India and China, which will be carried out in co-operation with the Oriental Bank Corporation.

The success of Joint Stock-Banks dealing in Exchange is evidenced by the present quotations of the shares of the undermentioned Companies: and it is somewhat remarkable that the Joint-Stock principle has not yet been adopted in the American trade, though presenting a wider field for its profitable operation than any other part of the world.

	Paid-up.	Present Prices.
Bank of Australasia...	40	69 to 71
New South Wales	20	49 — 51
Union of Australia	25	49 — 51
London Chartered of Australia	20	$26\frac{3}{4}$ — $27\frac{1}{4}$
Oriental	25	54 — 55
Agra and United Service	50	94 — 96
Mercantile Bank of India, London, and China	25	41 — 53
Ottoman	20	34 — 35
Colonial	25	41 — 43

The Corporation will have Offices both in London and Liverpool.

The Corporation is formed under "The Companies' Act, 1862," whereby the liability of the shareholders is strictly limited to the amount of their respective shares.

No promotion money will be given for originating the undertaking, and the preliminary expenses will be strictly confined to such as are indispensable.

Applications for Shares may be addressed in the annexed form to the Directors; or to the Brokers of the Corporation; and copies of the Prospectus may be obtained upon application to them, or to the Solicitors, or at the London and Liverpool Offices of the Corporation.

Brown Brothers Harriman & Co. Historical File)

By mid-February it was clear that the new corporation was not quite so ably managed as Hamilton had expected it to be. Collet reported, in Brown Shipley's private letter of February 14th, that the board of directors "has not figured very creditably" in the way they issued the corporation's shares, "which (if not improper) is deemed at least disingenuous & as designed to promote that speculation in the Shares which drove them to the ridiculous Premium of 11½ from which they have since relapsed to 8, and in which jobbings some of the Directors are believed to have had a Share." But even though these things had "not improved the Standing of the Concern," Collet admitted they involved "nothing to prevent the Company achieving all that the Board professes to aim at." And he had heard on good authority that "a second Bank of the same kind" was "being got up" —so profitable did the business promise to be.

Throughout succeeding months there are recurrent references in Brown Shipley's letters to the "wild speculation" in the shares of the British & American Exchange Banking Corporation, and by June 1864, most of the original directors had resigned, leaving the bank "in the uncontrolled management of Mr. Fernie & his nominees." Fernie had apparently headed a "Stock-jobbing clique" which got in trouble selling more shares than had been issued, and the bank appears to have quietly died late in 1864. Meanwhile, however, the threat to Brown Shipley's and Brown Brothers' business embodied in its original prospectus had precipitated a decision which marked a major turning point in the history of the Brown firms. On January 28, 1863—just eighteen days after Hamilton had sent the prospectus to the New York house—Collet wrote, in the firm's regular private letter, that "the effect on our business likely to follow from the establishment" of the new Exchange Banking Corporation, and "increasing competition we have to meet in various directions . . . had revived the question, often discussed before, of opening a House in London." After much discussion, he wrote, "we have come to the conclusion, subject to your full concurrence, that it will be for the interest of the House to open such an establishment. . . ."

The "Memorandum" on the setting up of a London house, included in the letter Collet wrote for the firm on January 28, 1863, indicated that the London office would be concerned with "the retention and extension of our existing business in Credits, Exchange & Commissions," leaving to Liverpool "its present Produce & forwarding business, and such part of the Bill business as is connected with Bills of Lading in Liverpool & in the neighbourhood."

So it was decided, and Collet went up to London to find suitable quarters for the new establishment. He found them in the shadow of the Bank of England, up a narrow passage off Lothbury known as Founders' Court (after the ancient and honorable Founders Company, formed in the fourteenth century to carry on the "mystery" of brass-founding). The ancient Founders Hall which long occupied the site had been replaced in 1848 by a building erected as the Central Telegraph Station of the Electric Telegraph Company. It was this building, whose entrance is shown above in a wood engraving from the *Illustrated London News* of January 22, 1848, that Collet secured for £22,000 as Brown Shipley's London office.

As the *Illustrated London News* said, in the 1848 article about the Central Telegraph Station accompanying the wood engravings on this page, the interior of the building was "remarkably elegant in arrangement and profuse in ornament." The "capacious Hall" which architect H. A. Hunt had provided for the "general business" of the telegraph company could with little change serve equally well for the general business of the banking house, and the rooms off the hall and off the balconies were as adaptable for the various managers and clerks of Brown Shipley as for the "electric correspondence" originally carried out in them. So, on December 15, 1863, Brown Shipley & Co. issued a circular announcing the opening of their London house, whose address would be—as that of Brown, Shipley & Co., Ltd., still is—"Founders Court, Lothbury, London, E.C."

American Rendezvous.

Prominent among those Anglo-American institutions which flourish in the English capital is the banking-house of Messrs. Brown, Shipley, & Co., of Founder's-court, Lothbury. It is the house which unquestionably transacts the bulk of the vast banking business between England and America. Americans coming to Europe, and Englishmen going out West, apply to Brown, Shipley, & Co. for their drafts and letters of credit, quite as a matter of course. The business premises of this great firm lie in the heart of the City, hard by the dingy, grimy building known as the Bank of England. Here of all places in the crowded bustling City may be obtained a fair idea of business London, and no visit to the metropolis is complete without a glimpse at least of such thoroughfares as Lothbury and Threadneedle-street. There are few, indeed, who miss the sight of the enormous traffic that surges through these narrow streets, for, as we have already said, Americans

INTERIOR VIEW OF MAIL DEPARTMENT: MESSRS. BROWN, SHIPLEY, & CO.'S, FOUNDER'S COURT, E.C.

come hither in their thousands to transact their banking business. Messrs. Brown, Shipley, & Co. are the financial agents to the United States Government, and this in itself is a recommendation, if such were needed, to citizens of the Great Republic. Their name, however, is as well known to Americans as the Bank of England itself, and the innumerable branches they have throughout the world render them, above other banks, the house *par excellence* for the wants of the traveling public. They have every facility for meeting the wishes of their customers in any direction, and telegraphic transfers of money from America to Europe are carried out in the course of a few hours. They also make a speciality of receiving accounts of American banks, firms, and individuals upon most favorable terms, and buy and sell bills of exchange on every country in the civilised world. The issue of travelers' credits in sterling, available in any part of the world, or in the various currencies required, is a special feature, and the enormous business done in this department speaks well of their banking arrangements abroad. In old London, or the City proper, there is much to interest the visitor. The old wall, the Cathedral, and the sight of the stupendous traffic that ebbs and flows from light to dark,—these things cannot be seen elsewhere; and if we add to them the banking house of Messrs. Brown & Shipley we but point to an institution which, in financial circles at least, stands second to none among the various objects of interest with which the City teems.

(Brown Brothers Harriman & Co. Historical File)

Some idea of how Brown Shipley modified the interior of the old telegraph station can be got from the rather crude half-tone illustrations published in the supplement to the July 10, 1896, issue of *The London American*. (The above picture, of course, shows the way teller's cages were put in the "capacious Hall.") Even though the pictures and the article accompanying them refer to a much later period than we have reached, they are amusing examples of eighteen nineties "puffery," and they call attention to a feature of the firm's business which for many years made Brown Brothers and Brown Shipley well known to people who had little if any interest in their less publicized but far more profitable operations in exchange and commercial credits. For the term "Letter of Credit" meant, to most Americans, a traveler's "Circular Letter of Credit," which —in the days before travelers checks—was the principal means of providing tourists with funds to spend abroad.

To get back to the 1850s and '60s, and see how generally travelers letters of credit were associated with Brown Brothers & Co. at that early date, we can turn to a book called *Notes from Plymouth Pulpit—A Collection of Memorable Passages from the Discourses of Henry Ward Beecher* (New York, 1859). Beecher (whose sister wrote *Uncle Tom's Cabin*) was by all odds the most popular preacher of the time. His triumphant revivalism packed the pews of Plymouth Church, on Brooklyn Heights, and an admirer named Augusta Moore took down the passages quoted in this volume. The passage we are concerned with begins near the bottom of p. 189, thus, and continues (as it does here) on the next page:

Suppose I were to set out on a pilgrimage to Jerusalem, and before I started were to go to Brown Brothers & Co., and obtain letters of credit for the cities of London, Jericho, etc. Then, with these papers which a child might destroy, which would be but ashes in the teeth of flame, which a thousand chances might take from me, I should go on with confidence and cheer, saying to myself, " As soon as I come to London I shall be in funds.

I have a letter in my pocket from Brown Brothers & Co., which will give me five hundred dollars there; and in the other cities to which I am bound I shall find similar supplies, all at my command, through the agency of these magic papers and pen strokes of these enterprising men." But, suppose that instead of this confidence I were to sit down on shipboard, and go to tormenting myself in this fashion: "Now, what *am* I to do when I get to London? I have no money, and how do I *know* that these bits of paper which I have with me mean anything, or will amount to anything? What shall I do? I am afraid I shall starve in the strange city to which I am going." I should be a fool, you say; but should I be *half* the fool that that man is who, bearing the letters of credit of the Eternal God, yet goes fearing all his way, cast down and doubting whether he shall ever get safe through his journey? No fire, no violence, nor any chance, can destroy the checks of the Lord. When he says: "I will never leave thee, nor forsake thee," and "my grace shall be sufficient for thee," believe it; and no longer dishonor your God by withholding from him the confidence which you freely accord to Brown Brothers & Co.

(Brown Brothers Harriman & Co. Historical File Library)

Since few readers nowadays can be supposed to know what "these magic papers and pen strokes of these enterprising men" looked like, or how they were used, the earliest known surviving example is pictured on this and the following three pages. The letter was a three-page circular which the traveler carried folded into an embossed leather case (below). The first page (reproduced at right) was the actual letter. Engraved on watermarked paper, with blanks to be filled in, it was addressed by Brown Shipley & Co. "To Messieurs The Bankers mentioned on the third page" and requested them to furnish the traveler (in this case George B. Atlee of Philadelphia, the author's maternal grandfather) "whose Signature is at the foot" with any funds he might require up to an amount written into a blank in the engraved text (in this case £300 sterling, or $1380 at the then rate of exchange). The bankers were to reimburse themselves by drafts on the Browns' London bankers, Heywood, Kennards & Co., Brown Shipley engaging "that the same shall meet due honor." Further, "Messieurs The Bankers" were asked to record on the second page of the circular the amounts of money the traveler "took up" at their banks so that there would be a record from which the next banker he approached could determine how much of the total was left. And finally the letter specified how long the credit ran (in this instance a little over five months, from July 18th to December 31, 1862). (*Author's Collection*)

GEORGE ALEXANDER BROWN, who signed the circular letter of credit "per procuration" for Brown Shipley & Co., was the brother of Stewart Brown, of the New York firm. Trained in the Baltimore house, he joined the Liverpool firm in 1847. In the days when Alexander and George Brown were helping to organize the Baltimore and Ohio Railroad, he is said to have had the distinction of riding with George Stephenson on the trial run of his famous *Rocket* on the Liverpool-Manchester Railway. (*Brown Brothers Harriman & Co. Historical File*)

The red morocco case, embossed with gilt designs, in which the 1862 letter of credit was folded, is more elaborate than the plain leather cases later supplied by the firm, several of which are in the Historical File. (*Author's Collection*)

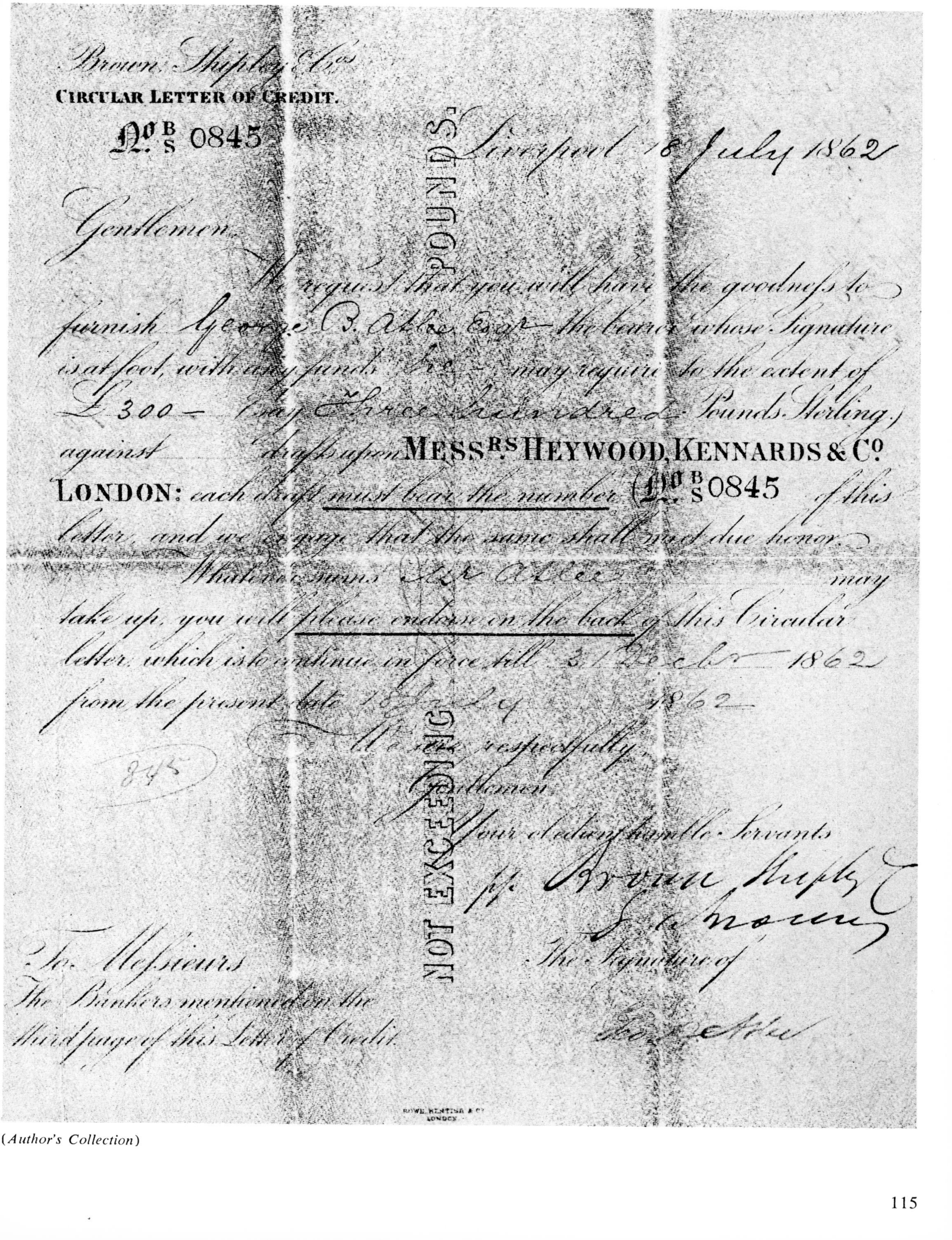

Brown Shipley & Co's

CIRCULAR LETTER OF CREDIT.

No. B/S 0845

NOT EXCEEDING POUNDS.

Liverpool 18 July 1862

Gentlemen

We request that you will have the goodness to furnish George B. Atlee Esqr the bearer whose Signature is at foot, with any funds he may require to the extent of £300 — say Three hundred Pounds Sterling, against drafts upon **MESSRS. HEYWOOD, KENNARDS & Co.** **LONDON:** each draft must bear the number (No. B/S 0845) of this letter, and we engage that the same shall meet due honor.

Whatever sums Mr Atlee may take up, you will please endorse on the back of this Circular letter, which is to continue in force till 31 Decr 1862 from the present date 18 July 1862

We are respectfully

Gentlemen

Your obedient humble Servants

pp. Brown Shipley & Co

845

To Messieurs

The Bankers mentioned on the third page of this Letter of Credit.

The Signature of

Geo B Atlee

ROWE, KENTISH & Co
LONDON

(*Author's Collection*)

Author's Collection

The second page of the circular (the back of the actual letter of credit) was left blank for the endorsements of "Messieurs The Bankers" who at various stages of the traveler's journey furnished him with sums of money to be deducted from the total amount of his credit. The endorsements on the back of Mr. Atlee's letter indicate that three days after he received the letter from George Alexander Brown in Liverpool he was in York, where he took up £10 at the bank of Messrs. Swann & Co. On August 1st he was in northern Scotland, and took up £20 at the office of the Bank of Scotland there. By the 16th he was in London, where he twice got £10 from Heywood & Co. Then, in September and October he took up similar sums from Lombard Odier & Co. in Geneva, S. & A. Blumenthal &

Co. in Venice, Robert de Froelich in Munich, Mendelssohn & Co. in Berlin, and John Monroe & Co. in Paris. All told, he took up only £140 of the 300 (well within the letter's time limit), and as there is no indication that the balance was paid to him, his grandson enjoys supposing that somewhere in the vaults of Brown, Shipley & Co., Ltd., Founders Court, London, E.C., there are one hundred and sixty pre-1914 gold-standard pounds, plus interest compounded for one hundred and six years, to which he is entitled by inherited right. But as Henry Ward Beecher might well have said under the circumstances, there was probably some magic in the pen strokes of the enterprising men at Brown Shipley's Liverpool office which arranged things otherwise.

AIX LA CHAPELLE..	C. Wintzens Oeler	
ALEXANDRIA	Tod Rathbone & Co.	
ALGIERS	Franqueville & Co.	
AMSTERDAM	Alstorphius & Von Hemert	
ANTWERP	Agie & Co.	
ATHENS	Paul Sculudi	
ABERDEEN	{ Bank of Scotland / National Bank of Scotland	
BAYONNE	F. J. Graham	
BADEN BADEN	F. S. Meyer	
BAGNI DI-LUCCA	Maquay & Pakenham	
BASLE	Passavant & Co.	
BATAVIA	Pitcairn Syme & Co.	
BARCELONA	Vidal y Quadras Hermanos	
BELFAST	Northern Banking Co.	
BERLIN	* Mendelssohn & Co.	
BERNE	Marcuard & Co.	
BEYROUT	Ottoman Bank	
BIRMINGHAM	Lloyds & Co.	
BONN	Jonas Cahn	
BOLOGNA	G. B. Renoli	
BOMBAY	Ewart Latham & Co.	
BOULOGNE s/m	Adam & Co.	
BORDEAUX	Barton & Guestier	
BREMEN	Evd. C. Delius & Co.	
BRESLAU	Eichborn & Co.	
BRIGHTON	London & County Bank	
BRISTOL	Stuckeys Banking Co.	
BRUSSELS	J. Delloye Tiberghien & Co.	
CADIZ	John D. Shaw	
CAIRO	Tod Rathbone & Co.	
CALCUTTA	Gillanders Arbuthnot & Co.	
CAMBRIDGE	London & County Bank	
CARLSRUHE	Haas Frères	
CANTON	Olyphant & Co.	
CAPE OF GOOD HOPE	James Searight & Co.	
CHELTENHAM	Gloucestershire Banking Co.	
CHRISTIANIA	Tho. Joh. Heftye & Son	
COBLENTZ	Deinhard & Jordan	
COLOMBO, CEYLON	Oriental Bank Corporation	
COLOGNE	{ Société de la Banque / A. Schaaffhausen	
CONSTANTINOPLE	{ Chs. S. Hanson & Co. / Ottoman Bank	
COPENHAGEN	Smidt & Le Maire	
CORK	National Bank	
DRESDEN	H. W. Bassenge & Co.	
DUBLIN	Royal Bank of Ireland	
DUNDEE	{ Bank of Scotland / National Bank of Scotland	
DUSSELDORF	Baum Boeddinghaus & Co.	
EDINBURGH	{ Bank of Scotland / National Bank of Scotland	
FLORENCE	{ Emanuel Fenzi & Co. / Maquay & Pakenham	
* FRANKFORT A/M	{ M. A. de Rothschild & Sons / Gogel Koeh & Co.	
FOOCHOW	Olyphant & Co.	

GALWAY	National Bank	
GALATZ	Ottoman Bank	
GENEVA	* Lombard Odier & Co.	
GENOA	Gibbs & Co.	
GIBRALTAR	Archbold Johnston & Powers	
GLASGOW	{ Bank of Scotland / National Bank of Scotland	
GOTHENBURG	James Dickson & Co.	
HAMBURG	{ Salomon Heine / J. Berenberg Gossler & Co.	
HANOVER	Adolph Meyer	
HARROGATE	Harrison & Co.	
HAVRE	C..Lataam & Co.	
HEILDEBERG	W. Köster & Co.	
HOMBOURG LES BAINS	{ Banque Privilegieé de / Commerce	
HONG KONG	Oriental Bank Corporation	
INTERLAKEN	Isidor Jackowski	
INVERNESS	{ * Bank of Scotland / National Bank of Scotland	
JERUSALEM	M. P. Bergheim	
KANDY, CEYLON	Oriental Bank Corporation	
KILLARNEY	National Bank	
KNARESBORO'	Harrison & Co.	
LAUSANNE	Felix Marcel & Fils	
LEAMINGTON	Warwick & Leamington Bank	
LEGHORN	{ Grant More & Co. / Maquay & Pakenham & Smyth	
LEIPSIC	Frege & Co.	
LIMERICK	National Bank	
LISBON	{ Duarte Carvalho & Co. / William Wynn	
LONDON	* Heywood Kennards & Co.	
LONDONDERRY	Northern Banking Co.	
LUCERNE	F. Knorr & Fils	
LYONS	Arlés-Dufour & Co.	
MADEIRA	John Blandy & Sons	
MADRAS	Arbuthnot & Co.	
MADRID		
MALAGA	{ Scholtz Brothers / John Clemens	
MALTA	{ P. Eynaud & Co. / R. Duckworth & Co.	
MANCHESTER	Sir B. Heywood, Bart., & Co.	
MANILLA	Ker & Co.	
MANNHEIM	Wm. Köster & Co.	
MARSEILLES	{ Rabaud Frères & Co. / Arlés-Dufour & Co.	
MAURITIUS	Oriental Bank Corporation	
MAYENCE	G. L. Kayser	
MELBOURNE	Oriental Bank Corporation	
MESSINA	Cailler & Co.	
MILAN	Carli & Co.	
MONTPELLIER	{ E. Blouquier Fils & Westphal / Bazille & Castelnau	
MOSCOW	A. Marc & Co.	
MUNICH	* Robert de Froelich & Co.	

NAPLES	{ Meuricoffre & Co. / C. M. de Rothschild & Sons / W. J. Turner & Co / Rogers Brothers & Co.	
NEUCHATEI	Pury & Co.	
NICE	Avigdor L'Ainé & Fils	
NOTTINGHAM	J. & J. C. Wright & Co.	
ODESSA	Ernest Mahs & Co.	
OSTEND	A. & J. van Iseghem	
OXFORD	London & County Bank	
PALERMO	I. & V. Florio	
PARIS	{ Hottinguer & Co. / John Munroe & Co. / Van den Broek Brothers & Co. / B. G. Wainwright	
PAU	Bergerot	
PISA	Maquay Pakenham & Smyth	
POINT DE GALLE	Oriental Bank Corporation	
PRAGUE	Leopold Laemel	
RIGA	Cumming & Co.	
ROME	{ Maquay Pakenham & Hooker / Plowden Cholmeley & Co.	
ROTTERDAM	Moses Ezechiels & Sons	
RYDE	Hampshire Banking Co.	
SEVILLE	{ Gomez & McPherson / Hartley & Co.	
SHANGHAI	{ Oriental Bank Corporation / Wetmore Williams & Co.	
SHEFFIELD	Sheffield Banking Co.	
SYDNEY, N.S.W.	Oriental Bank Corporation	
SINGAPORE	{ Ottoman Bank / Syme & Co.	
SMYRNA	{ Hanson & Co. / P. Homère	
SOUTHAMPTON	Hampshire Banking Co.	
SPA	Henry Hayemal	
STRASBURG	E. Klose & Co.	
ST. PETERSBURG	Thomson Bonar & Co.	
STETTIN	William Schlutow	
STOCKHOLM	Tottie & Arfwedson	
TOULOUSE	Courtois & Co.	
TRIESTE	Moore & Co.	
TUNBRIDGE WELLS	London & County Bank	
TURIN	Dupré, Père & Fils	
VEVEY	Genton & Co.	
VENICE	* S. & A. Blumenthal & Co.	
VIENNA	Henikstein & Co.	
WARSAW	S. A. Fraenkel	
WEISBADEN	B. Berlé	
WELLINGTON, N.Z.	Oriental Bank Corporation	
WATERFORD	National Bank	
YORK	* Swann Clongh &	
ZURICH	Bodmer Brothers	

OR ANY OTHER BANKER TO WHOM THIS MAY BE PRESENTED.

(Author's Collection)

On the third page of the circular there was a printed list of the banks and private banking houses that composed the world-wide network of banks with which Brown Brothers and Brown Shipley did business. Mr. Atlee placed stars by the names of those he dealt with, but it is interesting to note that the endorsements on the back of his letter include names not on the printed list. So universally respected was the name of the Brown firms that bankers everywhere in the world willingly accepted the assurance that drafts on Brown Shipley's account at Heywood, Kennards & Co., drawn with reference to their letters of credit, would "meet due honor." It was not an idle gesture for the firm to address their travelers letters of credit not only to their correspondents but also, as indicated at the bottom of the page, to "any other banker" to whom the traveler might present it anywhere in the world. Many of the banks listed—especially the private ones—went out of existence long ago, but more than thirty (some under other names) are included among the nearly one thousand correspondent banks with whom Brown Brothers Harriman & Co. does business today.

It is difficult to determine exactly when the Browns began issuing these travelers credits. As early as 1824, Alexander Brown & Sons in Baltimore addressed to the Liverpool house a letter lodging a credit of £250 in favor of a Mr. John M. Colston of Virginia "who crosses the Atlantic in search of Health & to see his Brother who resides in Paris." But this credit was available only at the Liverpool office. Circular letters, available wherever the traveler went, seem to have been developed in the 'fifties. Then, and until 1947 when Brown Brothers Harriman & Co. abandoned the circular credits business, Americans traveling on these credits used Brown Shipley's office as a rendezvous and a place where they could get their mail or arrange to have it forwarded. When Nathaniel Hawthorne's friend Herman Melville arrived in Liverpool in May 1857, one of the first things he did, according to his diary, was pick up his mail at Brown Shipley.

In that year the firm granted a total of £277,706 of such credits. Next year the total declined, but in 1859 picked up again and on February 22, 1860, Brown Shipley's private letter to Brown Brothers noted that although the totals for the past three years had been "small, compared with the amount that must be spent by Travellers in Europe," they expected that "there will now be a steady & progressive increase, when the additional facilities of your present system of Circular Credits become known."

As this suggests, Brown Brothers as well as Brown Shipley issued the circular letters. Mr. Atlee could have been provided with one at the firm's Philadelphia office, but apparently chose to take specie or bills of exchange with him on the ship to Liverpool and get the letter there.

Seated near William Brown at the banquet after the opening of the library was the Honduras Minister to the Court of St. James. His otherwise surprising presence is explained by the fact that in 1854, at the request of the British government, William Brown became involved in a project to build a Honduras Interoceanic Railway, linking the Atlantic and Pacific Oceans. A company was formed, of which William Brown was chairman. In the letter of which the first page is reproduced here William reported the difficulties the company was having wth a group of American engineers —headed by Trautwine, the great authority on bridges—who had been sent to Honduras to survey a line for the road.

Nothing much came of the railroad scheme, apparently, but the letter is reproduced here as evidence of the fact that William Brown as well as his brother James became involved in large enterprises not directly related to the firm's business. This sort of thing worried the junior partners— especially Hamilton and Collet in England.

Throughout the 1850s Collet's and Hamilton's letters express grave concern over the amount of capital "so invested as not to be immediately available for the purposes of business." The worst of these "lock ups" was, of course, the result of James Brown's involvement with the Collins Line. Brown Shipley's private letter of February 17, 1859 (written by Collet), points out that the balance sheets for 1858 showed that of the combined firms' total capital of something more than $4,500,000 almost $840,000 was locked up in "the Acct. connected with the Steamers." But there were considerable lock ups in railroads as well.

Soon after the sinking of the *Arctic*, William W. Gilbert, the young broker who had been so attentive to Millie Brown on board ship (p. 99), persuaded James Brown to buy almost $200,000 worth of stocks and bonds in two upstate New York railroads: the Canandaigua & Niagara Falls and the Lake Ontario. (To quote Hamilton's Brown Shipley letter of March 23, 1855: "Thus Mr. Gilbert to earn a Commission has palmed off upon Mr. Brown & the House some £42000 of *worthless Securities,* which

(Brown Brothers Harriman & Co. Historical File)

he *must have known* to be *questionable,* at all events, if he knew anything at all about them!! This is paying dear for his acquaintance.") At about the same time Henry Dwight, Jr., an exchange broker and railroad promoter whose office was in the 61 Wall Street half of Brown Brothers' building, was unable to pay a large debt he owed the firm, and Brown Brothers found itself the owner of a large block of Chicago & Mississippi Railroad stock which Dwight had put up as security for his loan. It had depreciated considerably in value since Brown Brothers accepted it as collateral, and in order to make the best of a bad bargain, the firm soon found itself involved in reorganizing the railroad. In the process they became heavily involved, making loans to pay for additional equipment and taking ownership of six of the road's locomotives as collateral security. By the fall of 1855, when the reorganized line was known as the Chicago, Alton & St. Louis Railway, Brown Brothers and Brown Shipley had about $384,000 locked up in it and the English partners were fearful that Brown Brothers would have to take over the road and operate it. As late as 1859 more than $250,000 was still locked up in the road. Ironically, perhaps, a considerable part of the capital presently available to Brown Brothers Harriman & Co. in 1968 resulted from a further reorganization of the Chicago & Alton, carried out forty years later by E. H. Harriman.

Perhaps the most disenchanted yet convincingly judicious estimate of Sir William Brown published after his death was by B. Guiness Orchard. Originally published in a Liverpool newspaper (in a version that substituted the name William Green for William Brown), the piece was later republished by Orchard in his *Liverpool's Legion of Honor* (Liverpool, 1893). "I cannot say that, apart from the acquisitive faculties, he had much intellect"; Orchard wrote, "though in a great merchant there is no small element of imagination, fancy, humor, sympathy—far more than is supposed by those literary men who have concentrated *theirs* on other objects." But Orchard stressed the fact that "from the commencement of his career . . . his mental grasp was capacious and firm. He saw clearly and widely, and never forgot. He knew at a glance, as if by instinct, the exact value of each element before him, whether material or emotional, . . . and never wasted in hesitating blindness his time or strength on what would not yield him profit."

Orchard also credited Sir William with "consummate prudence" which enabled him "to share the profits, yet avoid the losses, of whatever large enterprise he connected himself with," and the foresight to perceive, long before others began to consider the subject, "the true value of new projects or novel financing arrangements." But he also noted Sir William's skill in "selecting instruments": "His numerous staff of clerks was probably superior to any equal number of clerks in the town; and, though they found the work hard and the pay not liberal, they served him with unsurpassed faithfulness. His partners, too, were men of great talent." Orchard knew little about the partners of the early years (Shipley, Bowen, Frodsham, and Priestman), but of those who joined him later, "when his wealth entitled him to practically engage ambitious merchants as salaried and strongly controlled subordinates," Orchard spoke with firsthand knowledge: Collet "the sub-manager of a bank, who, when removed from a narrower post" justified the choice by becoming "an unsurpassed financial manager"; Stewart Henry Brown (Stewart's son), taken straight out of college, "soon mastered every detail" of the business and "rebuked the laughter of older men by showing almost superhuman tact and acuteness in judging markets"; and Hamilton, "a cotton broker, who, in the great firm, was infallible as a

Shortly before the Brown library was opened, when the British were worried about Napoleon the Third, WILLIAM BROWN had raised and equipped, at his own expense, the First Brigade of Lancashire Artillery Volunteers. He is shown here in his uniform as Lieutenant Colonel. (*Brown Brothers Harriman & Co. Historical File*)

judge of cotton, most estimable as a gentleman and philanthropist." Altogether, Orchard concluded, old Brown was "a marvellous man . . . and, regarded merely as a moneyspinner, he was admirable. Without intending to be so, he was a public benefactor. For these leaders of enterprise, these organizers of commerce, these centres of labour, are undoubtedly public benefactors." Liverpool had realized this, Orchard said, since the "memorable evening" back in 1837 when word came that the Bank of England had averted the stoppage of William & James Brown & Co. by giving them "such an advance as no other Liverpool firm has had before or since. This was the only time in his life, probably, when he was cordially cheered. On that day, for the first time, our general population recognized his importance to themselves; thenceforth he was known as Liverpool's foremost merchant."

In the months following the celebration of the opening of the William Brown Library, Hamilton and Collet were harassed with problems arising out of the approaching Civil War in America. South Carolina's secession from the Union in December 1860, and the establishment of the Confederacy the following spring, thoroughly disrupted the traditional cotton triangle trade by which the firm had prospered for so many years. In May 1861, the Confederate congress prohibited the payment of debts to Northern creditors and the shipment of cotton except through Confederate ports—but those ports, including New Orleans and Mobile, were under blockade by the Northern navy.

The pen and ink sketch (above), showing the "River and Levee at New Orleans from the North East Angle of New Custom House 4th Story," was made in October 1855 by Thomas K. Wharton, a New England architect who had superintended construction of the Custom House.

On June 8, 1861, the border state of Tennessee also seceded from the Union, closing the last of the great cotton ports on the Mississippi from which Northern merchants might have been able to get cotton for shipment abroad. The Memphis, Tennessee, levee is shown here in a wood engraving from *Harper's Weekly,* March 15, 1862. (*Author's Collection*)

OLD BATTERY AT THE NAVY-YARD   STEAMBOAT LANDING.

THE COTTON LEVEE.

This wood engraving of "United States Flying Artillery Going on Board the Steamship 'Atlantic' at New York, April 6, 1861" should be compared with the picture on p. 92, showing the same ship at the same Canal Street pier, when little Rollo embarked on his European travels and the name of a different steamship company was on the pier shed's gable. The text accompanying this picture in *Harper's Weekly* (April 20, 1861) records that the *Atlantic* sailed "under sealed orders" on the 6th with several hundred troops and 78 horses for whom stalls had been built in the bow of the ship.

(*Author's Collection*)

Eleven

THE AMERICAN QUARREL

In the spring of 1860 *Harper's Weekly* took occasion to drub the defunct Collins Line. "There was a time," it said in an editorial, "when Congress paid a large subsidy to the Collins steamers. Unhappily Mr. Collins and his associates had neither the sagacity nor the moderation which were requisite to retain the boon. Instead of relying on the patriotism and sagacity of Congress, it is loudly asserted that they undertook to buy up members and newspapers; and, as was to be expected, the result was the loss of their annual grant. An odor of corruption and roguery hung round the line to the day of its death. It was badly managed, badly officered, and badly engineered in every way."

Ironically, this blast was delivered in an editorial (March 10, 1860) arguing that America would need a steam navy in case of war, and that Congress should subsidize American steamers at least as well as England subsidized Cunard's. Ironically, too, it ignored the fact that whatever political skulduggery Collins and his associates had engaged in had been an effort to counteract the dubiously "patriotic" opposition of Jefferson Davis and his Southern colleagues to any subsidy for a Northern enterprise. Perhaps the greatest irony was that, about a year later, two of the "badly officered, badly engineered" ships of the "badly managed" line turned up in the *Weekly* as naval assets of some importance.

U.S. IRON CLAD STEAM-SHIP "ROANOKE,,
The first Turretted Frigate in the U S 1863.

(*Author's Collection*)

As noted earlier, Howard Potter had been secretary-treasurer of the Novelty Iron Works before becoming a partner in Brown Brothers, and he continued as a director after that, representing his father-in-law's majority interest. During the war, the Novelty Works built a good deal of naval armament for the federal government, including the turret for the first *Monitor*. This lithograph by G. Hayward for the 1863 edition of Valentine's *Manual of the Common Council* shows the Navy's first turreted frigate *Roanoke* being fitted out at the Novelty Works.

The issue of *Harper's Weekly* for April 20, 1861, contained two pictures of former Collins liners loading troops and military stores to be used in putting down the rebellion of Jefferson Davis's Confederacy—the one of the *Atlantic* on the preceding page and another of the *Baltic*. The latter sailed two days after the *Atlantic*, with five hundred troops and a cargo reported to consist of ordnance tools, muskets, foraging carts, forge vices, ammunition, and a "remarkable quantity" of spiritous liquors—or cases that were so labeled, at any rate. (One case was marked "58 bottles firemen's rum.") But the real giveaway—in those days of speculation about relieving Fort Sumter in Charleston harbor—were the large number of gunny bags put on board. As the canny New York *Herald*'s reporter noted, gunny bags were "very serviceable in protecting a boat's crew in approaching a battery." What he was hinting was true: this was the expeditionary force secretly organized by Assistant Secretary of the Navy G. V. Fox to relieve Major Anderson's beleaguered garrison.

When the war began, severe strains were, of course, set up between the English and American partners in the Brown firms and between the New York house and its agencies in Baltimore, Savannah, Mobile, and New Orleans. The chief burden of reconciling the divergent views which naturally arose fell upon James Brown, head of the New York house, who was in Paris with Mrs. Brown when the fighting started. Keeping in close touch with William L. Dayton, the American ambassador in Paris, with his brother William, and with the partners actively in charge at Liverpool and New York, he somehow managed to prevent what seemed for a while to be the imminent breakup of the partnership.

Some of the correspondence of those years has been published,[1] and a good deal of the unpublished material was gone through by Henry A. Davis during preparation of his unpublished thesis on "The Brown Partners in the Commerce and Politics of the Civil War" (Princeton University, Department of History, 1965). From these sources, and from additional letters now available in the firm's Historical File, it is evident that Brown Brothers, in

[1] See John Crosby Brown, *A Hundred Years of Merchant Banking* (New York, 1909), pp. 103–22 and 222–26. For Brown Brothers' participation, with other New York merchants, in efforts to preserve the Union during the 1850s, see Philip S. Foner, *Business and Slavery: The New York Merchants and the Irrepressible Conflict*, Chapel Hill, North Carolina, 1941.

New York, strongly supported the Union cause throughout the war, even when their immediate business interests conflicted with their political and social convictions, and even though their English partners—as well as their relatives and friends in the South—had strong Southern sympathies.

James Brown had been traveling on the Continent with Mrs. Brown since the library celebration in Liverpool the previous fall. Stewart Brown, James M. Brown, and Howard Potter were therefore in active charge of the 59 Wall Street office. Of James Brown's sons, the eldest—George Hunter Brown —was in New York, in poor health, and John Crosby Brown was beginning his two-year apprenticeship in the Liverpool office. So Clarence—the youngest, just back from England—was the only one free to enlist in the Army when Lincoln called for volunteers.

On July 8, 1861, CLARENCE STEWART BROWN (1840–1875) was appointed aide-de-camp to Brigadier General Irvin McDowell, the luckless first commanding general appointed by Lincoln. Major Brown is shown above (second from left) in a photograph of McDowell and his staff taken by Mathew Brady on the steps of Robert E. Lee's confiscated Arlington mansion, which served as McDowell's headquarters. The original print was cut in half for mounting in a family album of Civil War letters. Another print from the same plate, with the orderly and horse at left eliminated, appears in Roy Meredith's *Mr. Lincoln's Camera Man: Mathew B. Brady,* (New York, 1946).

Clarence Brown had returned from England on the same ship which brought to this country William Howard Russell, the London *Times* correspondent whose Civil War dispatches did much to mold British public opinion early in the war. Russell tells in *My Diary North and South* (1863) of his conversations on shipboard with Clarence Brown, whom he described as "an exceedingly intelligent, well-informed young merchant. . . . Without being violent in tone, the young Northerner was very resolute in temper, and determined to do all which lay in his power to prevent the 'glorious Union' being broken up."

After the war, Clarence Brown went to work in the New York office, and on January 1, 1867, was admitted to partnership. After two years, however, he resigned, apparently preferring to go into business for himself.

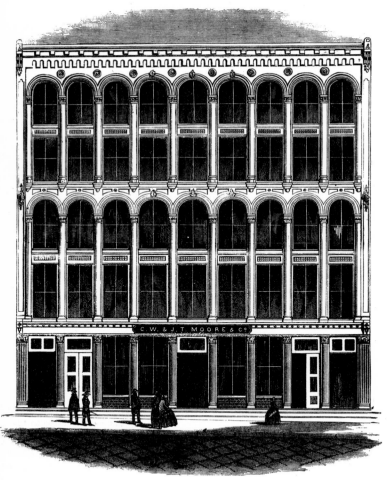

(Author's Collection)

Clarence Brown escaped injury in the war, but other members of the family were not so fortunate. One of Howard Potter's brothers was seriously wounded in battle, and Stewart Brown's son Milnor died heroically at Gettysburg. These are, to be sure, personal matters, not technically a part of the firm's history. Yet they are significant as evidence that the partners were not insulated from the harsh realities of war, as were so many well-to-do Northerners who could afford the $300 which bought exemption from the draft.

From the point of view of the business itself, the war brought all sorts of problems, in addition to the losses involved when Southern firms refused to pay their debts to Northern merchants. A typical instance involved the dry goods establishment of C. W. & J. T. Moore & Co., who had been clients of Brown Brothers and Brown Shipley since 1835. (During the panic of 1857, they wrote Brown Shipley: "We have been doing business with your house in this city during the past 22 years and almost daily & with so much satisfaction & punctuality that we should have no objection to its continuance for 22 years longer. . . ."

(Author's Collection)

When the *New-York Illustrated News* published the exterior and interior views of the Moores' new store, in the January 28, 1860 issue, the accompanying article described the building as "probably the most attractive and imposing structure on Broadway." Designed by Kellum & Son, architects, it was erected in 1859 on a T-shaped plot fronting on Broadway at No.'s 328 and 330 (east side, between Worth and Pearl), and with fronts also on the side streets. The *Illustrated News* was as much impressed by the "solid and substantial" yet "light and graceful" effect of the "Norman" architecture as by the way the basement, extending under Broadway, was lighted by "a patent illuminated iron platform" and "vault-lights in the flagging."

As for the firm itself, it was "the oldest general importing and jobbing house in the city," and the gentlemen comprising it were, "for business tact, judgment and industry, . . . examples of which our business world may well be proud." And yet, four days before the *Illustrated News* article was published, Brown Shipley wrote a letter to Brown Brothers expressing concern over the credits Brown Brothers had granted C. W. & J. T. Moore & Co.

What worried Brown Shipley was that Moore & Co. had drawn on them for sums in excess of the £50,000 ($240,000) which Brown Brothers' letter of credit authorized them to draw. To be sure, Brown Brothers had given the firm special authority to exceed their credit by as much as £5000 or £10,000, but the letter informing Brown Shipley of this special authority had not reached Liverpool until the Moores' English agent (one C. W. Browne) had already "transgressed the agreed limit."

Brown Shipley was somewhat reassured by Brown Brothers telling them that the Moores were in the habit of showing them their balance sheet each year, and that their capital at the beginning of 1859 had been "$529,000, besides private property worth $130,000." But though this was "no doubt . . . a handsome sum in New York" it seemed to Brown Shipley that a "£50,000 Clean Credit upon the strength of it" [i.e., a credit not requiring bills of lading or other documents to accompany the bills drawn] was "a large line."

Brown Brothers, however, felt there was "no greater risk involved" than the firm "ought willingly to run." There was, as James Brown wrote from Paris several months later, "such a thing in business as being over-careful and over-suspicious of the integrity of parties with whom we are dealing; it makes the house unpopular. Better to be taken in and lose a little occasionally than to be so rigid as to make parties afraid to approach you."

As it turned out, they were taken in by Moore & Co. Even after Brown Brothers reduced their line of credit to £30,000, the Moores' agent in Liverpool somehow managed to "work" the credit so that the account continued to stand at £55,000. And finally, in October, when the Moores suspended payment, it turned out that they had been less than candid about their assets when showing Brown Brothers their books on earlier occasions. The exhibit they now made of their affairs was, Brown Shipley wrote, "as little creditable to them, as it is annoying to us—as much perhaps, because of the Deception they have practiced, as for the actual loss we are likely to sustain."

The Browns' losses on account of Moore & Co. were no doubt directly traceable to the losses which the Moores incurred, along with many other jobbers in New York, when the Confederacy forbid payment of debts to Northern merchants. For it is almost certain that the Moores, like most prominent merchants, subscribed to Dun, Boyd & Co.'s Mercantile Agency, which provided—as its successor Dun & Bradstreet, Inc., still does—"information respecting the character, capacity and pecuniary condition of persons asking credit." The interior of Dun, Boyd & Co.'s establishment, a few doors south of Moore & Co.'s fine store, at 314 and 316 Broadway, had been pictured in the *New-York Illustrated News* for March 24, 1860, along with an article describing its activities. The Mercantile Agency had been established originally in 1841 by Lewis Tappan, formerly of Arthur Tappan & Co., silk merchants who failed in the panic of 1837. Under successive owners and managers the Agency had grown until in 1860 it had offices in eighteen cities and had become "an indispensable adjunct to the trade of the country" and "the great conservator of credit." But not even a good credit rating on Dun & Boyd's books assured payment of debts now that the Southern states had seceded.

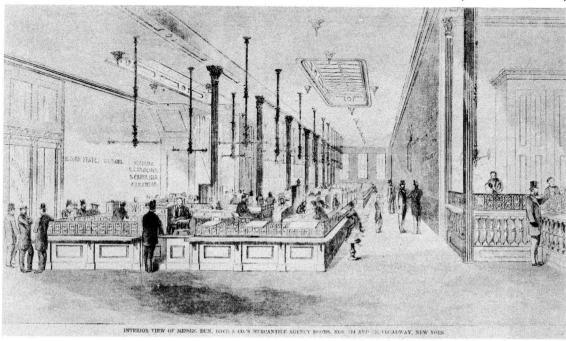

INTERIOR VIEW OF MESSRS. DUN, BOYD & CO.'S MERCANTILE AGENCY ROOMS, NOS. 314 AND 316 BROADWAY, NEW YORK.

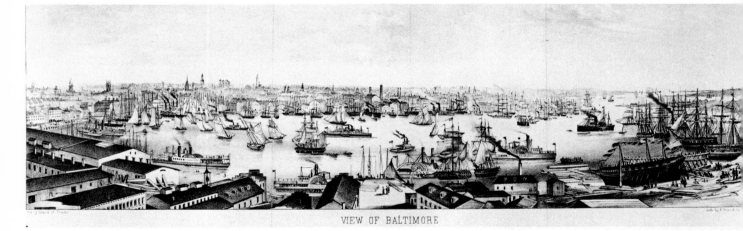

VIEW OF BALTIMORE

(*Brown Brothers Harriman & Co. Historical File*)

Baltimore, on the eve of the Civil War, was pictured in a handsome lithograph by A. Hoen & Co., published by the city's Board of Trade. Copies of it were supplied by the Board "in the most courteous and liberal manner" to *Hunt's Merchants' Magazine,* which distributed them folded into its April 1858 issue. The lithograph, reproduced here only about a quarter of its original size, gives a distinctly Board-of-Trade's-eye-view of the city as compared with the bucolic 1801 engraving reproduced on p. 21. Here the city's wharves and shipping occupy the foreground.

The location of Brown's Wharf, where the family's ships had tied up, is indicated by the group of sailing vessels on the waterfront just right of the center of the picture, above the flag at the mast of the tall ship moored on the near shore just to the right of the picture's title. But Alexander Brown & Sons had little to do with shipping any more. Though George Brown had kept the business alive for his son, George Stewart Brown (who became head of the firm after his father's death in August 1859), the firm was not very active, and the Baltimore agency of Brown Brothers & Co.—headed by William H. Graham, a brother-in-law of George Stewart Brown—now occupied the first-floor offices in Alexander Brown & Sons' building, the old firm having moved upstairs.

An episode involving the Baltimore agency gives some notion of the strains set up within the firm and between members of the Brown family by the passions involved in the Civil War. Baltimore was largely pro-Southern, and as Frank R. Kent says in his *Story of Alex. Brown & Sons,* there is no doubt that George Stewart Brown's personal sympathies were with the South, and the same was probably true of William Graham, his brother-in-law. But James Brown specifically ordered the Baltimore agency to fly the American flag above its door, as evidence of Brown Brothers' loyalty to the Union.

However, when the first contingent of federal troops (a Massachusetts regiment) arrived in Baltimore en route to Washington, the city's Mayor, George William Brown— a distant relative of George Stewart Brown—ordered the flag to be taken down, lest it provoke a riot. When news of this reached the New York office, there was great indignation, and a peremptory order to restore the flag was accompanied with severe condemnation of those who had

caused its removal—a rebuke to which George Stewart Brown apparently responded with a defense of the Mayor's order. "Those were trying days for families in the border states," as John Crosby Brown later wrote, "and it is a subject for devout thankfulness that while divergent views were held and expressed with characteristic earnestness by members of the family, . . . no serious break occurred."

(*Courtesy of the Library of Congress*)

Many of the firm's customers in Baltimore and throughout the Southern states supported the Confederate cause, but there were none who so well epitomized the fiery secessionist point of view as the slave-holding planter-aristocrat, COLONEL JOHN SMITH PRESTON, whose photograph reproduced opposite. A South Carolinian who came into possession of a huge Louisiana sugar plantation by marrying General Wade Hampton's daughter, Preston was one of the commissioners sent by South Carolina to persuade Virginia to secede from the Union. As a lieutenant colonel he fought at Bull Run with the Confederate forces that routed the troops under General McDowell (see p. 123) and later commanded a prison camp in Georgia and headed the Confederate Bureau of Conscription. After the war he remained bitterly hostile to the federal government and spent the rest of his life defending the Confederacy and the principle of states' rights.

The Browns and their London bankers had had a taste of his brand of "Southern Chivalry" in 1859. In a letter to Brown Shipley written at Fenton's Hotel in London on August 22nd that year, he informed them that having written them that morning asking them to give him a credit for £500 to use in Great Britain, he had gone round to Heywood & Co.'s office (without waiting for a reply) and asked them to take his draft on Brown Shipley for £50. Some "person" at the bank (he was sure it was a partner, not a clerk, who perfectly well knew who he was) apparently hesitated to give him the money until word came from Liverpool. Perceiving Preston's astonishment, the "person"—according to Preston—"attempted or was about to begin some explanation, but so gross, so wanton, so unexpected was the outrage that I left the house instantly fearing that I might be betrayed by my just anger to the commission of personal violence."

Early in the war, when it looked as if England might intervene on the side of the Confederacy, there was grave concern abroad about the capital English merchants had invested in America, and in November and December 1861, James Brown wrote several letters from Liverpool to Brown Brothers urging that they get a declaration from the Chamber of Commerce—or better still from Congress—"assuring the World, that Aliens property in the United States [would] be held safe and as sacred as it has been & is in Great Britain or in any other Country" even if England and the United States were at war. Unless some such assurance was given, he said, English and other European capital would be withdrawn from the United States, "thus weakening the resources of the Country as money is the sinews of War." Indeed, if the United States "could be guilty of such folly, madness & fraud as to confiscate aliens property in event of War"—as the Confederacy had confiscated all property of those living in the Northern states, including British subjects—they would, he wrote on December 5th, "be no better than Robbers in the eyes of the World and I would not desire to live amongst them and call America my home." Enemy property had always, he said, been "held sacred & never interfered with in England and the Interest on her public debt held by foreigners even those at War with her punctually paid," with the result that England could "borrow money lower than any country in the world," paying only 3% interest as against the 7% the U. S. government had to pay.

On January 3, 1862, Brown Shipley enclosed the clipping reproduced on this page in the firm's letter to Brown Brothers. The London *Times,* they wrote, had "hunted up" a letter Secretary Seward had written more than twenty years before to William Brown expressing "very strong views against the confiscation of Property," and Brown Shipley felt that publication of the letter would "give confidence" to those who had been apprehensive. William Brown "had forgotten the correspondence," they said, but the next day he wrote to Seward, referring to the clipping and urging him to make it clear that his ideas about confiscation had not changed. Seward replied in a letter dated January 31, 1862, in which he carefully avoided any commitment about confiscation, merely "recalling with great pleasure the memory of our ancient friendship and its incidents in this country and in your own," and asserting that, for his part, he had "never seen the occasion when [he] thought war between the two nations could be anything else than wrong in itself and mutually ruinous of both."

Certainly there was nothing in Seward's reply to change the opinion James Brown had expressed about him in a letter to Brown Brothers on November 30, 1861, after the "Trent Affair" involving the capture of Mason and Slidell, the Confederate envoys to Britain. "I have no *confidence in Seward,"* he wrote, "and never had, considering him a reckless politician, and its said sometimes in his Cups, so that it seems very important that *the Bankers and Merchants make themselves heard"* if war with Britain was to be avoided. What Seward thought of the Browns at that time we do not know, but if he had read the official dispatch sent him on September 6, 1861, by Charles Francis Adams, the American Minister in London, he knew that Adams had received "repeated visits from two of the older members of the house" (William and James, no doubt) who expressed "great anxiety at the then existing state of affairs." When one looks at the profit and loss figures on the partners' private accounts for 1861 and sees that Brown Brothers had to write off a loss of about $150,000 that year "for Southern paper" and another $50,000 for depreciation in the value of U. S. government securities, the partners' "anxiety" seems natural enough. But it should have impressed Seward that although they frankly admitted to Adams "that they had much property at stake in the seceding states," including, of course, personal property and the property of their agencies in Southern cities, Adams "did not receive the impression that they were sympathizers in the revolutionary movement."

His impression was certainly correct so far as James Brown was concerned. Just about the time Adams was presenting his credentials in London, James had written William that "Fort Sumpter [sic] & the indignity shown to the flag of the Union" had roused the North's patriotism at last; William could "depend upon it neither England nor France will get a bale of cotton (unless by accident) without permission of the north," if either of them interfered in favor of the Confederacy.

Among the most valuable unpublished records in the Historical File are the letters written by JOHN CROSBY BROWN (1838–1909) during his early years with the firm. Press copies of these letters are preserved in his private letter book covering the years 1861–69, the earliest dating from about the time when he posed for the unattributed photograph reproduced here.

It is impossible to give in brief excerpts more than a suggestion of the insights these letters give into the firm's activities and the characters of the people involved. As for John Crosby Brown himself, he obviously stuck at his post in Liverpool out of a sense of obligation to his father. To Clarence Brown, who had written him about the hardships of army life, he wrote on May 18, 1861: "You have a reputation to sustain, & you must not let either raw salt pork or hard bread damp your ardor. . . . Of course I take a deep interest in all your movements & if I were home, or if I felt it right to leave father & mother I should return directly and try to join some regiment. . . . From the Times correspondent Mr. Russell, it appears that the [Confederate] troops at Charleston are in good spirits & are faring sumptuously every day, champagne &c in abundance. But I would rather have hard bread & salt pork & be with you, on your side." And on August 19th he wrote his father saying that everyone in Liverpool was saying the "American quarrel" would soon be patched up because the North would not stand for the taxes required to prosecute the war and the government would be unable to raise the money. "As I cannot serve in person," he wrote, "I should like your permission to invest any funds I may have coming in, in U.S. securities, as I think every one ought to do his part." After the rout at Bull Run he wrote again to his father: "I hope Mother will not be so distressed by news from home as to write in such a way to Clarence as will induce him to abandon what may be his duty in this hour of trial. It does certainly require great faith in God to feel that all these things shall work together for our good, but we must feel that he is in God's hands, who will do what is right & just."

The most remarkable of these early letters about the war is one of sixteen pages written to his older brother George Hunter Brown, August 13, 1861, summarizing the opinions on American affairs then current in Liverpool—"of all places in England, perhaps the worst in which one can get a correct view of English popular feeling, as the society one meets is composed of cotton brokers & cotton dealers, whose opinions of things in general are proverbially governed by any circumstance that can affect the demand,

(*Brown Brothers Harriman & Co. Historical File*)

supply & price of cotton." Only after trying with scrupulous care to convey a fair impression of the pro-Southern arguments he encountered did young Brown express his own views. He believed that "if some check is not, in some way or other, put upon the slave-extending interest, that dreadful system of human bondage will be perpetuated, & I shall do all I can to prevent it." As for those who held "that our present condition proves that democracy is a failure" he had simply to say "that perhaps their judgment is premature, & that I am willing to suspend my judgment until we see the end of this contest."

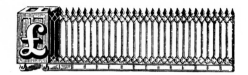

Copies of letters James Brown wrote to his retired partner Joseph Shipley at Rockwood during the war have recently been made available to the Historical File by Shipley's collateral descendants, Mrs. Henry W. Farnum and Mrs. Gordon Hargraves.

The letters are valuable because James Brown kept his old friend well posted on family matters, the state of the business, and his own personal investments. By May 1863 Brown Brothers had very few foreign credits out, and James Brown reported that "our business [is] now entirely buying & selling Ex[change], covering each packet as near as possible generally with a profit of not less than £500 per week and often running up to from £1000 to £2000 not often the latter figure but so far this year the Ex a/c shows well." Stewart Brown and James M. Brown, who handled the daily office work, "were becoming used up by the business excitement Gold & Ex jumping up & down from 1 to 3 or 4 per Cent even in [a] day."

To help with this exchange business Brown Brothers in that year hired Charles D. Simons, a young exchange broker who eventually became manager of the firm's Foreign Exchange Department. In the 1890s and early 1900s it was he who decided each morning what the rate of exchange for Sterling should be and posted the rate on one of the pillars in the banking house (see p. 136). For twenty years or more "Brown's posted rates" were accepted as the official rate of exchange, and were carried on the Stock Exchange ticker at 10:00 o'clock each morning.

It is interesting to note that Simons came to work at Brown Brothers just a year after young Edward Henry Harriman got his first Wall Street job up at No. 11 with a broker named Dewitt C. Hays. For it was Charles Simons, the manager of Brown Brothers' Foreign Exchange Department, who first achieved a "merger" with the Harriman family. The young lady he married some years later was E. H. Harriman's sister Lilly, and the earliest "Harriman" document in the firm's Historical File is a letter

Simons wrote on Brown Brothers stationery, January 29, 1906, to E. H. Harriman's chief clerk about some bills for "work done at Arden [Harriman's twenty-thousand acre estate in the Ramapo highlands] at the request of Mrs. Simons."

Though the articles of partnership under which Brown Brothers and Brown Shipley carried on their business in the 1860s specified, as had earlier articles, that they were "Merchants Factors and Bankers," the correspondence of the period indicates that they thought of themselves increasingly as "Exchange dealers and Bankers." Indeed, by mid-August, 1861, Brown Shipley raised the question whether they ought not to open a bank in Liverpool "on sound & legitimate principles" in order to provide "a good & profitable employment" of the capital they could not otherwise invest. Because of the war the credit business was almost at an end, and Brown Shipley was reluctant to invest in American securities.

"Undoubtedly a state of war will of itself produce a business of some kind or other," they wrote, "& in time probably we may find in America a safer & better business than has ever before existed." But this might take years; in the meantime, they noted, "the greater portion of our business is at an end."

The bank idea was eventually dropped, from a conviction that, to carry it on successfully, it would be necessary to give up the credit and produce business—"in fact everything but the Exchange business"; and that was more than any of the English partners was willing to recommend. But the opening of the London office tended to increase still further the importance of the firm's exchange and banking business, and by the late 'sixties Brown Shipley had to ask Brown Brothers to "do something quietly" to remove the misapprehensions caused by the fact that "the unfortunate appellation of 'Bankers'" led many of their correspondents "to suppose that *mercantile* business is out of our line." Just recently an old customer had assumed they would not "undertake the purchase of Plumbago."

This electrotype ornament, and the one at the top of this page, is reproduced from the *Abridged Specimen Book, Bruce's New-York Type-Foundry*, published in 1869. (*Author's Collection*)

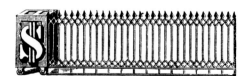

(*Both pictures courtesy of the Museum of the City of New York*)

After John Crosby Brown returned to New York in 1862, he joined with his brother-in-law Howard Potter in active support of the work of the U. S. Sanitary Commission, organized on a national scale to furnish medicines, food, clothing, and other supplies to the overcrowded and understaffed military hospitals, and to maintain a "Hospital Directory" through which relatives and friends could trace the hundreds of thousands of sick and wounded soldiers. In New York the medical supplies were assembled and distributed by the Women's Central Association of Relief, of which Howard Potter "of the firm of Brown Brothers & Co." was treasurer.

The photographs of the exterior and interior of the Women's Central Association of Relief headquarters at Cooper Union were taken in July 1865. The two ladies shown at right in the group above were Mrs. T. M. d'Oremieuex and Miss Ellen Collins (daughter of the manager of the ill-fated Collins steamship line), both of whom served with John Crosby Brown on the sub-committee of the Association's executive committee which had charge of "Receiving and Forwarding Supplies."

(*Author's Collection*)

Soon after Appomattox the U. S. Sanitary Commission set up a "Bureau of Employment for Disabled and Discharged Soldiers and Sailors" which in August 1865 distributed copies of the handbill reproduced at right. Both James Brown and Howard Potter were directors of the Bureau, and Potter was a member of the three-man executive committee along with William E. Dodge and Theodore Roosevelt—"three gentlemen," as *Harper's Weekly* observed in its September 9, 1865 issue, "whose names are identified with the most assiduous and faithful work during the war."

Roosevelt, a merchant of old Dutch stock, had a seven-year old son who was destined to be the twenty-sixth President of the United States. Dodge was an old client of Brown Brothers, whose loans to Phelps, Dodge & Co. during and after the panic of 1837 had (according to Richard Lowitt's scholarly biography of Dodge) saved the then struggling young metal-importing firm from going under.

U. S. SANITARY COMMISSION,

PROTECTIVE WAR-CLAIM ASSOCIATION,

Bureau of Employment for Disabled and Discharged Soldiers and Sailors.

PRESIDENT,

LIEUT. GENERAL WINFIELD SCOTT.

VICE-PRESIDENTS.

| HAMILTON FISH. | | ADMIRAL DUPONT. |
| JOHN J. CISCO. | | RUDOLPH A. WITTHAUS. |

TREASURER.

ROBT. B. MINTURN.

DIRECTORS.

EDWIN D. MORGAN,	WM. H. ASPINWALL,	GEORGE BANCROFT,
JAS. W. BEEKMAN,	HOWARD POTTER,	DANIEL LORD,
H. W. BELLOWS, D. D.	WM. E. DODGE, JR.,	WILSON G. HUNT,
JOHN JACOB ASTOR,	THEODORE ROOSEVELT,	ROBT. L. STUART,
JAMES BROWN,	JAS. GALLATIN,	ALFRED PELL.
	PETER COOPER,	

THIS BUREAU IS ESTABLISHED WITH THE FOLLOWING OBJECTS:

1. To aid those who have served honorably in the Army or Navy of the United States in obtaining employment.

2. To prevent the necessity of costly charitable institutions, such as exist in Europe, but which are foreign to our ideas, and repulsive to the innate dignity of American soldiers and sailors.

3. To lessen the pauperism and crime that follows war, and surely attends on large numbers of unoccupied men left to themselves, without employment or means of subsistence.

4. To save to the country a large amount of productive labor in this season of trial, when it can least afford to maintain idle hands.

The services of the Bureau *are given gratuitously*, both to employers and employed.

Information and suggestions are requested relative to labor adapted to maimed and disabled men—to men who have lost an arm or a leg—who are unable to walk, but have the free use of their hands—who are handless, yet can travel about on their feet—so that this Bureau shall be enabled to provide every disabled and deserving applicant with some kind of employment.

Employers are requested to send in applications for every class of employees. They are reminded that our army contains men of every trade and calling, and that our best and most trustworthy young men are in its ranks.

HOWARD POTTER,		*Address*,	COL. CHARLES C. NOTT,
WM. E. DODGE, JR.,	} *Ex. Com.*		Secretary of Bureau.
THEO. ROOSEVELT,			35 Chambers St., N. Y.

DIRECTIONS FOR EMPLOYERS.

1. State the nature of the work. 2. The locality. 3. The pay. 4. The time within which the application must be filled. 5. Any information which may be desired before giving the employment.

N.B.—The Bureau will transmit to employers the recommendations of character, etc., which it receives.

Twelve

RESPONSE TO CHALLENGE

Old Daniel Drew, the unscrupulous financial free-booter who plundered railroads with snuffling piety in the decades after the Civil War, had ideas about philanthropy that were widely shared though seldom expressed quite so crudely as he expressed them. "I calculate there are lots of business men who don't prosper," the ex-cattle drover wrote, "because they don't give to the Lord a slice of their profits. They try to hog it all. . . . They may think he doesn't know what they are doing, but he does. God wears gum shoes when he comes down here upon earth to spy. . . . To give a percentage to the Lord is just as good business policy as to pay the taxes on your house and lot. In either case, if you don't pay up good and prompt you'll sweat for it." So with promised gifts of a million dollars old Daniel founded a theological seminary that still bears his name (though most of the million was never given).

James Brown was also the benefactor of a theological seminary, but with a difference. Starting in 1865 he contributed generously to the Union Theological Seminary, but not for buildings to bear his name. Before his death in 1877 he had given more than $350,000 to endow higher salaries for its professors. His son John Crosby Brown became a member of the Seminary's board of directors in 1866 and served devotedly for forty-three years, the last ten as president. (Two of John Crosby Brown's sons served the Seminary for long periods of time: William Adams Brown, the eldest, for forty-two years as a member of the faculty; Thatcher M. Brown,

the youngest, for forty-six years as a member of the board, of which he became president in 1936, the year his older brother retired as Professor of Systematic Theology. On the present board there are two Brown Brothers Harriman partners, one of whom is James Brown's great-grandson Moreau Delano Brown.)

James Brown and his partners made no display of their philanthropies, though all were generous and all worked hard for the institutions they supported. Both James and Stewart Brown were among the founders of the New York Association for Improving the Condition of the Poor, a pioneering social agency organized in 1843 and incorporated in 1848. James Brown was its first president, serving from 1843 to 1875, and Stewart Brown was active on its board of managers. (It is pleasant to record that Howard Potter later served as president, and that a Brown Brothers Harriman partner is currently vice-chairman of the board of the successor organization, the Community Service Society.) James Brown also served on the board of the Presbyterian Hospital, and he and Howard Potter were among the founders of the New York Orthopaedic Dispensary and Hospital in 1868, while James M. Brown, from 1861 on, was a member of the board of governors of the New York Hospital, of which he later became president.

In addition to these and other non-controversial charitable activities, however, the Brown Brothers partners became involved in civic matters that were very controversial indeed. Both James Brown and James M. Brown were members of the council of the Citizens Association which in 1864 set up and financed the Council on Hygiene and Public Health —a committee of physicians who carried out a systematic, block-by-block fact-finding survey of living conditions throughout the city. Their *Report . . . upon the Sanitary Condition of the City,* crammed with shocking data on the city's disease-ridden tenements and slums, its unsanitary markets, and its inadequate provisions for the disposal of garbage and sewage, was submitted to James M. Brown, chairman of the Citizens Association, in 1865, and its prompt publication led directly to the enactment in 1866 of state legislation creating the first effective municipal Board of Health in the nation, and a year later to enactment of the first tenement house law.

Again, when the New York *Times* and *Harper's Weekly* began exposing the details of the Tweed ring's flagrantly corrupt administration of the city government, it was James Brown who presided at the huge citizens' meeting in Cooper Union on September 4, 1871, at which it was decided to set up the famous "Committee of Seventy" which finally brought the chief culprits to justice. James M. Brown was from the start a member of the "Committee of Seventy" and was its chairman from November 1872 until it wound up its work in October 1873. Charles O'Conner, special deputy attorney-general for the State, and the lawyers for the "Committee of Seventy" who prosecuted the ring, had their offices in Brown Brothers' building.

That the Brown Brothers partners had more than a superficially benevolent interest in contemporary problems is further witnessed by the fact that in 1865 both James Brown and Howard Potter helped E. L. Godkin found *The Nation,* America's first weekly journal devoted to the serious, non-partisan discussion of controversial political and social issues. The Browns had been impressed by Godkin's Civil War reporting for the London *Daily News,* and Howard Potter, one of Godkin's earliest friends in New York, had been in on his plans for the new journal from the beginning. He and his father-in-law were both among the original stockholders of the new periodical.

Nobody in Brown Brothers, however, had anything to do with the founding of an energetic and belligerent weekly called *The Revolution,* whose first issue appeared on January 8, 1868.

This photograph of E. L. GODKIN, founder and first editor of *The Nation,* was taken in 1863 and is reproduced from Rollo Ogden's *Life and Letters of Edwin Lawrence Godkin,* New York, 1907. (*Author's Collection*)

The Revolution.

PRINCIPLE, NOT POLICY: JUSTICE, NOT FAVORS.

VOL. I.—NO. 1.   NEW YORK, WEDNESDAY, JANUARY 8, 1868. $2.00 A YEAR.

The Revolution;

THE ORGAN OF THE

NATIONAL PARTY OF NEW AMERICA.

PRINCIPLE, NOT POLICY—INDIVIDUAL RIGHTS AND RESPONSIBILITIES.

THE REVOLUTION WILL ADVOCATE:

1. IN POLITICS—Educated Suffrage, Irrespective of Sex or Color; Equal Pay to Women for Equal Work; Eight Hours Labor; Abolition of Standing Armies and Party Despotisms. Down with Politicians—Up with the People!

2. IN RELIGION—Deeper Thought; Broader Idea; Science not Superstition; Personal Purity; Love to Man as well as God.

3. IN SOCIAL LIFE.—Morality and Reform; Practical Education, not Theoretical; Facts not Fiction; Virtue not Vice; Cold Water not Alcoholic Drinks or Medicines. It will indulge in no Gross Personalities and insert no Quack or Immoral Advertisements, so common even in Religious Newspapers.

4. THE REVOLUTION proposes a new Commercial and Financial Policy. America no longer led by Europe. Gold like our Cotton and Corn for sale. Greenbacks for money. An American System of Finance. American Products and Labor Free. Foreign Manufactures Prohibited. Open doors to Artisans and Immigrants. Atlantic and Pacific Oceans for American Steamships and Shipping; or American goods in American bottoms. New York the Financial Centre of the World. Wall Street emancipated from Bank of England, or American Cash for American Bills. The Credit Foncier and Credit Mobilier System, or Capital Mobilized to Resuscitate the South and our Mining Interests, and to People the Country from Ocean to Ocean, from Omaha to San Francisco. More organized Labor, more Cotton, more Gold and Silver Bullion to sell foreigners at the highest prices. Ten millions of Naturalized Citizens DEMAND A PENNY OCEAN POSTAGE, to Strengthen the Brotherhood of Labor; and if Congress Vote One Hundred and Twenty-five Millions for a Standing Army and Freedman's Bureau, cannot they spare One Million to Educate Europe and to keep bright the chain of acquaintance and friendship between those millions and their fatherland?

Send in your Subscription. THE REVOLUTION, published weekly, will be the Great Organ of the Age.

TERMS.—Two dollars a year, in advance. Ten names ($20) entitle the sender to one copy free.

ELIZABETH CADY STANTON, } EDS.
PARKER PILLSBURY, }

SUSAN B. ANTHONY,
Proprietor and Manager.
37 Park Row (Room 17), New York City.

(Courtesy of the New York Historical Society)

As the names of its proprietor and its editors suggest, *The Revolution* was militantly devoted to women's rights and the temperance crusade. Both Susan B. Anthony and Elizabeth Cady Stanton were already nationally known for their efforts in behalf of women's suffrage, so it was not surprising to read in the platform on page one of their new weekly that it would advocate suffrage "Irrespective of Sex or Color," "Equal Pay to Women for Equal Work," and "Cold Water not Alcoholic Drinks or Medicines." Even the advocacy of "Science not Superstition" in religion might have been expected. But the long fourth article in the platform would have puzzled anyone who did not know that the eccentric promoter-politician-reformer George Francis Train had financed the magazine on condition that he be allowed to express his opinions in its columns.

Associated with Train in writing the "Financial Department" of the new weekly was David Melliss, the financial editor of the New York *World*, who shared his "Down with Gold and up with Greenbacks" views and his belief that the new national banking system was a "Bank of England system of people-robbery." In the very first issue of *The Revolution* they went after "Messrs. Brown Brothers & Co. the eminent Anglo-American banking firm" with skillful innuendos about their involvements with the Novelty Iron Works and the Pacific Mail Steamship Company, and they promised that the next issue would discuss the matter further.

The promised article was not published, however, until June 11th, and it was not until early July that Brown Brothers got wind of the repercussions in England. On July 2, 1868, Brown Shipley's "Confidential" letter to the New York partners said that two days before "the writer Mr. Collet was asked openly at the Luncheon table at the Bank of England," by one of his fellow directors, "what could be the meaning of a violent onslaught on Brown Bros. & Co." which he had seen in a copy of *The Revolution* sent to him "by some unknown person." The article, he told Collet, charged that Brown Brothers' management had ruined the Collins Line and was now ruining the Pacific Mail Steamship Company.

At first, Collet "thought very little of the remark," and simply replied that it was "too notorious that Brown Bros. & Co. never had the management of the Collins Line, though Mr. James Brown paid for Mr. Collins' follies" and that they had as little to do with the management of the Pacific Mail line. But when he saw a copy of the magazine he found that it made other "reckless allegations, of which one—having a substratum of truth" especially troubled him. This was the reference to "a loan to the Novelty Works of $500,000" (see the next to last paragraph of the article, reproduced on p. 134) which, Collet adds, is "no doubt the same as is referred to in the Pacific Mail Co.'s Report as a Loan of $500,000 to Mr. James Brown upon approved Security." Even if *The Revolution*'s charges could be overlooked in the United States, Collet said, they wore "a different aspect" when distributed among "Houses of Standing" in England, "with Special passages marked." For a loan of the kind which the Pacific Mail Company's report was "intended to justify" was, in Collet's view, "just such an operation, which if it were ascribed to a leading Member of any first class House in this Country, could not easily be explained without its affecting the Credit of the House."

the Seventy-eighth Annual Meeting of the New Hampshire Medical Society, held in that city last week, admitted twelve new members ; that "Miss M. O. A. Hunt, by letter, asked for membership and her request was referred to the council." Does that mean to the Sleep of Death ?

Financial Department.

FINANCIAL AND COMMERCIAL.—*America versus Europe—Gold, like our Cotton, FOR SALE. Greenbacks for Money. An American System of Finance. American Products and Labor Free. Foreign Manufactures Prohibited. Open doors to Artisans and Immigrants. Atlantic and Pacific Oceans for AMERICAN Steamships and Shipping. New York the Financial Centre of the World. Wall Street emancipated from Bank of England, or American Cash for American Bills. The Credit Foncier and Credit Mobilier System, or Capital Mobilized to Resuscitate the South and our Mining Interests, and to People the Country from Ocean to Ocean, from Omaha to San Francisco. More organized Labor, more Cotton, more Gold and Silver Bullion to sell foreigners at the highest prices. Ten millions of Naturalized Citizens DEMAND A PENNY OCEAN POSTAGE, to Strengthen the Brotherhood of Labor. If Congress Vote One Hundred and Twenty-five Millions for a Standing Army and Freedman's Bureau for the Blacks, Cannot they spare One Million for the Whites ?*

THE REVOLUTION.

NO. XXIII.

EUROPE VS. THE UNITED STATES.

BROWN BROTHERS AND PACIFIC MAIL.

BEFORE the rebellion, it was the proud distinction of the United States to share the honors and profits of the ocean with Great Britain, as the maritime powers of the world. Our sole rival, Great Britain, was then rapidly giving way to us in the ocean-carrying trade. Our sailing packets and clipper ships were unrivalled, and the American flag crowded the pathways from New York to Europe and China. The rebellion, with its Alabamas, was the first check on this order of things, and misgovernment at Washington has given a severe blow to the prosperity of American shipping. Ocean steam navigation and the improvements and economy of iron hulls and screw propellers are superceding sailing vessels. In these, the United States have made no progress. Europe enjoys the monopoly of ocean steamship navigation. The only American lines afloat are between here and Cuba and Brazil, and the Great Pacific Mail Steamship Company from New York to San Francisco and China, with Webb's new opposition. The United States have no line of ocean screw steamers.

THE COLLINS LINE—THE GREATEST SUCCESS AND THE GREATEST FAILURE.

From New York to Europe the steamships average more than one for every day in the year, and they are all European lines. This is a remarkable fact, and by no means creditable to ourselves. It is not because we cannot build steamships, for no finer models have ever been afloat than the old Collins line, and their accommodations and speed inaugurated a new era

for the travelling public on the ocean. They stimulated the Cunard Company into improvements which were never thought of or attempted until the Collins line started. We are indebted to it for the increased speed and superior accommodations now to be had on the transatlantic route. The Collins line was at once the greatest success and greatest failure the ocean has ever seen. Successful beyond expectation in the patronage it obtained, and disastrous beyond imagination to conceive in its financial collapse. The flattering patronage the Collins line had received from the travelling public seemed to promise the cream of the ocean trade to the United States, and that promise would have been fulfilled to the letter, if the Collins line had not been ruined by gross and culpable, not to say corrupt mismanagement.

BROWN BROTHERS RUINED THE COLLINS LINE.

The Anglo-American banking firm, Messrs. Brown Bros. & Co., were the agents and managers of the Collins Steamship Company. Commissions were paid on outlay and disbursements, the furnishing of the ships was farmed out, and a system of reckless extravagance was carried on by that firm which finally ruined the Company, and by its ruin so frightened American capital from investing in ocean steamships as virtually to take from America the steamship transatlantic route, and make a present of it to Europe. This has been the logical, practical result of the ruin of the Collins Steamship Company. If Messrs Brown Bros. and Co. had been bribed by the Cunard line or Europe to sweep American steamships from the Atlantic, they could not have done it more effectually than they did, by their policy and management of the Collins line. Why ?

BROWN BROTHERS "COLLINS LINE POLICY" RUI- ING PACIFIC MAIL.

Not content with ruining one of the finest steamship fleets afloat, the Collins line, Messrs. Brown Bros. & Co. have fastened themselves like a barnacle on the Pacific Mail Steamship Company, with the same policy of exclusive insolence, favoritism, disregard of public wants, commissions on supplying stores, and reckless extravagance of expenditures, which would have ruined the Company long ago, if the route had not been one which pays extraordinary profits. A year ago, Pacific Mail, according to the sworn testimony of Mr. Howard Potter, the son-in-law of one of the Browns, and others, had cash assets of $14,000,000, and they stated the stock was worth 150 or $30,000,000. The last official statement published by the president, Mr. Louis McLane, tells the stockholders that the Company is running at a loss, can pay no dividend, and recommends that all dividends be postponed indefinitely. The capital stock of the Company is $20,000,000, but deducting that which the Company owns or has not issued, it is in round numbers $17,000,000. Of this amount $12,000,000 in money has been contributed within the last few years, and all that the Company has to show for this besides the original capital, are side-wheeled steamships, which would not sell for $6,000,000, and a business which the president coolly states is so ruinously bad as in his judgment to render dividends hopeless. In plain terms Pacific Mail, like the Collins line, is on the *verge of dissolution at the hands of the same doctors, the eminent bankers, Messrs. Brown Brothers & Co.* If this were simply the dissolution of a corporate steamship company, and its results were only loss to a body of stockholders who were stupid enough to entrust the management of

their property in such hands, then the ruin of Pacific Mail would be of minor importance. But unfortunately for the national prosperity that is not so. As the ruin of the Collins line gave the transatlantic route to Europe, so will the ruin of the Pacific Mail Company also give to Europe the monopoly of the Atlantic and Pacific oceans. For if Pacific Mail fails, it will frighten American capital from investing in that route. As the scandal of Messrs. Brown Bros. & Co.'s mismanagement of the Collins and Pacific Mail Steamship Companies is a matter of public notoriety, it behooves the merchants and shipowners of New York, as well as the Pacific Mail stockholders, for their own pecuniary gain, to take prompt and vigorous measures for saving this great national enterprise from ruin, *and the carrying steamship trade from passing into the hands of foreigners.*

THE NOVELTY IRON WORKS LOAN FROM PACIFIC MAIL.

The Novelty Iron Works, which are in reality the Brown's property, have borrowed $500,000 of the Pacific Mail Steamship Company on collaterals which no bank or money lender in Wall street would advance $50,000. Why do Messrs. Brown Brothers & Co., with their enormous wealth and transacting a *business of giving their sixty days paper for other people's money*, not advance this sum of $500,000 to the Novelty Iron Works, instead of borrowing it from a corporation of which they are trustees ?

FIRST CLASS FIRMS TO BE WATCHED.—"ALL IS NOT GOLD THAT GLITTERS."

The developments in the case of Overend, Gurney & Co., showing a condition of hopeless insolvency for years precedent to their avowed bankruptcy, are warnings that the highest standing and credit are no guarantees against irregularities, nor incentives to blind confidence. The recent decision in Paris that the Credit Mobilier had swindled its new stockholders out of $12,000,000 in gold, by "watering" its capital stock, and the decree that this sum was due to and should be paid back to them, are warnings which no prudent business man ought to neglect.

The article which so disturbed Mark Collet appeared in *The Revolution*'s "Financial Department" in the issue for June 11, 1868. Collet was no doubt right in suspecting that it "derived its inspiration from that reckless fellow Geo. F. Train." Brown Shipley had known about Train's recklessness ever since the 1850s, when he was a partner in his father's great ship-owning house, Enoch Train & Co. of Boston. On November 5, 1856, Brown Shipley had reported to Brown Brothers that the means of the Train house were "quite inadequate to the extent of the engagements they enter into." And later in the 'fifties they had again encountered Train when he was involved in a reckless railroad building scheme (the Atlantic & Great Western).

The reference in the last paragraph of the article to the swindles of the Credit Mobilier of France is ironic in view of the fact that Train, at the moment, was himself involved in the American Credit Mobilier, the construction company which was plundering the resources of the first transcontinental railroad, the Union Pacific, with the connivance of well-bribed government officials and congressmen.

Brown Brothers' connections with the Pacific Mail line were certainly no secret, for the name of the Pacific Mail Steamship Company was directly under their own above the entrance to the splendid new marble banking house James Brown had recently erected at Wall and Hanover Streets. (The original photograph is almost twice the size of the reproduction and shows both names clearly.)

The work of demolishing the old building had begun in the spring of 1864, at which time the firm moved across Wall Street to temporary quarters in No. 56. Most of the records concerning the new building have been lost, but we know from a letter John Crosby Brown wrote Howard Potter in 1868 that there was a year's delay in completing it, "which might certainly have been prevented by care and attention." John himself had been so busy "looking into and working up the detail office work of the house, especially in No. 56 where we started our new method of

keeping our exchange account," that he had been unable to look after the new building or any of his father's other property "outside the house" (which "so largely" exceeded what was "in" the firm). Finally Clarence Brown, back in the office after his army service, had been assigned full time to the supervision of the building's erection. By June 1866 Brown Brothers had apparently moved in, for on June 6th Brown Shipley wrote wishing them "much comfort & prosperity" in their new offices. The architect may have been Howard Potter's brother, Edward Tuckerman Potter (designer of the *Arctic* monument, p. 98), who later formed a partnership with James Brown Lord (a grandson of James Brown) and in the 1880s designed the building erected on Park Avenue at 69th for the Union Theological Seminary. (Among Potter & Lord's other buildings was the Delmonico restaurant that still stands at the corner of Beaver and South William Streets.)

This undated photograph, reproduced from John Crosby Brown's book *A Hundred Years of Merchant Banking*, seems to be the only available picture of the interior of what Matthew Hale Smith in 1871 called "the finest private banking house in the world." The electric lights suggest that the photograph was probably taken about 1900 and the paper affixed to the pillar at right was probably one on which Charles Simons had listed that day's "Brown's posted rates" for foreign exchange (see p. 129). But except for minor details the main banking room probably was much as it had been in 1866. (*Brown Brothers Harriman & Co. Historical File*)

---

iv.   **NEW YORK CITY.**

BROWN BROTHERS & CO.,

59 WALL STREET, NEW YORK,

211 Chestnut Street, PHILADELPHIA,   66 State Street, BOSTON,

ALEXANDER BROWN & SONS,

Corner Baltimore and Calvert Streets, BALTIMORE,

Issue against cash deposited, or satisfactory guarantee of repayment, CIRCULAR CREDITS FOR TRAVELERS, in *Dollars* for use in the United States and adjacent countries, and in *Pounds sterling* for use in any part of the world.

These credits, bearing the signature of the holder, afford a ready means of identification, and the amounts for which they are issued can be availed of from time to time, and wherever he may be, in sums to meet the requirements of the traveler.

Application for credits may be made to either of the above houses direct, or through any first class bank or banker in this country.

THEY ALSO ISSUE COMMERCIAL CREDITS,

MAKE CABLE TRANSFERS OF MONEY BETWEEN THIS COUNTRY AND ENGLAND,

DRAW BILLS OF EXCHANGE ON GREAT BRITAIN AND IRELAND,

AND MAKE ADVANCES UPON COTTON OR OTHER APPROVED MERCHANDISE

To the consignment of MESSRS. BROWN, SHIPLEY & CO., *London and Liverpool.*

Brown Brothers' advertisement in *The Banker's Almanac for 1873* is interesting evidence of the degree to which the firm's business had changed since before the Civil War. Advances on cotton and other merchandise "to the consignment of Brown Shipley & Co." were still made, but the advertisement features the firm's circular credits for travelers, its commercial credits, and its business in money and exchange.

Note also the prominence given to the name of Alexander Brown & Sons, who had resumed the Baltimore agency of the firm after the Civil War. (*Brown Brothers Harriman & Co. Historical File*)

The Pacific Mail line also advertised in *The Banker's Almanac for 1873,* and its address was still 59 Wall Street. According to Worthington Fowler's autobiographical *Ten Years in Wall Street* (Hartford, 1870), "He who visits the office of the company in the banking house of Brown Brothers, in which marble, iron, plate glass, black walnut and fresco, form a pleasing combination of solidity and beauty, will be reminded that he may here shake hands with China for a small consideration."

With the early history of Pacific Mail James Brown apparently had little to do, though the company was established in 1848 by his University Place neighbor, William Howland Aspinwall (whose cousin, Maria Howland Brown, had been widowed by the tragic Fourth-of-July accident that killed James Brown's eldest son). But in the 1860s both James Brown and Brown Brothers became heavily involved. According to Fowler's account Aspinwall, James Brown, and others in 1862 formed "a 'ring' of a new and singular character" which bought up 65 percent of the company's stock. This they "transferred to Brown Brothers, by an irrevocable stock power, as trustees to hold it for *five years*" for their joint benefit. The "ring" thereupon selected Leonard W. Jerome —"a leader of fashion, a prince of the turf," whose daughter Jennie became Lady Churchill and the mother of Sir Winston—to manipulate the stock. What followed, according to James K. Medbery's *Men and Mysteries of Wall Street* (1870), involved "some of the most startling and romantic phases of stock brokerage ever known in the street"—operations which stripped Jerome of much of his fortune and by February 1868 had reduced the value of James Brown's stock considerably. By the end of 1870 Brown Brothers had sold out all its interest.

That Brown Brothers did not, however, ruin the Pacific Mail Steamship Company is witnessed by the paragraph with which Fowler introduced his long and fascinating account of Jerome's and the "ring's" activities. True, the stock which in 1857 had sold for 50 sold for "what was equivalent to 700, on the basis of the increased stock;" but the line which had had only two second-class steamboats

PACIFIC MAIL STEAMSHIP COMPANY.

Steamers leave San Francisco as follows:

FOR JAPAN AND CHINA.

1st and 16th of every month, at noon, for Hong Kong, *via* Yokohama, connecting at Yokohama with the Company's steamers for Hakodadi, Hiogo, Nagasaki, and Shanghae.

FOR NEW YORK, *via* PANAMA.

7th, 17th, and 27th of every month, at noon, touching at San Diego and Acapulco. Steamers of 17th and 27th also touch at Cape St. Lucas, Mazatlan, and Manzanillo.

Connections at Acapulco with steamers for all Central American ports.

☞ When either of the above dates falls on Sunday, the steamer will sail on the preceding Saturday.

LOS ANGELES AND SAN DIEGO BRANCH.

For Santa Barbara, San Pedro, and San Diego every Thursday, at 9 A.M.
For Monterey, San Simeon, and San Luis Obispo, on alternate Wednesdays, at 9 A.M.

GUAYMAS BRANCH.

For Cape St. Lucas, San Blas, Mazatlan, La Paz, and Guaymas, every fifth Tuesday: viz., January 28th, March 4th, and April 8th, etc., etc.

☞ Through Tickets and through Bills of Lading between all principal ports of Europe and North and South America and Japan, China, and India.

ELDRIDGE & IRWIN,
General Agents for the Pacific,
SAN FRANCISCO.

A. B. STOCKWELL, *President,*
No. 59 Wall Street, New York.

(Brown Brothers Harriman & Co. Historical File)

in 1849, plying between San Francisco and Panama, in 1869 had twenty-three first-class ships plying between New York and Aspinwall on the Atlantic side of the isthmus, between Panama and San Francisco on the Pacific side, and across the Pacific itself between San Francisco and the Far East. Even *Harper's Weekly,* which editorialized on March 23, 1867, about the way "a well known steamship king, a powerful Anglo-American banking house, and a rich and daring financier" had inflated, cornered, watered, and doctored the stock, had to admit that the stock itself was "intrinsically valuable" and that the line had prospered. The Pacific Mail was, in fact, one of the longest-lived of all American steamship lines, and long after Brown Brothers had ceased to be interested in it, it became a part of the world-girdling transportation system which E. H. Harriman was building at the time of his death.

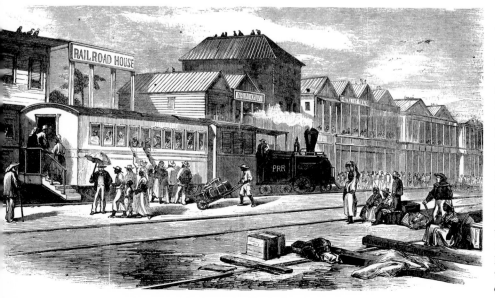

The sailings from San Francisco "For New York, *via* Panama" referred to in Pacific Mail's advertisement (above) were not, of course, "through voyages" in those pre-canal days. Passengers and freight crossed the isthmus by the Panama Railroad whose Atlantic terminus at Aspinwall (later Colón) is shown in this wood engraving from *Harper's Weekly* (January 27, 1866). Like the Pacific Mail line itself, the Panama Railroad was William H. Aspinwall's creation, but it was not until 1866 that the steamship line, with Brown Brothers' aid, got full control of the railroad. (*Author's Collection*)

In contrast with the Pacific Mail "ring," whose activities—however profitable—permitted the survival of a great steamship line, were other "rings" organized solely to manipulate the market for the profit of speculators, without regard for consequences. Probably the most infamous of these was the one headed by Jay Gould and Col. Jim Fisk, which tried to corner the nation's gold supply in September 1869—an attempt which pushed the price of gold from 133 to 162½ in about twenty days, and which ended in the disastrous collapse of "Black Friday" (the 24th). The scene on the gold exchange that day is shown in the anonymous wood engraving at right, from *Harper's Weekly*, October 16, 1869. It is worth noting that in the report of the congressional committee which investigated the events leading up to "Black Friday" James Brown shares credit with Secretary of the Treasury Boutwell for smashing the Gould-Fiske conspiracy. According to the report submitted on March 1, 1870, by James A. Garfield, chairman of the House Committee on Banking and Currency,

SCENE IN THE GOLD ROOM, NEW YORK CITY, DURING THE INTENSE EXCITEMENT OF FRIDAY, SEPTEMBER 24, 1869.

"The situation of all those whose legitimate business required the purchase of gold was exceedingly critical, and the boldest of them, under the lead of Brown, joined the great crowd of speculative bears in desperate efforts to break down the conspiracy and put down the price by heavy sales. . . . A few minutes before noon [on "Black Friday"], when the excitement in the gold-room had risen to a tempest, James Brown offered to sell one million at 162; then another million at 161; and then five millions more at 160; and the market broke. About ten minutes afterwards the news came that the Treasury would sell, and the break was complete."

"WHAT A FALL WAS THERE, MY COUNTRYMEN!"

(*Both pictures from Author's Collection*)

The result of "Black Friday," as the Garfield report went on to say, was that "half of Wall Street was in ruins." Thomas Nast's cartoon, in the same issue of *Harper's Weekly* that carried the picture reproduced at left, told the story of the slaughtered bulls and bears in graphic terms.

"Black Friday" brought ruin to many speculators, and suffering to their families, but the consequences for the country as a whole were not disastrous. The panic of 1873, however, was another matter. Again the crash came in September. Starting on the 8th several important Wall Street houses failed, and there were grave rumors of worse things to come. Then, unbelievably, on the 18th the New York house of Jay Cooke & Co., the nation's greatest banking house, closed its doors, shattering the last hopes that a complete collapse could be avoided. (The wood engraving at left, showing the closed doors of Jay Cooke's office on Nassau Street, was one of a group of "Scenes in Wall Street During the Panic" which were published in *Harper's Weekly,* October 11, 1873.) The actual panic was of relatively brief duration, but its aftermath brought months of suffering and hardship to countless thousands. Almost half a million laborers were thrown out of work, long bread lines appeared in the cities, and profound social unrest found expression in the increasing radicalism of various workers' organizations.

(Both pictures from Author's Collection)

A center of radical working-class demonstrations in New York during the depression years after the panic of 1873 was Tompkins Square, shown here in a wood engraving by C. Maurand from a drawing by C. S. Reinhart, published in *Harper's Weekly,* September 13, 1873. Reinhart, one of the greatest American illustrators, had a sharp but subtle eye for the kind of social contrast depicted in this drawing of a fashionable couple encountering the regular denizens of Tompkins Square when "Out for a Breath of Fresh Air."

It was in the basement of one of the crumbling buildings on Tompkins Square, three years after Reinhart made this drawing, that E. H. Harriman—by then head of his own brokerage house on Wall Street—founded the first of the now famous Boys' Clubs, where he and a group of his friends took turns spending an evening a week boxing and playing games with youngsters who otherwise would have had nothing to do but rove the neighborhood in disorderly gangs. Harriman's interest in the Boys' Club never flagged, and after his death his sons continued to support and direct its work. (Roland Harriman is currently chairman of the board, and three other Brown Brothers Harriman partners are active trustees.)

(Brown Brothers Harriman & Co. Historical File)

In the late 1860s the first generation of Brown Brothers partners began turning over the active management of the firm to younger men. In the spring of 1865, for example, STEWART BROWN took the first long vacation he had had in many years, visiting his son Stewart Henry in Liverpool and leaving the management of the New York office to James M. Brown and Charles D. Dickey, assisted by Howard Potter and John Crosby Brown, who had just been admitted to partnership. Prior to that, he told James M. in a letter from Liverpool, April 25, 1865, he thought he could claim to have been "as strictly at work *for a longer time* than any one in the concern," having read "every letter rec^d or sent out of the office" and been "always in conference with the credit clerk."

This letter was written at a moment when Stewart had just heard of James Brown's plans to increase the shares in the partnership assigned to the younger men, and Stewart seems to have feared that his own claims, based on previous service, were being overlooked. James was forgetting, he said, that "for the last 20 or 25 years he has come in & out of the office without knowing what was going on, devolving the whole responsibility on me." But Stewart's irritation was momentary. "Cousin J. B. has been always very kind to me," he concluded, "& if he had had his own way I know I should have had a much larger interest than I had at an earlier period & should now have been much better off, and I should be sorry that he could think for a moment I am not sensible of his goodness; but as he was prevented by his brother carrying out his generous intentions towards me & the other juniors I have thought it right to make this statement of facts."

James Brown had, indeed, had difficulties with his brother over the shares to be allotted the juniors. In a letter to Howard Potter, September 25, 1867, he noted that in 1853 Hamilton and Collet had felt that the seniors "had an over proportion of Shares, and as I concurred with them in that opinion I undertook to persuade my Brother William to increase the Juniors shares which he did with very great reluctance and it almost made a breach between my Brother W^m & myself."

(Original in possession of Mrs. John Crosby Brown II, Old Lyme, Conn.)

Stewart Brown's comment about James Brown's generosity reminds one of a touching letter John Crosby Brown wrote, December 10, 1862, to his sister Sarah, then living at Richmond Hill. Sarah had married her cousin Alexander Brown, son of William Brown, in 1838, and after Alexander's death in 1849 she lived on with her father-in-law uncle until his death in 1864. "What a pity it is," John Crosby wrote her, "that one, who has so much money, seems to know so little about its true use! I assure you I appreciate the feelings of anxiety in which you must constantly be kept & only wish Uncle was more like father. . . . I can't help being struck with the contrast between the two men."

In the spring and summer of 1868 the partners in England and America were involved in painful negotiations concerning the renewal of the articles of partnership, due to expire at the end of the year. But James Brown—a grandfather now—wisely left it to the juniors to work out the terms on which they would carry on the business. "The truth is," John Crosby Brown wrote on April 14, 1868, to Howard Potter (in England for consultations with Hamilton and Collet), "father's advancing years are be-

ginning to tell on him, and altho' his mind is as clear & his judgment as sound as ever, yet he cannot take up any such subject as the present, which might involve a difference with those with whom he has been so long associated. . . ."

The Eastman Johnson painting above (reproduced from a color transparency by John T. Hill) shows Mr. and Mrs. Brown with their grandson in the parlor of the University Place house (see Brady's photograph, p. 85). Though undated, it must have been done in 1868, since the grandson (John Crosby Brown's son William Adams Brown) was three in that year, and in the following year the family moved uptown to a new house at 37th Street and Park Avenue.

Of Mrs. Brown about this time we get a glimpse in a letter Thomas B. Curtis, of the Boston agency, wrote to his son Louis on February 23, 1870. Louis Curtis (later to become Brown Brother's first Boston partner) had just gone to work for his older brother Daniel S. Curtis in the Boston office. "I hope you will someday go to New York," his father wrote, "and will cultivate all the Browns, especially Mrs. *James* who always seemed to possess much influence with the heads of the firm in business matters."

The wreathed date, above, and the watercolor drawing of the decorated dining room, both date from 1875 in the first of the "Brighthurst Chronicles." The dining room is shown hung with garlands for the fortieth wedding anniversary of Mrs. Brown's parents, the Reverend and Mrs. William Adams. Dr. Adams had been the pastor of the Madison Square Presbyterian Church for twenty years when, in 1873, he was elected president of the Union Theological Seminary, of which he had been one of the original projectors. (*Both pictures from Brown Brothers Harriman & Co. Historical File*)

The watercolors reproduced on this page were selected from the various scrapbooks in which John Crosby Brown and his wife, Mary Elizabeth Adams Brown, lovingly recorded their lives with their family and friends. The two above, both dating from 1875, are from volume one of the elaborate "Brighthurst Chronicles," memorabilia of their country home, Brighthurst, near Orange, New Jersey. The one below, dated 1881, is from the "Brighthurst Visitors Book." Nine volumes of the "Chronicles," covering the years 1874 to 1901, are now in the firm's Historical File, along with a number of other albums, scrapbooks, and diaries, providing fascinating glimpses of the domestic "world" of the man who became head of Brown Brothers & Co. in 1877 after the death of his father, James Brown, and of the

The 1881 sketch of John Crosby Brown at left, entitled "Our President's Greatest Catch except M.E.B.," was drawn for the Brighthurst "Visitors Book" by William Adams Delano, the son of Mrs. Brown's sister and Eugene Delano. The Delanos and Browns spent part of each summer at Pasque Island, which had been bought in 1866 by John Crosby Brown and some of his friends and was controlled by them as a "club." Eugene Delano, a merchant of considerable experience, had joined the staff of Brown Brothers' Philadelphia house in 1880 (and was to become a partner in 1894). His son, who drew this picture, became one of the country's most successful architects and head of the firm of Delano & Aldrich which in 1928 designed two of the buildings Brown Brothers Harriman & Co. now occupies (see pp. 196 & 221). (*Brown Brothers Harriman & Co. Historical File*)

world into which his son Thatcher M. Brown, first senior partner of Brown Brothers Harriman & Co., was born in 1876.

In his history of the firm, published in 1909, John Crosby Brown records that until Sir William Brown's death in 1864 "the ownership and control of the business rested absolutely with William and James Brown; and after William Brown's death, with James alone until 1868. They decided when and what partners were to be admitted and what interest they should have in the business. . . ." But when the new articles of partnership were drawn up in 1868, it was not possible to keep the firm under the absolute control of the Browns. Sir William's sons were dead, and his grandsons were not yet old enough to enter the business. Of James' sons, only John Crosby and Clarence were in the firm, and neither had the necessary experience to assume "the power of seniority."

Howard Potter went to London in the spring of 1868 as representative of James Brown and his sons, to work out the details of the new articles in discussions with the English partners, and the letters he wrote and received at that time reveal how close the firm came to dissolution before acceptable compromises were arrived at. It was clear to Potter from the start that a "reconstruction" of the firm was necessary, but, as he wrote Clarence Brown retirement, or limitation of his liability to a Special on March 3, "I think anything so radical as Father's partnership, would be fatal to the credit of the House— It might go on in the Howland & Aspinwall, perhaps even in the Duncan Sherman & Co 'form'—to use an English racing word—, but it would not be Brown Brothers & Co., the first House in the United States, any longer." By July 3 he was writing to John Crosby Brown: "I would give a thousand Dollars for an hours quiet talk with you —five thousand, ten thousand, if you would come over here & arrange this business to suit yourself— I feel in fact as if I was handling a business ready to drop to pieces in all directions— You do not care to remain in the House having your fortune &

your books & your home— Clarence does not care to stay in the House having his fortune & his Novelty Works . . . & his underground railroad [the first New York subway scheme], & his Pacific Mail. Mr. Hamilton does not care to stay in the concern, having buried his hopes & his heart in the grave of his boys [both his sons had recently died]. . . . Mr. Collet would see things wound up with great philosophy if it came to that—" Furthermore, Herman Hoskier, who had served in the Mobile agency with Charles D. Dickey before the Civil War and had recently been admitted to partnership at Founders Court, "carries a heavy load & works hard here," Potter said, and was "disposed to stand for what he considers his rights & to go if he does not get them." And there were serious disagreements about the advisability of continuing the Liverpool house with Stewart Henry Brown as partner in residence. Altogether it is a wonder that by the end of August new articles had been drawn up and agreed to, embodying—as John Crosby Brown later said—changes which, while retaining "the ideals and traditions" that had contributed to the success of the firm when it was "merely a family affair," made the organization "more elastic and better adapted to modern conditions."

Within three years the business of the reorganized firm had expanded so greatly that—as John Crosby Brown said in a letter of February 17, 1871—it was "afflicted with too much prosperity." When the new articles of partnership had been signed no one, he said, had "imagined that our credit business would develop & increase as it has done & that a cash capital ample to work it comfortably as it then was" would prove to be "plainly insufficient" a few years later. The immediate problem was solved by having each of the partners put some of his "outside" investments into the working capital. Then in 1875 William Brown's grandson, Alexander Hargreaves Brown, became a partner, strengthening the family connection and bringing back into the firm a considerable share of Sir William's estate. A new era for the firm had begun.

(Brown Brothers Harriman & Co. Historical File)

The "modern conditions" to which the re-organized partnership responded were in part the result of the fact that in 1866 Cyrus W. Field had finally succeeded in laying a successful transatlantic cable. As Ellis points out in his history of Brown Shipley, it was the cable, more than anything else, that "put an end to the intervention of the merchant in the cotton trade," since British manufacturers could now cable orders direct to brokers in Southern cities, after inspecting cotton samples sent directly to their factories. But at the same time that the cable limited the firm's merchanting activities, it vastly accelerated foreign exchange transactions.

When Field gave a dinner 1879 to celebrate the twenty-fifth anniversary of the founding of his first cable company, one of the invitations (designed and engraved by Tiffany & Co.) naturally went to John Crosby Brown of Brown Brothers. The Brown firms had been large stockholders in the enterprise from 1856 on, and William Brown was for a time the president of Field's Atlantic Telegraph Co. of Great Britain. One wonders if John Crosby Brown remembered the letter Brown Shipley had written to Brown Brothers, back on September 27, 1865, shortly after Field sailed on the *Great Eastern*'s cable-laying voyage. The price of Atlantic Telegraph Co. shares having recently been depressed by news that another company was going to lay a cable via the Azores, Field had visited Brown Shipley, they said, and "so strongly expatiated" on their duty to retain their interest in the company "on public grounds" that they decided not to sell their shares even though they felt "but little confidence in the mercantile success of the Undertaking." Since then they had learned that Field himself had nevertheless "sold out all his shares in the old Company just before the *Great Eastern* sailed."

In June 1868 Brown Shipley was asked to bring out the bonds of another company, which was to lay a cable from Brest to New York, but they turned the proposition down. "Profitable as the negotiation of Bonds & the launching of Companies may be, we would rather confine ourselves to our \steady Banking business, unless indeed [and this must have caused wry smiles in the New York office, where the Civil W... disagreements were still fresh in mind] some good loans to a first class State, or the U. S. Government were to come in our way; these do not involve the risk of compromising our position, as the connexion with private companies necessarily does."

(Brown Brothers Harriman & Co. Historical File)

Yet in the days of electricity's first great triumphs even the "steady Banking business" involved risks of embarrassing "connexions," as can be seen in the notice printed vertically in the right-hand margin of the undated advertisement reproduced here.

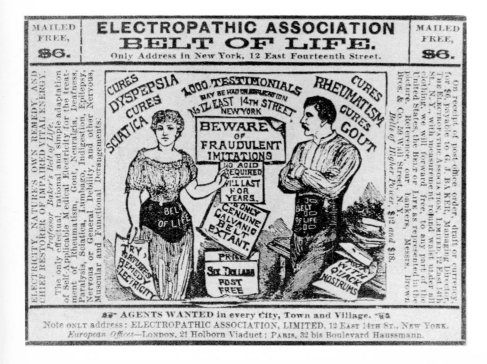

COMPLETION OF THE PACIFIC RAILROAD, MAY 10, 1869—THE GREAT LINK CONNECTING EUROPE WITH ASIA ACROSS THE AMERICAN CONTINENT.—[See Page 341.]

(Author's Collection)

When the promoters of the new Atlantic telegraph cable asked Brown Shipley to "launch" their company by negotiating the sale of its bonds, they did so, as Brown Shipley said in their letter to Brown Brothers, because of the interest the firm was "justly supposed to have in multiplying & cheapening facilities for intercourse." That interest had been shown first by their building their own ships, then by their contribution to the development of regular transatlantic sailing packet services, then by their investments in the Cunard and Collins steamship lines and in Field's first Atlantic cable.

All these had been transatlantic enterprises, but early in the 1860s —as Brown Brothers' involvement with the Pacific Mail Steamship Co. indicated—the American partners had turned their thoughts westward toward California and they must have shared in the nation's excitement and pride when the first transcontinental railroad was completed on May 10, 1869.

Notice that when *Harper's Weekly* published its two-page wood engraving celebrating completion of the Pacific Railroad (in the issue for May 29, 1869), its caption referred to the road as "The Great Link Connecting Europe with Asia," and that the decorative border exploited the same theme. Surely that ship, framed between the American and Chinese merchants at the bottom center of the border, is a Pacific Mail steamer leaving San Francisco "for Hong Kong, *via* Yokohama" as the advertisement on p. 137 says.

The imagery of the ornamental title page of the first *Tourist's Guide* to the Pacific Railroad also emphasizes the road's presumed destiny as a route for commerce with Asia. Again we have the American and Chinese merchants (at top this time), and the three cars on the train headed across the plain at lower right bear the names (not legible in this reduced reproduction) Omaha, California, and China. It may well have been a copy of Crofutt's *Great Transcontinental P.R.R. Tourist's Guide* that John Crosby Brown took along on his first journey over the line, when Mrs. Brown accompanied him on a business trip to California in 1873. If so, they were lucky; it still makes excellent reading. In any event, when the Browns passed Promontory Point, Utah, and got on the section of track that had been built eastward from California by the Central Pacific company, it may have occurred to them that all the rails and other equipment used in its construction had had to be imported from Europe or the East—much of it in Pacific Mail steamships. And John Crosby Brown may also have remembered that in Brown Brothers' "General Gold Ledger" for 1868 there was an item reading:

"Union Pacific R.R. Co. Option Account $849,722.33." That was a sizable gold transaction by any standards.

GREAT TRANS-CONTINENTAL P.R.R.

CALIFORNIA IN 1849   CALIFORNIA IN 1869

TOURIST'S GUIDE

GEO. A. CROFUTT & CO., Publishers,
21 Park Row N. Y.

Entered according to Act of Congress, in the year 1870, by GEO. A. CROFUTT, in the Clerk's Office of the District Court

(Author's Collection)

GREAT TRAVELING WORLD'S FAIR FOR THE CAMPAIGN OF 1873.

P. T. BARNUM TO THE PUBLIC.

LADIES, GENTLEMEN, FAMILIES, CHILDREN, FRIENDS:

My career for forty years as a public Manager of Amusements blended with Instruction is well known. You have all heard of my three New York Museums; my appearance before kings, queens, and royal courts, with Gen. Tom Thumb; my great triumphal tour with Jenny Lind, the Swedish Nightingale; and my immense Traveling Exhibitions. Every body concedes that I give ten times the money's worth, and always delight my patrons. I now come before you with the **LAST GRAND CROWNING TRIUMPH OF MY MANAGERIAL LIFE.**

Notwithstanding the burning of my last museum, in December (which, however, did not destroy any of my great traveling chariots, vans, cages, or horses, nor duplicates of most of my living wild animals, which were then on exhibition in New Orleans), I have been enabled, through the aid of cable dispatches, electricity, and steam, and the expenditure of nearly a million of dollars, to place upon the road by far the largest and most interesting Combination of **MUSEUM, ME-NAGERIE,** and **HIPPODROME** ever known. Indeed, it may fairly be called a great **TRAVELING WORLD'S FAIR.**

No description will convey an adequate idea of its vastness, its beauty, and its marvelous collection of wonders. After our *Grand Opening* in the buildings of the American Institute, Monday, March 31, where we will remain for about ten days, we shall commence the campaign of 1873.

It will travel entirely by railroad, and be exhibited this season in nearly every large town in New England, Canada, and the States east of the Mississippi River and north of the Ohio. It requires more than one hundred cars, besides *fifty of my own*, made expressly for this purpose, and five or six locomotives, to transport it. My daily expenses exceed $5000. We can only stop in large towns, and leave it to those residing elsewhere to reach us by cheap excursion trains, which they can easily get up.

Among some of my novelties are a **FREE FULL MENAGERIE OF WILD ANI-MALS,** including all, and more than are usually seen in a traveling menagerie, which I now open to be seen by every body, **WITHOUT ANY CHARGE WHATEVER.**

Although I have consolidated more than twenty shows in one, containing nearly one hundred gorgeously magnificent gold and enameled cages, dens, and vans, requiring the services of nearly ONE THOUSAND MEN and OVER FIVE HUNDRED HORSES, the price of admission to the entire combination of exhibitions is only the same as is charged to a common show, viz., 50 cents; children half price.

My great Hippodrome Tent comfortably seats 13,000 persons at one time, while my numerous other tents cover several acres of ground.

The Museum Department contains 100,000 Curiosities, including Prof. Faber's wonderful **TALKING MACHINE**, costing me $20,000 for its use six months. Also a NATIONAL PORTRAIT GALLERY of 100 life-size Oil Paintings, including all the Presidents of the United States, our Statesmen and Military Heroes, as well as foreign Potentates and Celebrities, and the entire Collection of the celebrated John Rogers' Groups of Historical and Classic Statuary. Also an almost endless variety of Curiosities, including numberless Automaton Musicians and Mechanicians, and Moving Scenes, Transformation Landscapes, Sailing-Ships, Running Water-Mills, Railroad Trains, &c., made in Paris and Geneva, more beautiful and marvelous than can be imagined, and all kept in motion by a Steam-Engine. Here also are Giants, Dwarfs, Feejee Cannibals, Modoc and Digger Indians, Circassian Girls, the No-Armed Boy, &c.

Among the Rare Living Animals are **MONSTER SEA LIONS**, transported in great water-tanks; the largest **RHINOCEROS** ever captured alive, and 500 Wild Beasts and Rare Birds, Elephants, Elands, Gnus, Lions, Tigers, Polar Bears, Ostriches, and every description of Wild Animal hitherto exhibited, besides many never before seen on this Continent.

In the Hippodrome department are **THREE DISTINCT RINGS**, wherein three sets of rival performances are taking place at the same time, in full view of all the audience. Here will be seen performing elephants, horse-riding goats, educated horses, ponies, trick mules and bears, and three distinct equestrian companies (with six clowns), including by far the best male and female bare-back riders in the world, with numerous athletes and gymnasts who have no equal. Every thing is perfectly chaste and unobjectionable.

I regard this with pride as the culminating triumph of my amusement career, and I hazard nothing in saying that **the like will not be seen again in this generation.**

THE GREAT STREET PROCESSION, three miles long, takes place every morning at half-past eight o'clock. It is worth going one hundred miles to see. It consists of trains of elephants, camels, dromedaries, zebras, and elks in harness; nearly one hundred gold, enameled, and cerulean chariots, vans, dens, and cages; Arabian horses, trick ponies, three bands of music, and a most marvelous display of gymnastic, automatic, and musical performances in the public streets.

☞ THREE FULL EXHIBITIONS will be given each day at 10, 1, and 7 o'clock. Clergymen of all denominations, and their wives, admitted free. Parties from the country are earnestly advised to see the Grand Procession, and attend the first morning exhibitions, while every thing is fresh, and seen to the best advantage, thus avoiding the immense crowds of afternoon and evening.

The public's obedient servant,

P. T. Barnum

438 FIFTH AVENUE, March 15, 1873.

(*Author's Collection*)

As P. T. Barnum's splendid advertisement (opposite) shows, everyone and everything headed west by rail in 1873—the year Mr. and Mrs. John Crosby Brown made their first trip on the new transcontinental railroad. The advertisement, which occupied a full page of *Harper's Weekly* for March 29, 1873, is worth reading if the type is not illegible in this reduced reproduction. By means of "cable dispatches, electricity, and steam," Barnum says he has assembled a Traveling World's Fair which "will travel entirely by railroad" as far west as the Mississippi.

Records of the John Crosby Browns' Western trip are preserved in Mrs. Brown's "Journal" and a scrapbook containing pictures and other memorabilia. Their first stop was Chicago, where Mr. Brown undoubtedly called on the officers of the First National Bank, with which Brown Brothers dealt in Sterling Exchange on Joint Account in the later 'seventies.

It is interesting that one of the Chicago pictures the Browns pasted in their scrapbook showed some Illinois Central Railroad freight cars and one of the railroad's grain elevators. Back in the 1850s, despite the English partners' objections to "locking up" the firm's capital, Brown Brothers had taken more than $200,000 worth of Illinois Central Railroad bonds—"simply for the purpose of helping" a concern that had "no kind of claim for such selfsacrifice on our part," as Mark Collet complained in a private letter to Stewart Brown, February 9, 1855. [The Chicago partner of Brown Brothers Harriman, Stephen Y. Hord (p. 215) is currently a director and a member of the executive committee of the Illinois Central.]

(*Brown Brothers Harriman & Co. Historical File*)

The photograph, showing the lake steamer *Muskegon* tied up near the elevator, was taken from the roof of one Illinois Central freight car (right foreground) and shows another (at left) beyond two ox-drawn wagons—one belonging to Miller Brothers & Keep, Hardware & Cutlery dealers, the other to the Chicago White Lead & Oil Co.

rown Brothers Harriman & Co. Historical File)

One of the San Francisco pictures in the Browns' scrapbook of the 1873 trip is this photograph of California Street, looking eastward from near Webb Street. Though Mrs. Brown's "Journal" gives no details of her husband's business contacts on the Western trip, there is little doubt that John Crosby Brown renewed contacts that had been originally made by his brother Clarence, who had been in San Francisco on Brown Brothers' business in 1863, after leaving the army. And he must certainly have conferred with the men who had been visited—just a year before—by Brown Shipley's newest partner, Mark Collet's brother-in-law Frederick Chalmers. Chalmers had written to Brown Brothers from San Francisco, May 31, 1872, telling of arrangements he had made with Sather & Co., one of San Francisco's largest private banking houses, and of successful talks with W. C. Ralston, of the Bank of California, who had been "exceedingly civil & hospitable."

The year after the California trip, John Crosby Brown journeyed through the Southern states, visiting the firm's agencies in New Orleans and elsewhere. While in New Orleans, he and Mrs. Brown stayed at the home of W. F. Halsey, who headed the agency there from 1865 to 1887. The photograph reproduced at left (from one in the Browns' scrapbook) shows Canal Street, where Samuel Nicholson's pre-Civil War agency had had its offices in a large bank building at the corner of Exchange Place. The New Orleans agency was the only one of the firm's Southern agencies that proved to be very profitable after the war. According to Charles F. Hoffman, who served with Halsey for many years, "the local Banks came out of the war period in an impoverished condition, and the facilities furnished by the Agency, through means of the unlimited funds placed at its disposal by Brown Brothers & Company, of New York, for moving the annual cotton crops, were greatly appreciated by the business community." (Quoted in *A Hundred Years of Merchant Banking,* pp. 271–72.)

Mrs. Brown's "Journal" of the 1874 Southern trip gives a very interesting account of a trip she and her husband made with the Halseys up the Mississippi to Natchez and back. At five in the afternoon of a "fearfully sultry day" they left New Orleans on the *Thompson Dean* an "immense" boat, "four stories high, above water," which could carry "immense loads of cotton & freight." The Browns had "a lovely room some ten or twelve ft. square, & it was quite fun to be on such a big boat & have no sea sickness." Their arrival at Natchez the next day, at eight o'clock in the evening, was "like a scene in an opera," with the brilliantly lighted *Robert E. Lee* just leaving and "the dark night lighted up by an immense light wood torch from the front of our boat, the lights of the town shining in the distance, & the band of music playing."

After several days in Natchez during which John Crosby Brown had business with "the Marshall brothers" and a Mr. Ogden (at whose "queer old fashioned one story house" he and Mrs. Brown stayed), they returned to New Orleans on the *Ames*—a much less agreeable boat, which stopped so often to "wood up" and to discharge freight or take on cotton that it seemed "almost impossible we should ever arrive."

The picture of a cotton steamboat reproduced here is a wood engraving from a drawing by J. Wells Champney, who accompanied Edward King on a tour of the Southern states in 1873 and 1874, and illustrated King's book *The Great South* (Hartford, 1875).

In Charleston, South Carolina, the Browns got this photograph of the Charleston House, where they stayed during their visit. They found several of their acquaintances at the hotel when they arrived, and they saw a good deal of the Adgers. James Adger, the Browns' first Charleston agent (p. 49), had died in 1858, but his son Robert Adger had succeeded him and had charge of the agency until it was discontinued in 1879.

Mrs. Brown's "Journal" tells of a visit with her husband and Robert Adger to a rice mill, "to see the different processes the rice goes through before it is ready for market," but she apparently did not accompany the men on their visit to the phosphate works shown in the scrapbook photograph reproduced here. Robert Adger had become interested in "water phosphate mining" soon after the Civil War, and he and George Stewart Brown (head of Alexander Brown & Sons) were the principal stockholders in the Coosaw Mining Co., which had acquired from the South Carolina legislature the sole right to mine phosphate rock in the streams and navigable rivers of the state. The manufacture of phosphate fertilizers was Charleston's principal industry for some years, until the discovery of even more profitable phosphate deposits in Florida. All told, John Crosby Brown's Western and Southern trips had given him a broad view of the industrial and agricultural

(*Brown Brothers Harriman & Co. Historical File*)

resources which were contributing to the nation's unprecedented economic growth. For, as Allan Nevins said (in *The Emergence of Modern America 1865–1878,* New York, 1932), "the South showed where the reconstructive energies of the nation were working most vigorously" and the Far West "showed where its capacities for new construction were being most effectively expressed."

Brown Brothers Harriman & Co. Historical File)

(*Brown Brothers Harriman & Co. Historical File*)

When the Browns were not traveling they lived either in their forty-foot town house at 36 East 37th or at their country home near Orange, New Jersey. The city house, shown here in an undated photograph, was built in 1871 from designs by Edward Tuckerman Potter (see pp. 98, 135). William Adams Brown, the son who became a professor at Union Theological Seminary, recalls in his autobiography (*A Teacher and His Times,* New York, 1940) that the house was one of four erected by James Brown for himself and members of the family. "My father's house was the most westerly. His sister, Mrs. James Couper Lord, occupied the southerly part of the plot facing Park Avenue, my uncle, Howard Potter, the lot immediately opposite on the north side of the street. In the middle, on the corner site [37th and Park], lived my grandfather in truly patriarchal style, surrounded by his children and grandchildren."

(*Courtesy of Mrs. Harold T. White*)

This photograph of the drawing room in John Crosby Brown's house at 36 East 37 Street was taken by John H. Tarbell, sometime in the early 1890s. Notice that the mantel piece, the ornaments and clock on the mantel shelf, and the elaborate mirror above it are the ones Leon Marcotte had designed back in the 1840s for James Brown's house on University Place (p. 85). When James moved uptown to the corner of 37th and Park in 1869, the Marcotte decorations were installed in the drawing room of his new house, "in order that he might feel perfectly at home," as John Crosby recorded in his unpublished "Reminiscences." Then, when James' house was sold in 1890, after Mrs. James Brown's death, John Crosby had the mantel piece transferred to his house.

(*Courtesy of Mrs. Harold T. White*)

Over the mantel in the dining room at 36 East 37 Street hung the picture Eastman Johnson had painted in 1868, showing John Crosby's father and mother with his son William Adams Brown (see p. 141). A copy of this painting, made by Johnson in 1869, was given by John Crosby Brown in 1870 to his English cousin James Clifton Brown (grandson both of William Brown and James Brown). It now hangs in the home of a director of Brown, Shipley & Co., Ltd.—Mr. Ion Garnett-Orme, whose wife is a granddaughter of James Clifton Brown.

About the time the 37th Street house was built, John Crosby Brown acquired a tract of forty acres on Orange Mountain, near Orange, New Jersey, and built the summer home shown here in a photograph of the architect's original wash drawing, mounted on page one of the first volume of the "Brighthurst Chronicles." The original drawing is now in possession of John Crosby Brown Moore, a New York architect who is a grandson of the owner of Brighthurst. Though the original is unsigned, it was probably the work either of Edward Tuckerman Potter (who designed the house in the city) or of James Brown Lord, a son of James Brown's daughter Margaretta, who was also an architect and became Potter's partner.

Characteristically, the first party given at Brighthurst was one for the carpenters, masons, plumbers, and others who had built the house and worked on the grounds. They and their families were entertained at a supper and dance, and John Crosby Brown made a little speech praising them for their work and assuring them that "as long as he enjoyed the comfortable house which their hands had prepared for him" he hoped they would "feel an interest in the place, and be free to come and see it whenever they liked." Mrs. Brown recorded in the "Chronicles" that the master builder, as he left, said, "We have built hundreds of houses, Mr. Brown, & we have never before even had anyone say thank you."

This photograph and the one on the following page are from a series taken at Brighthurst by an unidentified photographer sometime in the late 1870s or early 1880s. This one shows what William Adams Brown described as "the ample living room with a glorious view of the distant city, a room lined with books and with oaken rafters each bearing its appropriate inscription."

The mottoes and quotations carved and painted on the beams were in English, French, and German, and each had been carefully chosen by the Browns for its appropriateness to their home. One of them, for instance, read: "A tout oiseau son nid est beau." And another, visible in this photograph, said that "Home, like a delicate, sensitive Instrument can only be kept in perfect Tune by constant Care."

The music room at Brighthurst contained a small reed organ (not visible in the picture) on which, William Adams Brown said, "my mother persuaded my father, himself no musician, to learn to play so that we might sing hymns at family prayers." It also housed a collection of musical instruments, assembled by Mrs. Brown from many countries, often with the help of Brown Brothers' correspondents. Some of these instruments can be seen in the photograph—a rack full of reeds and pipes in the left background, an African drum at right. In 1889, when Mrs. Brown gave the collection to the Metropolitan Museum of Art, it consisted of "about 270 instruments, chiefly those of Oriental Nations & Savage Tribes, with a few interesting European specimens." Later acquisitions made the Crosby Brown Collection (as it is called) "one of the richest collections of musical instruments in the world." (See the Museum's 1961 booklet on *Keyboard Instruments,* by Emanuel Winternitz, Curator of Musical Instruments.)

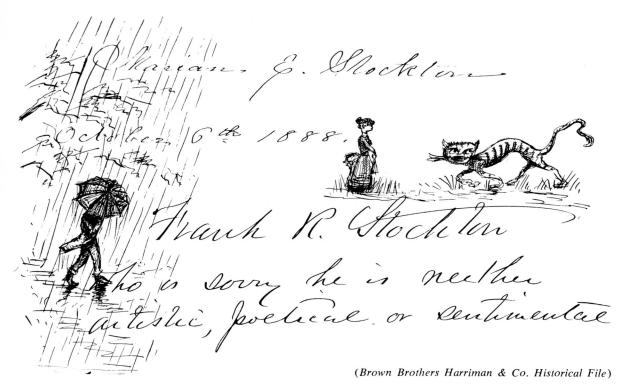

Marian E. Stockton

October 6th 1888.

Frank R. Stockton

who is sorry he is neither artistic, poetical, or sentimental

Brighthurst was a hospitable home. William Adams Brown tells of "Bankers and business men from the city; students and professors from the Theological Seminary; visitors from other lands; missionaries from the ends of the earth," pouring into Brighthurst "in ceaseless succession." But there were artists and writers, too—such as Daniel Chester French, whose fine statue of Lincoln broods in the shadows of the Lincoln Memorial, and Frank R. Stockton, author of "The Lady or the Tiger?", who decorated the page on which he and his wife inscribed their names on a rainy October day in 1888. And every Wednesday, from early June until late autumn, a group of twenty or thirty mothers and children from the New York tenements were brought to Brighthurst early in the morning, given a hot meal, left free to roam and play all day in the gardens and fields or in the log cabin playhouse, fed again before leaving, and each given a fresh bouquet to take back to the city when the day was over. With that sort of family background it is not surprising that the Browns' daughter Mary (called May) studied nursing and became one of Lillian Wald's chief aides at the famous Henry Street Settlement.

Nor is it surprising that, when the Browns celebrated their fifteenth wedding anniversary at Brighthurst, on November 14, 1879, none of the guests to whom these round trip tickets on the Hoboken Ferry and the D. L. & W. Railroad were given bore a name which can be found on the sycophantic Ward McAllister's list of "The 400" who composed Society in 1892. Nor can any of the names be found in the index of that entertaining saga of the self-indulgent rich, Lucius Beebe's *The Big Spenders* (Garden City, 1966).

PASS Del., Lack. & Western R. R.
PASSENGER over
Hoboken Ferry from Hoboken.

DEL., LACK. & WESTERN R. R.
MORRIS & ESSEX DIV.
This TICKET entitles the holder thereof to a First Class Passage
ORANGE TO HOBOKEN
On NOV. 14th 1879.
Train leaves Orange at 5.34 P. M.

102

DEL., LACK. & WESTERN R. R.
MORRIS & ESSEX DIV.
This TICKET entitles the holder thereof to a First Class Passage
HOBOKEN TO ORANGE
On NOV. 14th, 1879.
Train leaves New York at 1.10 P. M.

102

PASS Del., Lack. & Western R. R.
PASSENGER over
Hoboken Ferry from New York.

Thirteen

TO THE GOLDEN DOOR

In the same year that Mr. and Mrs. John Crosby Brown celebrated their crystal wedding anniversary, a young Wall Street broker went up to Ogdensburg, New York, to marry Miss Mary Williamson Averell, daughter of Ogdensburg's leading banker, William Averell. Since Mr. Averell was also president of a railroad company, he provided a special train for the newly married couple, who found, when they arrived at the station after the ceremony, that the workmen in the railroad's shops had painted a new name on the locomotive's nameplate—the bridegroom's name: E. H. Harriman.

As Harriman's biographer, George Kennan, rather coyly put it, this was the first time Harriman's name "appeared in connection with a railroad." But two years later he and a couple of his Wall Street associates bought a small, run-down upstate line called the Lake Ontario Southern. By October 1883 he was practically sole owner of the

road, and by June 1, 1884, he had put it in such thoroughly good working condition that both the Pennsylvania Railroad and the New York Central wanted it, and Harriman sold (at a handsome profit) to the highest bidder, the Pennsylvania.

Meanwhile, probably at first through his old acquaintance Stuyvesant Fish, Harriman had become interested in the Illinois Central Railroad, of which Fish was vice-president at the time. Harriman had bought a good many of the railroad's bonds, and early in 1883 he "seems to have made up his mind," as Kennan says, to become a director of the road. By May 30, he was on the board, and in the next five years played a large part in acquiring and building profitable feeder lines (in one instance—the Dubuque & Sioux City road—snatching a prize from J. P. Morgan in a way Morgan never forgave him for). On September 28, 1887, after Stuyvesant Fish had moved up to the presidency of the road, Harriman became vice-president.

(Courtesy of the Harriman Estate Office)

The undated photograph at left, showing Harriman with a group of Illinois Central officers at Rockford, Illinois, was probably taken about the time he became vice-president. The man in the center of the front row, with a cigar in his left hand, is E. T. Jeffrey, general manager of the railroad (later president of the Denver & Rio Grande). The tall man with the derby, left of Jeffrey, is president Stuyvesant Fish. Between and behind them, standing on the steps, is Harriman.

In 1899, when he was in the midst of converting the Union Pacific railroad from "two streaks of rust" across the plains into what even his enemies conceded was the finest railroad property in the world, Harriman decided to get a little rest by hunting Kodiak bear in Alaska. But what started out to be a mere vacation characteristically turned into an expedition—the famous Harriman Alaska Expedition. As his guests on the chartered steamship *George W. Elder,* in addition to his family and a few friends, he took along twenty-five distinguished scientists, selected in consultation with Dr. C. Hart Merriam, Chief of the U. S. Biological Survey, plus two photographers and three artists. The pictures on this page are all reproduced from a two-volume photograph album, "A Souvenir of the Harriman Alaska Expedition May–August 1899," in the library at Arden Homestead. The one at right was taken during a fire drill on the *Elder,* and includes John Burroughs, the naturalist (at far left); Mr. Harriman at center; the Harriman boys, Averell and Roland; and (at far right) Harriman's daughter Cornelia.

(All pictures on this page courtesy of E. Roland Harriman)

This photograph by E. S. Curtis, one of the expedition's photographers, is captioned "The Admiral" in the souvenir album. It shows young Roland Harriman on the roof of the *George W. Elder*'s deck house. John Muir, one of the most distinguished scientists and writers in the party, says, in his account of the expedition: "One of the telling sights that comes to mind as I write is Mr. Harriman keeping trot-step with little Roland while helping him to drag a toy canoe along the deck with a cotton string."

Another of photographer Curtis's pictures shows Mr. Harriman (at right), John Burroughs (with the flowing white beard), and Captain Doran of the *George W. Elder* (left of Burroughs in the vizored cap), at Dutch Harbor on the return voyage. The others in the party are not identified in the album, but among the scientists on the expedition were Dr. G. K. Gilbert of the U. S. Geological Survey; Daniel G. Elliot, zoologist of the Field Museum in Chicago; Robert Ridgeway, ornithologist of the National Museum in Washington; and Dean Fernow of the Cornell University School of Forestry. Twenty-two scientific papers published in the *Proceedings* of the Washington Academy of Sciences were devoted to the expedition's findings, and the Academy also published thirteen large illustrated volumes of Burrough's narrative and eleven special monographs.

156

A CONFERENCE OF AMERICA'S GREATEST RAILROAD MAGNATES

E. H. HARRIMAN   GEORGE J. GOULD   J. PIERPONT MORGAN   J. J. HILL

THIS DRAWING WAS MADE FROM PHOTOGRAPHS AND SKETCHES FROM LIFE, AND REPRESENTS A SPECIAL BUSINESS SESSION HELD IN THE OFFICE OF J. PIERPONT MORGAN, WHERE THE GREAT RAILROAD DEALS WERE CONSUMMATED

(Courtesy of the Harriman Estate Office)

In 1901 Harriman was engaged in a fight with J. P. Morgan and James J. Hill for control of the Northern Pacific also. (John Crosby Brown, writing to Collet about the struggle on May 21, 1901, thought "neither party . . . has gained in reputation" and that "much bitterness would result.") The picture above, "imagined" by W. R. Leigh for *Collier's Weekly,* November 30, 1901, purports to show Harriman (at left) in Morgan's office with Hill (at right) and George J. Gould. The picture accompanied an article by Ray Stannard Baker on "The Great 'Northern Pacific Deal.'"

Though Harriman seems to lurk offstage in Leigh's *Collier's Weekly* picture, and J. P. Morgan dominates the imagined scene at the conference, J. T. McCutcheon's cartoon for the front page of the Chicago *Tribune,* August 1, 1908, reflects a big change in the public's view of Harriman's position. The copy of the cartoon reproduced here was given to Harriman by McCutcheon.

(Courtesy of E. Roland Harriman)

MR. HARRIMAN'S PLANS FOR REORGANIZING THE RAILWAYS OF THE COUNTRY

157

In 1902 Harriman's Union Pacific had acquired 45.49% of the stock of the Southern Pacific Railroad, giving him control of its 9000 miles of track as well as its subsidiary, the Pacific Mail Steamship Company which James Brown had once controlled (see p. 137). This photograph was first published in *The Southern Pacific Bulletin*, August 1928, with an article saying that it was taken in 1906, when Harriman was living "in a tent camp in the environs of San Antonio," directing the operations of the railroad while trying to recuperate from an illness by outdoor living. Those seated with Harriman in the front row are Julius Kruttschnitt, his chief operating aide (at left) and H. F. Anderson, superintendent of the Southern Pacific.

ROBERT SCOTT LOVETT, the Texas attorney who became E. H. Harriman's legal counsel in 1904 (see p. 17), probably knew Harriman as well or better than any of his associates in the last years of his life. A wise and shrewd observer of men, he was by no means blind to Harriman's faults. ("He would not understand public resentment or why he had public opposition in many cases," Judge Lovett is quoted as saying.) Yet, as he said in a letter to Harriman's biographer, George Kennan, he was convinced that Harriman was "a genius, as pronounced and unique as Napoleon," who possessed "insight, resourcefulness, boundless courage, command of the confidence of others, persistency and yet endless patience when necessary, and above all, push, drive, and determination. . . . He never arrived at his conclusions by reason or argument, or any deliberative process that I could observe. His judgments seemed to be formed intuitively. The proposition was presented and he saw it. It was much like turning a flashlight on an object. If interested, he *saw* it; and did not care and probably did not know how it was revealed."

But Lovett felt that any biography which omitted Harriman's family life would miss the point and lose "the light of the whole story." Those associated with him in business soon learned "that no business, however great its magnitude nor how urgent its importance, caused him to neglect his home or his household, or to forget the most unimportant engagement with his wife, or the smallest plans for his children." His attitude toward Mrs. Harriman, Judge Lovett wrote, "was more than devotion. It was profound admiration, respect, and unfailing attention and courtesy. . . . And as for the children, their welfare and education came before everything."

All of which tells us something of Judge Lovett, as well as of Harriman.

This delightful picture of the interior of a Pullman car is one of the illustrations in the *Railroad Picture Book,* one of those books for young children, printed on thick, almost indestructible linen pages, that were published by McLoughlin Bros., of New York. This one, telling of the adventures of Jessie and Frank on their first train ride (from Chicago to New York) was originally published in 1898, just about the time E. H. Harriman decided to take over and reorganize the Chicago & Alton Railroad—a controversial but profitable episode he might never have become involved in had Judge Lovett been his partner at the time. (Clarence W. Barron quoted Judge Lovett as having said later that there was "never any explanation made" of Harriman's actions in reorganizing the Alton, "and I do not think that there could be any made. He [Harriman] declared it was the blot on his record.")

It was on the Chicago & Alton that George Pullman's first experimental sleeping car had been put into service in 1858, back in the days when Brown Brothers & Co. were involved in an earlier reorganization of the railroad (see p. 118). The chances are that the train on which that first Pullman saw service was pulled by one of the six Chicago & Alton locomotives then owned by Brown Brothers.

As noted earlier (p. 18) Judge Lovett's son, Robert A. Lovett, has carried on his father's association with the Harriman family in the railroad business, having been a director and member of the executive committee of the Union Pacific Railroad since 1926 (with time out on several occasions for government service). As chairman of the executive committee he was the chief administrative officer of the road from 1953 to 1966. Even in his role as an amateur painter (a hobby he took up for relaxation some years ago), he has the eye of an observant railroad man. His oil painting of "Track Worker's Cottage, Florida East Coast Railroad, Hobe Sound, Florida" was done in 1957.

There were impressive displays of Pullman cars, loco-motives, and other railroad equipment at the Chicago World's Fair (properly the World's Columbian Exposition) in 1893. And there was a sort of accidental appropriateness in the fact that, at a moment when transportation was revolutionizing America's social and industrial development, the only building at the "White City" which was not designed in the tradition of academic classicism was Louis Sullivan's Transportation Building. Its colorful entrance, the famous "Golden Door," is known today chiefly through black and white photographs that give no clue to its name. The plate reproduced here is in *Picturesque World's Fair,* Boston, 1894.

Only one automobile—a foreign one—was exhibited at the Chicago fair in 1893, but on September 20th in that year Frank Duryea made what was probably the first trip ever made in an American-built automobile, driving the machine he and his brother had developed a total of 225 feet. By 1900, when the first National Automobile Show was held in Madison Square Garden, the nation was on the verge of another revolution in transportation.

In the December 1905 issue of *Harper's Magazine* there were advertisements of thirteen different makes of cars. The only one in color announced the 1906 models available at the Olds Motor Works in Lansing, Michigan—the first automobile plant to achieve quantity production. Edward Penfield's two-color plate entitled "Giving St. Nicholas a lift with an Oldsmobile" showed a Model S, described as "a rangy four-cylinder Touring Car at $2,250."

(*Author's Collection*)

(*Author's Collection*)

The series of pictures on the facing page, "A practical illustration of what can be done with a horse scared by an automobile," appeared as a two-page feature in *Harper's Weekly,* July 1902. If the narrative captions are illegible in this much reduced reproduction it would be worth trying a magnifying glass.

1.—The first sight the horse had of the motor. The motor was moving at 12 miles an hour, and was more than 300 feet away. The coachman raised his hand and signalled distress

2.—Motor 50 feet away, with the horse backing fast, and almost beyond the driver's control. The motor was kept at 12 miles an hour on the far side of the road

3.—Motor just abreast of the horse, with the animal thoroughly frightened and backed well off the road. This was the fourth time the motor passed him, and the case appeared hopeless; but from that time an improvement began

4.—After several trials the horse was set on the macadam on one side, and another pony, saddled, on the other side. The motor was then run between them at 30 miles an hour. Both horses jumped off the road, but the result was a distinct improvement on No. 1

5.—The chauffeur was then sent out ahead to hold the animal, and he stood reasonably still with the motor going at 25 miles an hour. In ordinary courtesy an automobilist should use his chauffeur thus on such occasions

6.—Again holding the horse, the Panhard was run close in to him, moving very slowly, and making much more noise than when moving swiftly. The horse stood absolutely still, and watched the motor with increasing interest

7.—After fifteen minutes of experimenting as above, the chauffeur led the horse up to the motor as it stood still and perfectly silent. The animal hesitated for a few moments, and finally began to sniff at the car

8.—Finally, absolutely cured of his fright, the horse was driven quietly up to the car, which, though standing still, was vibrating, and making all the noise that could be produced by the engine. At the same time the horn was tooting constantly

THE AUTOMOBILE AND THE HORSE

These photographs were taken of a horse which had run away and broken a cart on meeting an automobile, and in less than half an hour he was cured

Photographs by Peter A. Juley

The picture reproduced here is a detail from an anonymous photograph taken in 1889, soon after the statue of Washington was erected on the steps of the Sub-Treasury (formerly the Custom House) at the head of Broad Street. It shows the three-story Mansard addition to Brown Brothers' building at 59 Wall Street, just beyond the former Merchants Exchange (which served as the U. S. Custom House from 1863 to 1907).

Fourteen

END OF A CENTURY

During the final decades of the nineteenth century, while E. H. Harriman was building his railroad empire, John Crosby Brown and his partners were presiding over the modernization of the old banking firm. Hitherto Brown Brothers' business had been largely confined to "foreign banking"—the purchase and sale of sterling exchange, making advances against shipments of cotton and other produce consigned to Brown Shipley & Co. for sale, granting credits to merchants for the importation of goods, and issuing circular letters of credit to travelers. The partners of James Brown's generation had had little interest in domestic banking, and deposit accounts from domestic concerns were discouraged. "The only deposit accounts of any moment on the books of the firm at the time I became a partner," John Crosby Brown wrote in *A Hundred Years of Merchant Banking*, "were from concerns engaged in foreign business."

But in the years after the Atlantic cable provided rapid communication with Europe, the firm faced increasing competition for foreign business from domestic banks and bankers, and—as Mr. Brown wrote—"it became evident that, if the firm was to hold its own, new lines of business must be sought and cultivated. It was, therefore, at the earnest solicitation of Howard Potter and the writer that the firm began to equip itself for more varied operations, and to build up a conservative investment business."

The resulting increase in business required more office space, not only in New York but also in Philadelphia. Three additional stories were added as a Mansard-roofed superstructure on the 59 Wall Street building in 1886, and in Philadelphia the site of Matthew Carey's bookstore and publishing house at the corner of Fourth and Chestnut Streets was purchased (see p. 22) and a fine new banking house was erected in 1887.

During the 'eighties office procedures were modernized and up-to-date equipment was introduced. In 1885 the old methods of longhand bookkeeping and accounting were abandoned and "printed forms with blanks to be filled" were substituted. "The departments in the office were divided and subdivided, each with its respective head, and the records of original entries were kept by these departments, totals only being entered in the cash books of the day," thus eliminating much copying and reducing the chances of error. In that same year stenographers (male) were hired and the first typewriter was introduced in the New York office (though it "met with little favor from the older partners" and Thatcher Brown later recorded that in 1897, when he went to work in the bank, most letters were still handwritten). It was in 1885 also that the New York house was for the first time connected by private telegraph wire to the offices in Boston, Philadelphia, and Baltimore. By 1891 a private long-distance telephone line was introduced (one wall telephone in each establishment), and in 1899 the desks in all the firm's offices were connected by a private telephone exchange. By 1909 the New York office had four male stenographers and twelve women, and from then on—as John Crosby Brown put it—"no head of a department [was] allowed to waste his time in writing letters with his own hand."

The first stenographer ever employed by Brown Brothers & Co. was hired in 1879, when a complaint from Brown Shipley about the illegibility of John Crosby Brown's handwriting led, as he said, to this "concession to his infirmity." But the first female stenographer was not hired until 1897. Thatcher Brown, in his informal historical sketches of the firm, records that—unlike the young lady in this very un-Brown Brothers series of postcards—"she was put in a frosted glass cage, right opposite the Manager's desk in the left-center of the office, and the male members of the staff were entirely barred from going into that enclosure."

Judging from the clothes and the typewriter, the postcards in the narrative series must have been made about 1907—and certainly not in a respectable banking house.

(Courtesy of the Reverend C. Frederick Buechner)

164

One of the first women employed by Brown Brothers & Co. was Miss MAY E. GOSMAN, who got a job as a stenographer at 59 Wall Street sometime in 1898 or early 1899, and who appears in this photograph dressed in what she referred to sixty-eight years later as her "Brown Brothers un-form." The proper attire for young ladies in Wall Street in those days was "a long black skirt with a dust ruffle" and a plain white shirtwaist with long sleeves whose cuffs were protected by paper shields to keep them from getting soiled. It was only after she had been at the bank for several months that Miss Gosman (like the young lady in the postcards opposite) "spiced up" her uniform with a ribbon bow at the neck—a touch that was considered "very new and daring."

Not even the names of the other young ladies who worked at Brown Brothers before 1900 are known, and it was only a series of fortunate chances that led in 1966 to the discovery of this charming picture of Miss Gosman. In the summer of 1952, Lawrence W. Simonds of Brown Brothers Harriman & Co.'s Boston office wrote a memorandum to Thatcher M. Brown, head of the firm, in which he told of meeting at a New Hampshire inn, a Mrs. F. Luis Mora, widow of a distinguished painter whose work is in the Metropolitan and other museums. Mrs. Mora, when she was still May Gosman, had gotten her $10-a-week job at Brown Brothers through the recommendation of a friend who was in charge of the Crosby Brown collection of musical instruments at the Metropolitan Museum. After only a few months in the office she had been asked to go to Brighthurst to help Mrs. John Crosby Brown with a book she was working on. It was her recollections of life at Brighthurst that prompted Simonds to send his memorandum to Thatcher Brown.

By chance that memorandum was preserved and turned up in 1966. By chance it occurred to us to see if Mrs. Mora was in the New York telephone book, and by chance she was. By chance, also, she had preserved the somewhat battered print of this photograph, taken in the garden at Brighthurst in the summer of 1899.

Mrs. Mora enjoyed reminiscing about her experiences at 59 Wall Street and Brighthurst. At the bank she remembered being hidden away with the other stenographers on the mezzanine. It was reached by a circular iron stair with an open railing which had been closed in when the young ladies were hired, lest the young men in the bank should get a glimpse of female ankles as the stenographers climbed the stairs. She remembered how, on her first day at the bank when she was called to the partners' room to take dictation from Mr. Eugene Delano, she froze with fright after getting as far as "Dear Sir," so that when he asked her to read back what he had said, she had nothing to read. And she remembered how kindly he said "You are new here, aren't you? . . . Well, let's begin again, more slowly." She remembered John Crosby Brown as "a dear little old man" with very white hair and a white beard, "the human incarnation of Santa Claus."

In April 1966, Mrs. Mora came to the bank for lunch and won the hearts of all who met her. At eighty-six she was a beautiful woman, full of apparently unquenchable vitality. But in the autumn, after a brief illness, she was unbelievably dead.

(*Photograph courtesy of the late Mrs. F. Luis Mora*)

At the time May Gosman and other young lady stenographers were starting out at $10 a week, young men who entered the Brown Brothers office as clerks got a starting salary of $250 per year. Even the boss's son, Thatcher M. Brown, got no more than that when he started out in 1897, the year before Miss Gosman came to the office. But an exception was made for one clerk who came to work at 59 Wall Street in 1895. This was Montagu Collet Norman, a grandson of Sir Mark Collet of Brown Shipley & Co.; as a foreigner he was paid $500 a year.

Norman, who was to be one of the firm's London partners from 1900 to 1915, had worked briefly in London at Martins Bank (where his father was a partner) and at Brown Shipley before coming to New York in September 1895. His first visit to the Browns' home, judging from the sketch he drew in the "Brighthurst Visitors Book" was on a weekend as inclement as the one Frank R. Stockton had encountered (see p. 154). The other visitors on the "watery Sabbath" were cousins of Mrs. Brown, and the next visitor, John Henry Hammond, was a young lawyer, just out of Yale, who would become a partner in Brown Brothers twenty-one years later (see p. 206).

Norman's was a complex, subtle, insular personality, and his twenty years in Brown Brothers and Brown Shipley (fifteen as a partner in London after 1900) were not easy for him or for his partners. Things were especially difficult for him in the early years at Founders Court, where Francis Hamilton and Mark Collet, now in their eighties, naturally showed little inclination to accept new ideas or embark on new enterprises. Charles D. Dickey, Jr., who was in London in 1898, after Norman's return from New York, reported in a letter to John Crosby Brown on July 29th that "There is no concealing the fact that Norman is not liked personally either in the inside or outside office at Founders Court, & much as I regret it, I believe it will be a long time before he is given the opportunity to Show the ability which we all know he has, not only for doing business but for creating it. So far as I properly can, I shall do my best to urge Norman's return to America until such times as changes *must* be made in the inside office here."

Everyone at Brown Brothers wanted Norman to return, and John Crosby Brown felt (as he told Sir Mark Collet in a January 20, 1899, letter) that Norman would be much happier at 59 Wall Street where "he would be associated with us in the inside office & have a part in the management & inauguration of the business." But that did not work out. Changes were made in the "inner office" at Founders Court and Norman stayed. By 1907 (about the time the photograph at right was taken) he had built such a fine reputation as a banker that he was elected a director of the Bank of England. Like his grandfather, Sir Mark, he went on to be Deputy Governor and then Governor of the Bank, serving in the latter capacity for an unprecedented twenty-four years, from 1920 to 1944.

(*Brown Brothers Harriman & Co. Historical File*)

166

Early in 1904 Norman acquired an old house named Thorpe Lodge, at Campden Hill, then in London's outskirts, and completely rebuilt and redecorated it, designing some of the furnishings himself. In the spring of 1908 Thatcher Brown stayed for two months with Norman in his new house while working at Founders Court and learning at firsthand, how the business was run in England. This photograph of the house, with several others, is mounted in Thatcher Brown's scrapbook and may have been taken by him. In a letter to his wife, written at Thorpe Lodge on March 26, 1908, he enclosed the "Kodaks" he had taken to date, noting that "The ones of Mont's house (except perhaps 2) are not really good."

The friendship between Norman and Thatcher Brown had begun, of course, in 1895 at Brighthurst, and there was a close bond between the two men. "However I may get along with the others here, I know I have come closer to Mont than ever before," Thatcher wrote his wife. "What a wonderful man he is—I know no one like him." And the next day: "I feel it is really

(Courtesy of Thatcher M. Brown, Jr.)

a great privilege to get to know Mont as I am having a chance to do—not only on a/c of business but because personally it is such a pleasure & inspiration."

As to the house itself, Thatcher wrote enthusiastically in a letter of March 14th: "In the first place one wouldn't know you were in London at all. The place is about 2 acres in size with the most enchanting garden. . . . The house is a long low 2 story brick building—the bricks being covered with rough cement—most attractive in effect. The living room is very large & has 2 grand pianos on a platform at one end where he has his musical entertainments. . . . The feature is the fireplace—an enormous stone one which he bought in Italy many years ago. The diningroom & parlor are most attractive too—each room is in different wood & all are panelled almost to the ceiling. . . . The bedrooms are also different kinds of woods, all finished beautifully & with old fashioned furniture. There are 2 large bathrooms—exceptional for England!"

(Courtesy of Walker Evans)

BANK OF ENGLAND AND ROYAL EXCHANGE   A344/1073

The postcard reproduced here was published about 1908 by W. & C. Lane, and shows the financial heart of London as it was when Thatcher Brown was staying with Montagu Norman at Thorpe Lodge and working at Brown Shipley & Co.'s Founders Court offices (behind the Bank of England at left). "Do you remember the joys of the London bus?" Thatcher wrote to his wife on March 18, 1908. "I enjoy getting about that way more than any other & never get sick of it. The new motor busses [sic] are not nearly so nice, tho faster, because they bounce you about so, & I almost always try to get one of the old horse busses which are really so much nicer."

167

No.L 945
Philadelphia 26 May 1892

Mess Carlowitz & Co. at Shanghai, China are hereby authorized to value on Brown, Shipley & Co London. at four months sight.

for account of Miller & Tattersfield of this city for any sum or sums not exceeding in all Twenty five hundred pounds Stg. for merchandise to be shipped to Philadelphia or new York by vessel or vessels.

The Bills of Lading to be filled up to Brown Brothers & Co

The shipment must be completed and the Bills drawn within Six months from this date, and the advice of them to Brown, Shipley & Co London (in duplicate) must be accompanied by Bill of Lading, with an abstract of Invoice endorsed thereon, on receipt of which documents the Bills will be duly honored.

And Brown, Shipley & Co London hereby agree with the drawers, endorsers and bona fide holders of Bills drawn in compliance with the terms of this Credit that the same shall be duly honored on presentation at their counting house.

Drafts under this Credit to contain the clause drawn under Credit No. 1.945 dated Phila 26 May 1892 for £ 2500 Stg.

The user of this credit will please send Invoice properly certified & B/Lading by the vessel under cover to Mess. Brown Brothers & Co Philadelphia and advice of draft when drawn

The Insurance will be effected here. pp BB & Co.

This credit issued in duplicate

Brown, Shipley & Co
by their partners in Philadelphia
pp Brown Brothers & Co J M Duane

(Brown Brothers Harriman & Co. Historical File)

In his history of Brown Shipley & Co. (*Heir of Adventure*), Aytoun Ellis notes that one reason Montagu Norman found little to interest him at Founders Court in the 1890s was that the work "was largely confined to giving acceptance credits to American customers of Brown Brothers; thus the really interesting part of the job—the examination of applications for credits and the gauging of credit worthiness—was undertaken in New York"—or, he might have added, in Philadelphia or Boston, where a great deal of the firm's commercial credit business was done, then as now.

The document reproduced here is a commercial credit issued by the Philadelphia house on May 26, 1892, to finance the importation of merchandise from Shanghai, China, by the old Philadelphia firm of Miller & Tattersfield. (It would be a document similar to this against which the "bankers acceptance" on pp. 14 and 15 was to be drawn.) It authorized Carlowitz & Co., the Shanghai merchants, to draw on Brown Shipley & Co. "at four months sight" for sums "not exceeding in all" £2500 sterling, and specified that bills of lading consigning the goods to Brown Brothers & Co. (with an abstract of the invoice indicating the contents of the shipment) must accompany any bills of exchange sent to Brown Shipley & Co. for acceptance. The document was signed, *per procuration,* for Brown Brothers by James May Duane, who became a partner in Philadelphia four years later (see p. 180).

(Courtesy of Edward A. Doelp)

Many of the bank's commercial credit customers in those days are still among its valued clients, including the tea importing firm whose establishment at 50 South Street, Philadelphia, is shown in this photograph, taken about 1895. Andrew Pollock Irwin, founder of the firm, is at his desk (second from right). Mr. Albert G. Richardson, who retired several years ago as treasurer of Irwin-Harrisons-Whitney, Inc. (the present company), remembers that back in 1916, when he first went to work at 50 South Street, "We were always happy in our office, to have Mr. Davis Lewis [a manager in Brown Brothers' Philadelphia house] drop in on us as he went about calling on customers, and he always enjoyed having a cup of tea with us. Some time before his retirement he used to be accompanied by his young assistant, Mr. Wm. Hess. Then, in later years, Mr. Moreau Brown and Mr. Hess would visit us. . . . My personal contacts became closer with Mr. Hess and Mr. Llewellyn, and during the hectic period of the [Second World] war, and also when the devaluations of the pound Sterling were under way, Brown Bros. Harriman was a great help to us in many ways. . . . I shall always remember that they were able to save us a substantial sum by their prompt action in connection with some Japanese tea drafts at the outbreak of hostilities." (See p. 222.)

Faced with increasing competition and major changes in the industrial and commercial community, Brown Brothers again adapted its business to the new conditions. Competition was becoming more challenging every year and was coming from quite different directions. Baring Brothers, the firm's greatest rival in the old days, had gone down in the financial panic of 1891, but new rivals had appeared. As John Crosby Brown wrote on March 21, 1895, to Howard Potter: "the competition which is growing & which is cutting into our regular business comes from the great Life Insurance Companies with their affiliated concerns, the Trust Companies with their enormous capital & cheap money, concerns manned by active & competent men always on the lookout for business." What Brown was acutely aware of here was a financial development which was to be a major factor in business a few years later. The assets of insurance companies had not generally been regarded by Wall Street as available for industrial financing, or speculation until in the middle 'nineties a method to tap their rich treasuries was found. Insurance companies were allowed, by law, to invest in trust companies, and trust companies in turn were legally permitted to invest the proceeds of their banking business in the underwriting of new financial schemes. So each of the major insurance companies acquired control of trust companies, and the millions of dollars in the treasuries of the insurance companies began to flow into highly speculative enterprises forbidden to the insurance companies themselves. By 1905, when the New York legislature investigated the situation, it had led to serious abuses, and remedial laws were soon passed. But in the meantime merchant banking firms like Brown Brothers & Co., which were extending their securities underwriting business, had to cope with the powerful competition from this new quarter.

The Brown firms had, of course, had considerable experience in the securities business even before it became an important part of their activities. As early as 1857 Brown Brothers had had what would now be called "investment advisory clients." Correspondence of that period shows, for instance, that a Mr. Thomasson, "a rich spinner" of Bolton, England, "sold out part of his English Stock investments" and asked Brown Brothers to invest for him £32,000 (something over $153,000) of the

(Author's Collection)

This advertisement, which was published in a special "New York Number" of *Harper's Weekly*, November 15, 1902, seems to be the earliest to feature Brown Brothers' "Investment Securities" business and its functions as a bank of deposit. The travelers credits and commercial credits which dominated the earlier advertisement reproduced on p. 136 are here relegated to a secondary position. The emphasis now is on the firm's brokerage business and upon its readiness to receive the accounts of "Banks, Bankers, Corporations, Firms, and individuals." (Notice, by the way, the use of initial capital letters in that series.)

proceeds in American securities "with a view of their *resale* when they shall recover their fair value." But this sort of thing was done in those days only as a sideline, to accommodate good customers. As Brown Shipley said, in a letter to Brown Brothers, May 11, 1858: "We have always been particular to impress on parties wishing to purchase securities through you, that you could not take the least responsibility. Still with all our care responsibility will attach to us, & for the trumpery commission we get the business of itself is scarcely worth attention, but it is an awkward thing in the position we hold, to refuse to purchase stocks for our Friends or Correspondents." By the end of the century, however, the buying and selling of "first class Investment Securities on commission" had become a major part of Brown Brothers' business, as the advertisement reproduced on this page shows.

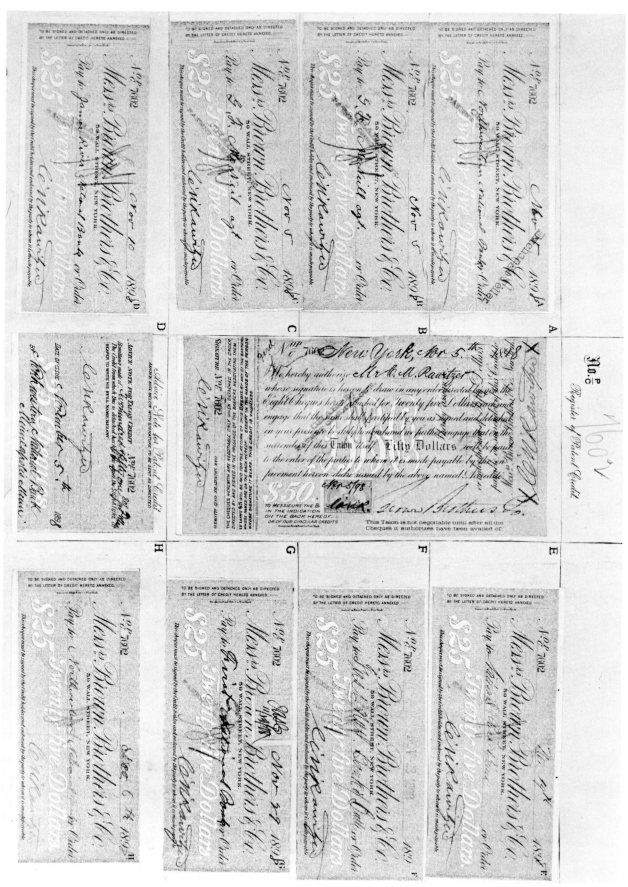

Even in the field of travelers credits there was strong competition, and in 1891 Brown Brothers developed a form of travelers checks especially for use in the United States, Canada, and Latin America. A set of these checks is shown in the illustration opposite, about half their original size. (The patent, applied for in 1891, was registered December 22, 1892.)

As originally issued the eight checks, numbered A to H in the upper right corner, were printed along with the "talon" (at center right) and the "advice note" (at center left) on a single sheet of paper. Sheets like that were sent to Brown Brothers' correspondent banks in North and South America, which sold them to their customers. This particular sheet was sold by the Northwestern National Bank of Minneapolis to a Mr. C. N. Rawitzer. After the purchaser had signed the "talon" and the "advice note" (providing specimens of his signature), the advice note was sent back to Brown Brothers' Patent Credit Department where it was pasted on a "Register" sheet like the one illustrated here.

Meanwhile the purchaser, Mr. Rawitzer, had the eight checks, worth $25 each, and the "talon," worth $50, which he could cash after all the checks had been cut off and cashed. As the checks were cleared at Brown Brothers they were pasted on the register sheet, and finally the talon itself was pasted in, closing the credit transaction. (Mr. Rawitzer paid $251.80 for his $250.00 worth of checks—a commission of $1.80 for the convenience of being able to carry around $250 in the form of checks that were valueless until he endorsed them in the presence of the bankers who detached them from the talon.)

A simpler form of travelers checks, like those we are familiar with today, was introduced by the American Express Company in 1896, four years after Brown Brothers' talon credit checks were patented, and that fact no doubt influenced the foreign travelers checks which Brown Brothers introduced in 1900. (The patent on these checks was applied for June 2, 1900, and registered on May 6, 1902.)

Notice that these travelers checks for use primarily in Europe were issued at a time when it was taken for granted that the rate of exchange between the principal currencies of the world would remain constant. The "wheel" at lower left indicates the precise sum—in pounds sterling, francs, lire, roubles, kroner, marks, or dollars—that Brown Brothers guaranteed the traveler he would receive from Brown Shipley & Co. in London, "or any banker" anywhere in Europe.

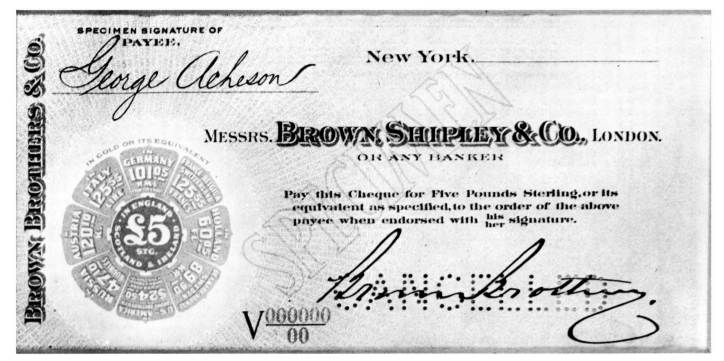

(*Brown Brothers Harriman & Co. Historical File*)

The banks listed in this "Letter of Indication" were Brown Brothers & Co.'s correspondent banks in the Americas in the late 1890s. The "Letter" is reproduced, slightly larger than the original, from the back of the "talon" on the sheet of travelers checks shown on p. 170. Why Honolulu in the Sandwich Islands was put under "South America" is hard to explain, but where else, after all, should it have gone?

It is interesting to note that the Minneapolis bank which issued the sheet of checks to Mr. Rawitzer in 1898 is not on this list, and that a number of the banks where he cashed the checks are also not on the list. Probably the list is incomplete, though the checks could no doubt be cashed at any bank which had an account with one of those on the list.

LETTER OF INDICATION.

UNITED STATES.

ALABAMA.
Birmingham....Alabama National Bank.
Mobile..........First National Bank.

ARKANSAS.
Little Rock.....German National Bank.

CALIFORNIA.
Los Angeles.....Farmers' and Merchants' Bank
Pasadena........First National Bank.
Sacramento..National Bank of D. O. Mills & Co.
San Diego.....First National Bank.
San Francisco..Bank of California.
San Jose.........Bank of San Jose.
Santa Barbara.First National Bank.

COLORADO.
Colorado Spr'gs.First National Bank.
Del Norte.....Bank of Del Norte.
Denver........First National Bank.
Greeley.......First National Bank.
Leadville........American National Bank.

CONNECTICUT.
Hartford.......Hartford National Bank.
New Haven....First National Bank.
New London...Union Bank.

DAKOTA.
Fargo.....Red River Valley National Bk.

DIST. OF COLUMBIA.
Washington....Lewis Johnson & Co.

FLORIDA.
Jacksonville....National Bank of the State of Fla.
Orlando.........State Bank of Orlando.
Palatka........East Florida Savings & Trust Co.
St. Augustine...First National Bank.
Tampa.........First National Bank.

GEORGIA.
Atlanta.........Atlanta National Bank.
Augusta.......Georgia Railroad Bank.
Brunswick.....National Bank of Brunswick.
Macon.........I. C. Plant & Son.
Savannah......Savannah Bank & Trust Co.
Thomasville...Bank of Thomasville.

ILLINOIS.
Chicago ....First National Bank.

KENTUCKY.
Louisville.......Louisville City National Bank.

LOUISIANA.
New Orleans...Louisiana National Bank.

MAINE.
Bar Harbor,.....Bar Harbor Banking and Trust
Company.

MARYLAND.
Baltimore......Alex. Brown & Sons.

MASSACHUSETTS.
Boston.........Brown Brothers & Co.,
50 State Street.
Lenox...........Lenox National Bank.

MICHIGAN.
Detroit..........Detroit Savings Bank.

MINNESOTA.
Duluth.........American Exchange Bank.
Minneapolis....Security Bank of Minnesota.
St. Paul.........First National Bank.

MISSOURI.
Kansas City.....United States Trust Co.
St. Joseph......First National Bank.
St. Louis.......State Bank of St. Louis.

NEBRASKA.
Lincoln........American Exchange Nat. Bank.
Omaha.........Omaha National Bank.

NEVADA.
Reno..........Washoe County Bank.
Virginia City...Branch Bank of California.

NEW YORK.
Albany.........Mechanics' & Farmers' Bank.
Buffalo.........Bank of Buffalo.
New York......Brown Brothers & Co.,
59 Wall Street.
Niagara Falls..Bank of Niagara.
Saratoga Sp'gs.First National Bank.

NORTH CAROLINA.
Asheville.....First National Bank.

OHIO.
Cincinnati......National La Fayette Bank.
Cleveland.....National Bank of Commerce.
Sandusky......Moss National Bank.
Toledo.........Second National Bank.

OREGON.
Portland........First National Bank.

PENNSYLVANIA.
Philadelphia....Brown Bros. & Co., corner of
4th and Chestnut Streets.
Pittsburg......Bank of Pittsburg.

RHODE ISLAND.
Newport........Union National Bank.

SOUTH CAROLINA.
Charleston ....James Adger & Co.

TENNESSEE.
Chattanooga....First National Bank.
Memphis......Union & Planters' Bank.
Nashville.......American National Bank.

TEXAS.
Dallas.........National Exchange Bank.
El Paso........First National Bank.
Galveston......Ball, Hutchings & Co.
Houston........First National Bank.
Laredo.........Milmo National Bank.
San Antonio....Lockwood National Bank.

UTAH.
Salt Lake City .Walker Brothers.

VIRGINIA.
Norfolk........Norfolk National Bank.
Richmond.....First National Bank.

WASHINGTON.
Seattle.........Puget Sound National Bank.
Spokane.......Exchange National Bank.
Tacoma.......Pacific National Bank.

WISCONSIN.
Milwaukee....Wisconsin Marine & Fire In-
surance Co. Bank.
Second Ward Savings Bank.

WYOMING.
Cheyenne.......Stock Growers National Bank.
Laramie........First National Bank.

CANADA.

BRITISH COLUMBIA.
Vancouver......Bank of Montreal.
Victoria.........Bank of British Columbia.

CANADA EAST.
Montreal.......Bank of Montreal.
Quebec.........Bank of British North America

CANADA WEST.
Brantford.......Bank of British North America
Hamilton.......Bank of British North America
Kingston.......Bank of British North America
London.........Bank of British North America

MANITOBA.
Winnipeg......Bank of Montreal.

NEW BRUNSWICK.
St. John.........Bank of British North America

NEWFOUNDLAND.
St. John's......Bank of Montreal.

NOVA SCOTIA.
Halifax.........Bank of British North America

ONTARIO.
Toronto........Bank of Montreal.

MEXICO, CENTRAL AMERICA, WEST INDIES, &c.

BAHAMAS.—NEW PROVIDENCE.
Nassau.........Bank of Nassau.

BERMUDA.
Hamilton.......Hon. N. T. Butterfield & Son.

CUBA.
Havana.........H. Upmann & Co.
Matanzas......Heidegger & Co.
Santiago de Cuba..Brooks & Co.

MEXICO.
Guadalajara...Bank of London and Mexico.
Guanajuato.....Bank of London and Mexico.

Mazatlan........F. Echeguren Hna. y Sobs.
Merida.........Banco Nacional de Mexico.
Mexico (City)...Bank of London and Mexico.
Monterey.......Patricio Milmo e Hijos.
Morelia.........
Puebla.........Bank of London and Mexico.
Queretaro......Bank of London and Mexico.
San Luis Potosi.Bank of London and Mexico.
Tampico........Federico T. Schutz.
Vera Cruz......Bank of London and Mexico.
Zacatecas......Racom C. Ortiz.

WEST INDIES.
Any of the Agencies of the Colonial Bank.

SOUTH AMERICA.

BRAZIL.
Any Agencies of London and Brazilian Bank.

VENEZUELA.
Caracas........H. L. Boulton & Co.
Maracaibo.....H. L. Boulton, Jr. & Co.

U. S. of COLOMBIA.
Panama.........Henry Ehrman.

ARGENTINE REPUBLIC.
Buenos Ayres ..London & River Plate Bank.
Rosario........London & River Plate Bank.

URUGUAY.
Montevideo....London & River Plate Bank.

SANDWICH ISLANDS.
Honolulu.......Bishop & Co.

(Brown Brothers Harriman & Co. Historical File)

(Brown Brothers Harriman & Co. Historical File)

Fifteen

THE POWER TO MOVE

The financing of railroad construction, and the financial reorganization of railroads, was an important part of the firm's business at the turn of the century. Not that Brown Brothers ranked with E. H. Harriman or J. P. Morgan in the field of railway consolidations. They had their reservations about such big business—as witness John Crosby Brown's comment quoted on p. 157. Many passages in the partners' correspondence of the period reflect a similar uneasiness about the "bigness" of big business. When one of the partners wrote John Crosby Brown that Andrew Carnegie wanted to talk with him, Brown's reply (October 6, 1896) was characteristically lukewarm: "He & the concerns he represents are very rich & his business is very ably managed. At the same time they are large borrowers & somewhat difficult to deal with. When I know what he has in mind, I will see if BB & Co & BS & Co can serve him. We are good friends & I can usually get on well with him." J. P. Morgan had little difficulty dealing with Carnegie four years later, when he bought him out to form the United States Steel Corporation. But then, John Crosby Brown could not be John Pierpont Morgan, and showed no signs of wishing he could. Nor could B.B. & Co. have put its hands on anything like the $447 million Morgan paid Carnegie for his steel company.

Brown Brothers could, however, and sometimes did join with Morgan or other bankers in railroad financing projects. The first of these, apparently, was the reorganization of the Chesapeake & Ohio Railroad in 1887 and 1888 (see clipping at left).

This clipping, from an unidentified Cincinnati newspaper, was pasted into the "Brighthurst Chronicle" for 1888. Note that, as usual, Mrs. Brown accompanied her husband on the inspection trip over the Chesapeake & Ohio. When the party divided at Maysville, however, she went directly on to Cincinnati with Mrs. George Bliss and the others, while Mr. Brown went on to inspect the whole length of the newly constructed section of the road. Brown, George Bliss, and Morgan were the voting trustees of the five-year trust into which more than a majority of the railroad's stock had been put during the reorganization.

(*Brown Brothers Harriman & Co. Historical File*)

It was also in 1888, in May and June, that John Crosby Brown, accompanied this time by his eldest son, William Adams Brown, made a tour of inspection on the Rock Island line. He is shown here (sixth man from the right, with his son bareheaded behind him) with the party that accompanied the railroad's president, R. R. Cable, on his private train. In his autobiography (*A Teacher and His Times,* 1940) William Adams Brown tells of accompanying his father on this trip "into what was then the Great West, Kansas, Nebraska, Oklahoma, the Dakotas and Montana." He remembered especially "the newly opened territory of Oklahoma where the first settlers were already breaking up the spacious areas of the prairie into town lots which were offered us for sale." As for the other men on the trip, they were "typical businessmen of the period with an eye to the main chance."

Brown Brothers again participated with Morgan in 1894, during the reorganization of the Reading Railroad. The correspondence at this time between John Crosby Brown and his partner in Philadelphia, Eugene Delano, makes it quite clear that Brown Brothers' "participation" was by no means mere acquiescence in plans Morgan conceived. "Probably it will not do for us to oppose Mr. Morgan," Delano wrote at one point in the difficult negotiations; "we would scarcely wish to do so unless really necessary, but we can hold different views and if wise express them frankly to him." They did frankly express their different views, and that was how a reorganization that had bogged down twice previously was finally worked out.

Brown Brothers' interest in railroads was not, however, confined to reorganization and consolidation of lines. One of the most interesting railroad enterprises with which the firm became involved in the 'nineties was the building of a new road—the Bangor & Aroostook Railroad, which railroad historian Alvin F. Harlow has called "one of the soundest little rail developments in America." (*Steelways of New England,* New York, [1946].) In 1890 almost all of Aroostook County, in northern Maine, was without rail connection with the outer world except through Canada via the Canadian Pacific. But in that year two Maine men who saw a future in Aroostook's lumber, pulp, and agriculture, combined forces to create a railroad which would make that future possible. One was a well-to-do civil engineer named Albert Burleigh, who had served as County Commissioner; the other was Franklin W. Cram, an experienced railroad manager.

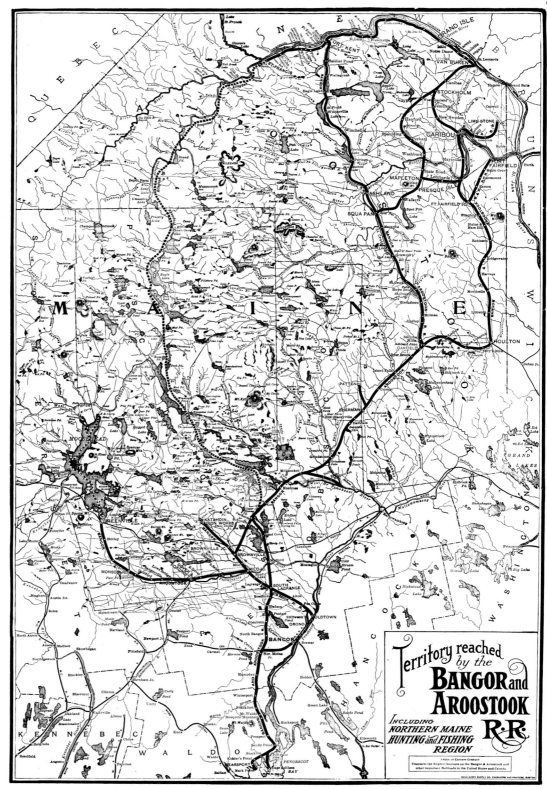

(All pictures courtesy of the Bangor & Aroostook Railroad Co.)

This map of the "Territory reached by the Bangor and Aroostook R. R." was engraved and printed by the Rand Avery Supply Co., Boston, and published in the 1913 edition of the railroad's promotion booklet, *In the Maine Woods*. The first stretch of road, completed by the end of 1893, ran from Brownville (near center of map, about 2¼ inches up from the bottom) to Houlton, near the New Brunswick border (near the right edge of map, about midway between top and bottom). By November 1894 the road was opened as far as Caribou (upper right). From Brownville down to Bangor (about level with the top of the titlebox) the road used the track of the old Bangor & Piscataquis Railroad, which had been acquired before construction of the new road began.

The Bangor & Aroostook Railroad Co., incorporated in Maine in 1891, was financed, according to Harlow, "mostly with money from outside the state." Just how or when Brown Brothers & Co. became involved is not certain. Years later, Thatcher M. Brown told Joseph C. Lucey, a Brown Brothers Harriman manager, that the company "was formed in his father's house." At any rate, John Crosby Brown certainly had some part in the early financing of the road. Franklin W. Cram, in a letter written as president of the company (June 17, 1911), told James Brown (head of the firm since his uncle's death in 1909) that "your uncle stated to some of the Directors, in my presence, (winter 1894–5), in effect: 'We have interested ourselves out of regard for, and confidence in, Mr. Cram, and we propose to stand by him.'" And there is a letter in the Historical File written by John Crosby Brown on November 25, 1894, at the Bangor House, just after his return "from a three days trip to the northern part of Maine" over the newly finished track to Caribou (see p. 175). By 1904 Brown Brothers controlled a majority of the railroad's stock.

Railroad building in northern Maine at the turn of the century was rugged work. Picks, shovels and strong backs, wheelbarrows and horse-drawn carts, did the work that is now done by mechanized earthmoving equipment. The pictures on this and the three following pages were selected from a large collection of photographs documenting the construction work in the early 1900s. The prints, made from some recently discovered glass plate negatives, were presented to the Historical File by Richard W. Sprague of the railroad's Public Relations Department.

(All pictures courtesy of the Bangor & Aroostook Railroad Co.)

The three pictures on the opposite page show grading work on the line from Ashland to Fort Kent (top center of map on p. 175). Those on this page are a record of some of the men involved: an Italian water boy, the driver of a dump cart, senior engineers inspecting a bridge, and a group of younger engineers and surveyors at their tent headquarters. (*All pictures courtesy of the Bangor & Aroostook Railroad Co.*)

The glass plate negative of the photograph above is identified only as "Nixon's camp" at Winchell, October 1903; the one below as the "Dining Tent" at the "first crossing." Note the bouquets of daisies on both tables, and the netting thrown over everything to keep off flies.

The picture at the bottom of the opposite page was taken on October 7, 1906, "opposite Burnt Land," somewhere along the line. The locomotive pulling the "Flanger" work car is the Bangor & Aroostook's No. 5—one of the road's earliest engines, built in the middle 1890s.

The picture above is not one of the photographs made from the recently discovered glass plate negatives. It is reproduced from a halftone illustration in the 1901 edition of the railroad's promotion booklet, *In the Maine Woods. A Guidebook for Sportsmen.* The accompanying text explains that while the company does not want "to overdraw the facts concerning the kind and quality of hunting," it wants to give as "straightforward" an account as possible "without unduly favoring any given locality." Hence this station is not named.

(Both pictures on this page courtesy of the Bangor & Aroostook Railroad Co.)

In 1910 the Bangor & Aroostook's hard-driving president, Franklin Cram, began laying plans to build a branch line up through western Maine, along the Allagash River. (The route is indicated by a dotted line on the left side of the map, p. 175. At Cram's invitation, therefore, three Brown Brothers partners made a canoe trip down the Allagash, June 24–July 2, 1910, to inspect the proposed route and the economic resources of the country through which it ran. The snapshot reproduced here was taken at one of the camps set up on this trip. Eugene Delano stands at the right. Seated in the middle is Delano's son, Moreau Delano, who had become a partner in 1907. At the left is James May Duane, who had been closely associated with Delano in many of the firm's railroad financing operations. The snapshot was preserved by Duane's son, Richard B. Duane, who accompanied his father on the trip.

Pleasant as the trip was, Delano and his partners were not convinced of the wisdom of building the Allagash branch, and Brown Brothers decided not to undertake the financing. The branch was never built.

This photograph of EUGENE DELANO was taken by Pach Brothers about 1905. A brother-in-law of John Crosby Brown (he had married Mrs. Brown's sister), Delano did much to shape and direct the policies of the firm until his death in 1920. There are many letters in the Historical File which demonstrate his sound business judgment and his extraordinary capacity to understand, and appreciate the merits of, conflicting views without compromising the integrity of his own austere allegiance to high principles. Anyone who reads this correspondence will feel the truth of the concluding paragraph of an editorial published in the *Commercial and Financial Chronicle* after his death. "He represented the best of his day. His associations were with men who did fine things for other men and who sought to serve rather than be served. If we analyze the confidence and respect for certain institutions or business houses [held] by the public we generally find that these are due to some strong and upright personality, like Eugene Delano, whose attributes as an individual have been engrained in the policies of the organization to which he is attached and whose success along right lines is his strongest desire."

If the Brown Brothers partners went camping because they wanted to know if a railroad should be built, E. H. Harriman built a railroad because he went camping. That, at least, is the story as told by Samuel M. Evans in *Sunset. The Magazine of the Pacific and of all the Far West*, October 1911. "Harriman, in search of a wilderness resting-place, established his lodge on the shores of Pelican Bay, an arm of Upper Klamath lake. . . . But the restless spirit of the railroad man soon asserted itself and Harriman asked himself the question, 'What would this country be with adequate transportation facilities?' He came away from Pelican Bay, not with a picture of the wilderness he had gone to seek, but with a vision of a new empire equal in extent to four New England states, awaiting the steel rail to awaken it to industrial life. Then followed surveys. . . . Soon the line from Weed to Klamath Falls was put through and a construction gang is now at work pushing the line along the shores of Upper Klamath lake.

. . . When the building of railroads into this country has ceased, Klamath Falls will be connected with San Francisco and Portland on the main line of the Southern Pacific; . . . and with the East direct by a Harriman cut-off through Nevada."

The picture of Harriman's lodge (below) was one of the illustrations of Evans' article. The snapshot above shows Harriman at a picnic in the Klamath country, in the summer of 1907, with his sons Roland (at left) and Averell (at right). The man sitting left of Mr. Harriman was his physician, Dr. William G. Lyle.

Lest any members of the Sierra Society take umbrage at the thought of Harriman's bringing railroads into the wilderness, it is well to point out that their patron, the great naturalist John Muir, profoundly admired and liked Mr. Harriman and was at Klamath Lodge, working on one of his books, when the snapshot above was taken.

BROWN IN TOWN

IS INSPECTING HIS ST. LOUIS STREET RAILWAYS.

Patrick Calhoun, His Representative, With Him.

WENT OVER THE RECENTLY PURCHASED SCULLIN SYSTEM.

The Head of the Syndicate Which Now Controls Most of the St. Louis Street Railway Systems Is on His Way to California—Was Escorted by Mr. Harry Scullin.

John C. Brown, of Brown Brothers, New York, who engineered the sale of the big street railway systems of St. Louis to Eastern capitalists, is in St. Louis.

With him is Mr. Patrick Calhoun, also of New York, who first called the attention of the Knickerbocker millionaires to the fact that St. Louis street railways were good-paying properties.

Mr. Brown, escorted by Mr. Harry Scul-

John Crosby Brown.

lin, went on a tour of inspection over the Union Depot or Scullin system this morning. Brown Bros., representing clients, resently bought the system for about $4,500,000.

The New Yorkers quietly slipped into town last Sunday. Mr. Brown, who was accompanied by his wife, secured a suite of rooms at the Planters.

He was in conference Monday with the street railway men of St. Louis, from whom he recently purchased millions in stocks, and discussed plans for a general consolidation of the various systems.

The trip over the Scullin system to-day was in line with this. The different branches of the road were inspected and the electric power house examined.

The inspection, it is said, will probably result in some changes and improve-

(Brown Brothers Harriman & Co. Historical File)

(Brown Brothers Harriman & Co. Historical File)

This article in the St. Louis *Star,* March 7, 1899, calls attention to another kind of railroad in which Brown Brothers became interested. This transaction, ultimately profitable, at first gave trouble. A letter to John Crosby Brown written by his English partner Lawrence E. Chalmers on January 4, 1901, indicates that "but for the [St.] Louis Street Railways" the firm's "Investment Account" for 1900 would have shown a small profit "in spite of the year being one of the worst for Stock business in London except as an intelligent 'bear.'"

One of the most important developments in transportation and in industry generally at the end of the nineteenth century was the development of electrical technology. The first successful electric trolley car system, developed and put into operation in Richmond, Virginia, in 1887–1888 by Frank J. Sprague, started a revolution in urban transport. By 1895 there were 850 trolley lines operating in cities all over the country, on a total of more than 10,000 miles of track. The effective consolidation of these lines was important to their efficient operation, and Brown Brothers had a part (not always profitable) in several consolidations.

The long-distance transmission of hydroelectric power, upon which the development of modern industry was largely dependent, was inaugurated in 1894–1895 when George Westinghouse installed three of his large alternating current generators at the Niagara Falls power plant. The international advisory committee of experts had favored using the Edison-General Electric direct-current generators, but Westinghouse got the contract because of the spectacular success of his lighting effects at the Chicago World's Fair. Characteristically, John Crosby Brown was one of the first visitors to inspect the new installation.

This photograph, preserved in the "Brighthurst Chronicles" for 1895, shows John Crosby Brown at Niagara Falls with other businessmen inspecting the world's first hydroelectric plant capable of generating power for long-distance transmission. Mr. Brown is at the center of the group, standing somewhat behind the others.

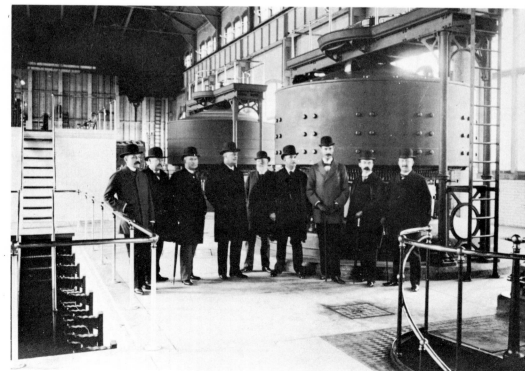

Sixteen

SCRAPBOOK OF A NEW ERA

The period between the financial panic of October 1907 and the stock market crash of October 1929 was a time of vast economic and social change, and the correspondence and other records of the firm during those years tell a story of continuous adaptation to new challenges: the "Dollar Diplomacy" of the 1910s, the establishment of the Federal Reserve System, the First World War, the post-war depression, and the great boom of the late 'twenties.

At the beginning of the period Brown Brothers & Co. was a transatlantic partnership dominated by members of a single family. "The firm has always been substantially a family concern & is so still," John Crosby Brown reminded one of his junior partners in a letter of May 8, 1906. As of January 1, 1907, seven of the fourteen partners were Browns, including the heads of the firm in New York and London. (A complete list of those who have been partners in the firm since 1818, with notations of family relationships, is given in the Appendix, starting on p. 229.) Before the period was half over

the transatlantic partnership had been dissolved and Brown Brothers & Co. was a wholly American concern. By the time, just prior to the 1929 crash, when Ellery James seems to have first discussed with Roland Harriman the possibility of a merger (as recounted in chapter one), only three of the twelve Brown Brothers partners were Browns: the senior partner, James Brown, and his cousins James Crosby Brown (who died before the merger took place) and Thatcher M. Brown.

This photograph is reproduced from one of the halftone illustrations in an article on "Manhattan Lights" by Edward S. Martin, published in *Harper's Magazine,* February 1907, eight months before the panic that closed so many banks and trust companies. It was with unintended irony, therefore, that Martin (himself a banker) wrote: "Usually six o'clock finds Wall Street all but deserted, and the lights that burn so faithfully are like so many candles burning to the better repose of Business, dead and laid out in a great narrow high-walled church."

A series of letters written to John Crosby Brown, ill at his home, by Thatcher Brown during the panic indicate that Brown Brothers weathered the storm without difficulty. "We have $1,500,000 in banks tonight and are keeping very strong," he wrote on October 23rd, and the next day: "Everyone keeps serene here, though you can imagine these days take it out of one. Brown, Shipley & Co. have been kept fully informed and apparently have kept cool."

(Author's Collection)

(*Brown Brothers Harriman & Co. Historical File*)

The year before the panic of 1907 the aging head of the firm's London house, Sir Alexander Hargreaves Brown, came over to America for the first time in many years to visit the John Crosby Browns at Brighthurst and to discuss plans for the renewal of the articles of partnership. This snapshot of him with Lady Hargreaves Brown (at right) and his daughter Gladys, is reproduced from the original in the Brighthurst "Visitors Book." John Crosby Brown had written to Sir Alexander on January 31, 1906, urging him to come to the United States and "see & know something of the country as it is, so as to be able to form a correct judgment of the opportunities & safety of business on this side the Atlantic. It is quite a different country from the America of your boyhood"—or of his own, he might have added.

"The old firm is certainly in many respects in a stronger position than at one time seemed possible," John Crosby continued, "& the fact that as a firm we have not been connected with any of the late deplorable Insurance Scandals has certainly worked to our advantage & to our credit as a conservative Banking House." Indeed he had heard last week in Washington, from his old friend John W. Foster, ex-Secretary of State, that one of the lawyers retained to defend a director of one of the insurance companies said "Brown Brothers & Co. were the only prominent banking house in New York not mixed up in the Insurance Scandals."

The question of renewing the articles of partnership was complicated in 1906 by the fact that both Sir Alexander and John Crosby Brown, the principal "capitalist partners," were getting on in years. This snapshot of JOHN CROSBY BROWN was taken four years before Sir Alexander's visit, and was preserved in one of Thatcher Brown's scrapbooks. Mrs. Brown is seated next to him in the carriage, though only a part of her bonnet shows. Some of the younger and more aggressive members of the firm were openly critical of current policies. George Harrison Frazier, one of the ablest Philadelphia partners, wrote frankly about his dissatisfaction with his current status in the partnership. In a letter dated May 15, 1906, Brown replied with equal frankness. Though he himself had consistently tried "to improve the status of the junior partners," increasing their "share interest" in the firm and "affording them greater liberty of action in the conduct of the business," he was "not prepared to see the control either of the share interest or of the management pass into their hands." It was doubtless true, he added, that "we in New York are not so closely in touch with many great enterprises as such firms as Kuhn Loeb & Co., Speyer & Co., Blair & Co., but we have neither the capital to handle such large [underwriting] ventures as they undertake, nor any great wish to rival them in their special lines of business." He was not "so wedded to old forms of business" that he wished to retain them when they became unprofitable, but he was "not prepared suddenly to abandon lines of business upon which the reputation & business of the firm have been built up.

. . . I do not believe it either wise or prudent suddenly to cut our London acceptances in half." The "old forms of bread & butter business, valuable as an expense payer in dull times" must be sustained. "Most of us," he wrote, "are not in business solely for all we can make out of it. There are other considerations that appeal to us." (See p. 188 for quotations from Frazier's reply.)

(*Courtesy of Thatcher M. Brown, Jr.*)

184

(Courtesy of the Harriman Estate Office)

It is one of the striking coincidences in the historical background of Brown Brothers Harriman & Co. that John Crosby Brown, the second-generation head of the house of Brown Brothers & Co., and E. H. Harriman, creator of the Harriman fortune, died in the same year, 1909.

The photograph above shows Harriman arriving at the Arden station on August 24, 1909, on his return from Bad Gastein, in Austria, where he had spent the summer with his family in a fruitless attempt to regain his health. Now he was returning to live for the first time in the recently completed mansion he had erected on a mountain top in his vast domain at Arden. Mrs. Harriman is at the right, and Harriman, with one of his daughters, is approaching Judge Lovett (back to camera). Two weeks later, on September 9th, he was dead.

A STUDY OF HARRIMAN.
Master of Railroads,
AND HIS METHODS OF WORK

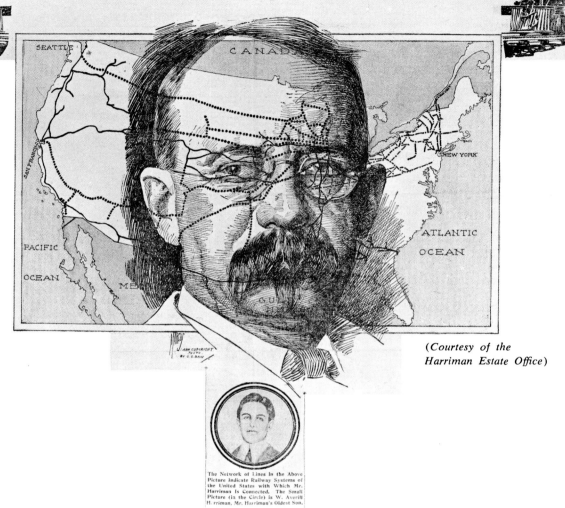

(Courtesy of the Harriman Estate Office)

The Network of Lines In the Above Picture Indicate Railway Systems of the United States with Which Mr. Harriman Is Connected. The Small Picture (in the Circle) is W. Averill Harriman, Mr. Harriman's Oldest Son.

This is the elaborately contrived heading of an article by E. J. Edwards published in the *New York Times* on August 1, 1909—just about a month before Harriman's death. The small circle at the bottom of the design contains a picture of Harriman's eldest son, Averell, then just nineteen years old. The implication of the design, at a time when Harriman was known to be ill, was clearly "Here is the heir to this vast empire." In a sense, perhaps not a very precise one, the implication was just, though Harriman's will—surely the simplest and most direct document that ever disposed of so much wealth—consisted of a single sentence by which he bequeathed all his property "real and personal, of every kind and nature," to his wife, Mary W. Harriman, "to be hers absolutely and forever." Nevertheless, the obligations and responsibilities that descended upon Averell Harriman were grave ones for a young man just about to enter college as a freshman.

Eleven years later (October 30, 1920) B. C. Forbes, editor of *Forbes* magazine, published an interview with Averell Harriman entitled "New Business Star: Harriman the Second." It makes interesting reading, in the light of what has happened since. "The rich man," young Harriman told Forbes, "who uses the dollar as the yardstick to measure the success, or non-success, of his activities, and who doesn't take very much broader—national—considerations into account is not the highest type of citizen, nor does he get the fullest satisfaction out of life. I am striving to do the thing which I believe is the best and most important thing I can do for the interest of America. I love work—I cannot see how anyone could prefer to be idle."

(*Courtesy of the U. S. Lawn Tennis Association*)

"Our veteran leaders have been passing on at an unusual rate," Forbes wrote, in a cover blurb for his 1920 story about Averell Harriman. Who, he asked, are "the coming men."

Anyone in 1920 who wanted to spot those who would be "coming men" at Brown Brothers in the years ahead could have done pretty well, it seems, just by picking the top men in the field of sports. When the firm opened its Chicago office on May 15, 1929, the resident manager was Charles S. Garland, who had been a member of the United States Davis Cup Team in 1920, and with R. Norris Williams won the world's doubles championship that year at Wimbledon.

This photograph of the Team, on the ship that took them to England, is reproduced from the cover of *American Lawn Tennis,* June 15, 1920. Garland stands at the right, next to William T. Tilden. Williams is at the left, next to William M. Johnston. Captain Samuel Hardy is in the center.

Garland became a partner in Brown Brothers Harriman & Co. on January 1, 1933, but resigned the following year to go into the investment banking business.

(*Courtesy of the late Francis D. Ouimet*)

Certainly the most eminent golfer in Brown Brothers Harriman & Co. was FRANCIS D. OUIMET, who was in the Securities Department of the Boston house from 1954 until his death on September 2, 1967. He is shown here at the Brookline Country Club in 1913, being congratulated by the British professionals Harry Vardon and Ted Ray whom he had just defeated in a spectacular playoff for the championship in the United States Open Tournament.

The Boston house also claims the firm's most eminent oarsman—Louis Curtis, Jr., who is now a limited partner in the firm. In the picture at left, below, he is shown (standing behind the challenge cup) with the Harvard Varsity crew that won at the Henley Regatta in 1914—the first American crew ever to win the Henley challenge cup. The other photograph was taken in 1964, and shows the same crew (not a man missing) exhibiting their skill at Henley fifty years later.

Just three years before the Henley victory Louis Curtis's father, Louis Curtis, Sr., had become Brown Brothers' first partner resident in Boston. The year following the regatta Louis Curtis, Jr., went to work in the Philadelphia house. In 1922 he became a partner resident in Boston (where his grandfather had established the agency in 1844—see pp. 78, 79).

(*Both pictures courtesy of Louis Curtis, Jr.*)

(Courtesy of Moreau D. Brown)

In the 1920s there was a good deal of friendly rivalry between the baseball teams of the New York and Philadelphia houses. These were not softball teams, like those that play for the firm in contemporary leagues. They played hardball baseball, and their games got good newspaper coverage, including this cartoon by Hugh Doyle, sports cartoonist of the Philadelphia *Bulletin,* who covered the game played on the Haverford College field in 1921. James Crosby Brown, elder brother of Thatcher Brown and head of the Philadelphia house, is the lanky, Panama-hatted figure on the bench at right. Willet C. Roper, a manager in the New York office, is caricatured at lower left. Oh—Philadelphia won.

GEORGE HARRISON FRAZIER (1867–1934) became a partner in Philadelphia in 1898, after a successful career as a merchant and head of the Franklin Sugar Refining Company. It seems to have been in large part owing to Frazier's aggressive insistence that the articles renewing the partnership in 1907 gave more authority to the junior partners. On p. 184 there are quotations from one of John Crosby Brown's letters to Frazier. In his reply Frazier pointed out that, as then constituted, "the majority of the members of our firm are comparatively inactive, either from choice or from inability to produce results. . . . I am of the opinion that those of us who do not feel the necessity or have the desire to keep apace with our Competitors, should either retire or submit to a substantial reduction in their interest in the firm. . . . I appreciate the position of association with the firm, but aside from an increase in profits, I do not think the firm have to any extent improved their position in the banking community, and this is due to a lack of all hands pulling a strong oar." It is not surprising to read, in the brief history of the house published at the time of its hundredth anniversary,* that "Mr. Frazier brought to the firm renewed activity and the business of the Philadelphia house has expanded greatly under his guidance."

* *Experiences of a Century, 1818–1918,* privately printed, 1918. The book was probably written by James Crosby Brown.

(Brown Brothers Harriman & Co. Historical File)

Look carefully at the signature of the "Presidente" of Banco Nacional de Nicaragua on this example of Nicaragua's paper currency in 1912. It is the signature of James Brown, senior partner of Brown Brothers & Co., and it is there because of developments which led Oswald Garrison Villard, E. L. Godkin's successor as editor of *The Nation* (see p. 132 for Brown Brothers' part in founding the weekly), to publish in his June 7, 1922, issue a caustic editorial entitled "The Republic of Brown Brothers." Attacking the "new imperialism" of the United States in Central America and the Caribbean, specifically in the form of the "Dollar Diplomacy" developed by Secretary of State Philander C. Knox during President Taft's administration, the editorial pointed to Nicaragua as an example of how the American government in the past dozen years had reduced Haiti, Santo Domingo, and Nicaragua "to the status of colonies with at most a degree of rather fictitious self-government."

Upon these three countries the United States was said to have "forced ruinous loans, making 'free and sovereign' republics the creatures of New York banks." Just why the State Department and the American Minister in Managua should have been, as Villard asserted, "agents for these bankers, using American Marines when necessary to impose their will," the editorial did not make clear. The extant records in the firm's Historical File (including the private diary of James Brown and an unpublished account of the whole affair by Thatcher M. Brown—the two partners who handled the negotiations) suggest that it was quite the other way around.

Brown Brothers & Co., in association wih J. & W. Seligman & Co. had, indeed, loaned money to Nicaragua. They did so in 1911, at the request of the Department of State which, in order to restore order in the turbulent republic, "was anxious," as Thatcher Brown related, "to have a small one-year loan made to Nicaragua, with the terms subject to the approval of the State Department, for the purpose of currency reform in that country and the formation of a bank, which would be headed by Americans, to manage the currency."

(Both pictures from Brown Brothers Harriman & Co. Historical File)

The original of this photograph of the head office of the Bank of Nicaragua, in Managua, is framed with specimen bills and coins issued by the bank, and hangs in a private hallway at 59 Wall Street.

(*Courtesy of the New York Society Library*)　　　　　　　　　　(*Courtesy of the J. G. White Engineering Corp.*)

The complicated story of Brown Brothers' venture in Nicaragua cannot even be summarized here. (It is quite fully reviewed in a pamphlet published by the World Peace Foundation in 1927, entitled *Nicaragua and the United States 1909–1927,* by Professor Isaac Cox, and from a slightly different point of view in Harold Norman Denny's *Dollars for Bullets,* New York, 1929.) Here we can only add a passage from Thatcher Brown's account, telling of the Senate investigation that followed publication of Villard's attack in *The Nation:*

"Mr. James Brown and Mr. Albert Straus [of the Seligman firm] repaired to Washington and spent a couple of days on the stand being grilled by Senators. None of these Senators believed that the bankers had originally loaned money without security [on Nicaraguan one-year notes] to a Central American country at 6%, and [they] wanted to know what there was in it for the bankers. The bankers, of course, stuck to the truth; namely, that the loans carried 6% interest—no more, no less, and there was no gravy on the side. . . . When the hearing concluded, Senator Williams walked away between James Brown and Albert Straus and said, 'Look here, gentlemen, the hearing is over and the record is 6% and no perquisites. Please tell me now what there was in it for you and why

(*Courtesy of the New York Society Library*)

you made the loan at that figure.' Both protested their testimony was truthful—nothing in it but 6%. 'Well,' said Senator Williams, 'I always knew Wall Street bankers were crooks, but this is the first time I ever realized they were damn fools as well.' "

"To conclude the Nicaragua story," Mr. Brown wrote, "we were finally paid off, principal and interest, in 1924." Then he added: "Incidentally, the Bank of Nicaragua was well managed and successful, and Nicaragua came through the First World War, unlike most Central American countries, with a stable currency and able to finance its exports and imports by use of the gold reserve of the bank in New York."

The two larger pictures on this page are reproduced from rather poor halftone illustrations of an article on "The Knox Mission to Central America" by the distinguished journalist William Bayard Hale, who covered Secretary Knox's "good will" tour in March and April of 1912. The article appeared in *The World's Work,* July 1912. The one at the top shows the heavily guarded train in which Knox traveled from the port of Corinto to Managua. The heavy guard was necessary because the United States government was supporting the unpopular President Adolfo Díaz, whom the rebel General Mena was trying to oust by force without waiting for an election. The popular hero "who would be the next president if a fair election could be held," according to Hale, was General Emiliano Chamorro, shown at left.

The small picture of a Nicaraguan train was originally published in a report of the J. G. White Engineering Co., which was employed by Brown Brothers and the Seligmans to get the country's railroads into operating condition.

(Courtesy of Roger, Lord Cunliffe)

Soon after the outbreak of war in Europe in the summer of 1914 James Brown of Brown Brothers & Co. was elected to serve with Ben Strong, Jr., then president of the Bankers Trust Co., and Albert H. Wiggin, president of the Chase National Bank, as a committee of three to formulate a report and make recommendations to the Federal Reserve Board on ways of regulating the international exchange situation. As a result of the report James Brown and H. P. Davison of J. P. Morgan & Co. were sent to England early in December 1914 to confer with the Chancellor of the Exchequer, DAVID LLOYD GEORGE (later Prime Minister), and LORD CUNLIFFE, Governor of the Bank of England—shown together in the photograph above in Whitehall, probably just outside the Horseguards, with an unidentified Army captain in amused attendance. James Brown had several discussions with Lord Cunliffe and Montagu Norman, which are carefully reported in a long "strictly private" memorandum among his papers in the Historical File. He found Lord Cunliffe (at left in the photograph) "a very reserved and taciturn man, but . . . very cordial and absolutely frank in his expressions and in the confidential information he imparted. It was not until afterward I learned that he had seen all the cable and mail correspondence between M. C. N[orman]. and myself, and that it had received his personal approval step by step. In other words he treated me and the firm as confidentially allied with the Bank, and therefore worthy of and entitled to full information. All this had a decided bearing on my interview at the Treasury, and subsequent interviews."

(Brown Brothers Harriman & Co. Historical File)

The first financing undertaken by any American bank for France during the war, and the first commercial export credit in dollars (not pounds sterling) ever issued by a syndicate, was the $20,000,000 credit arranged in August 1915, by Brown Brothers & Co., as managers of a syndicate of American banks, and the Credit Lyonnais (of Paris) as managers of a syndicate of French banks. This credit worked in essentially the same way as the one described in some detail in the first chapter of this book (pp. 14, 15). It permitted France to pay for the food, munitions, and commodities she was purchasing in the United States without having to export goods needed at home in order to get foreign exchange with which to make the purchases.

A credit of this sort, involving a syndicate that included national banks, would not have been possible before the setting up of the Federal Reserve System in 1914, for until then the acceptance of bills of exchange was not permitted to national banks. Indeed, so unfamiliar with the commercial credit business were some of the participating banks that they refused to sell their acceptances on the New York market; they simply "locked them up," as Thatcher Brown records, and considered their participation as if it were a cash advance. It was Brown Brothers' long experience as merchant bankers that qualified them to negotiate the credit and manage the syndicate. The document shown here is the back of the first "Bankers Acceptance" arising from this credit, a draft for $22,500 drawn by de Rothschild Freres on the Bank of New York, August 26, 1915. Brown Brothers & Co.'s signature guarantees the de Rothschild Freres endorsement just above it.

This advertisement appeared in *The Bayonet,* Camp Lee, Virginia, September 27, 1918—and in many other similar publications. By that time Brown Brothers & Co. and Brown Shipley & Co. were no longer a single partnership, as they had been for so many years, though—as the advertisement indicates—the two firms and Alexander Brown & Sons still acted as one another's agents in connection with travelers letters of credit and other business. Even before the war serious strains had developed in the partnership. As early as April 14, 1906, John Crosby Brown had suggested to Sir Alexander Hargreaves Brown the possibility that "it may be better for the two concerns to separate, working together in harmony on joint account as do J. S. Morgan & Co. and J. P. Morgan & Co." New complications were added by the war. From 1914 to 1917, for instance, the American partners, though citizens of a non-belligerent nation, were limited to the line of conduct prescribed for British subjects, lest their associates in London should be held responsible. Furthermore, war taxes levied on both sides of the Atlantic made continuation of the old arrangement impossible. As of January 1, 1918, the English and American firms became completely independent of one another. In 1946, the London firm ceased to be a partnership and was incorporated as Brown, Shipley & Co., Limited.

Financial Facilities *for* U.S. Forces in the West End *of* London Brown, Shipley & Company

(*Brown Brothers Harriman & Co. Historical File*)

(*Courtesy of Time, Inc.*)

As mentioned earlier (p. 17), Robert A. Lovett served during the First World War as a pilot in the U. S. Navy Flying Corps. In this photograph he is shown with the other members of the famous "Yale Flying Unit" (Aerial Coast Patrol Unit No. 1) which he helped organize in 1916. Front row: Wellesley Laud Brown, Ella (mascot), and Henry P. Davison, Jr. (whose father was with James Brown at the conferences with Lord Cunliffe and Lloyd George, p. 191). Back row: John M. Vorys, Artemus L. Gates, Albert J. Ditman, Jr., Allan W. Ames, David McCulloch (instructor of the group), F Trubee Davison, Lovett, and Erl C. B. Gould.

On November 12, 1918, the day after the Armistice was signed, Thatcher Brown and W. E. Blewett, manager in Brown Brothers New York house, boarded the small Danish ship *Oscar II*—the ship Henry Ford had chartered during the war for his Quixotic expedition "to get the boys out of the trenches by Christmas." (The snapshot reproduced here is in one of Mr. Brown's scrapbooks.) "It had been apparent for some weeks previous that the war was drawing to a close," Thatcher Brown wrote in 1950, in his informal history of the firm, "and it became necessary to send a partner to Europe promptly to trade and negotiate out and settle many war casualties involving the shipment of commodities to Europe and particularly to the Scandinavian countries under our Commercial Letters of Credit."

The trip was a success. "Of the numerous cases which Mr. Blewett and I traded out with our Scandinavian friends in Norway, Sweden, and Denmark, only one resulted in a law-suit and, as the amount ($5,000) was small, we felt our trip was well worth while." They were welcomed at Stockholm by Marcus Wallenberg, executive director of Stockholms Enskilda Bank (at whose country estate, adjoining one of the King's palaces, Mr. Brown had been a guest in 1913), and on January 19, 1919, Mr. Wallenberg took Mr. Brown to call on King Gustaf, who had expressed an interest to meet "the first American business man to reach Sweden since the end of the war." There were discussions also with the head of the Skandanaviska Bank and the Governor of the Bank of Sweden, and in Christiana (now Oslo), with the director of the Norges Bank and the president of Andresen's Bank.

(Courtesy of Thatcher M. Brown, Jr.)

(Brown Brothers Harriman & Co. Historical File)

Another traveler who went to Europe in November 1918, on a Brown Brothers circular letter of credit was President Woodrow Wilson, en route to the peace conference at Versailles. The original document (shown here less than half its original size) is made out in favor of, and signed by, both the President and Mrs. Wilson. The endorsements on the back indicate that the Wilsons used up only $4500 of the credit between December 18th, when they drew $300, and May 2, 1919, when they drew $2500. All the payments were made at the Paris office of the London County and Westminster Bank.

Just two years (minus a day) after the Wilsons drew the first sum under this credit, Jacob Wallenberg (successor to Marcus, above) wrote a letter to Thatcher Brown beginning: "The Stockholms Enskilda Bank today had the pleasure of remitting your honorable firm a check issued in favor of Mr. Woodrow Wilson, President of the United States of America. This check represents the amount of the Nobel Peace Prize which has been awarded your President to which I most respectfully congratulate."

(*All pictures on this page from Brown Brothers Harriman & Co. Historical File*)

The three pictures on this page, all taken in 1920 by J. C. Maugans & Co., were used as illustrations in a booklet entitled *59 Wall Street,* published by the firm in December 1920 at the time of the opening of a five-story white marble extension of the 1865 building, covering five recently acquired lots on Hanover and Beaver Streets behind the original corner plot. The new structure, designed by Delano & Aldrich (see p. 142), was made necessary by the great expansion of the business during the war.

At upper left is the Stenographic and Translation Department—the only one in which women were employed. (See p. 165 for first women employees.) Those in the front row are Miss Charlotte Mason (standing), Miss Bessie Plimpton, and (at right) Miss Mae Evarts, the Head Stenographer. Miss Alice Dippel is in the second row, between Miss Plimpton and Miss Evarts. Above at right is a view of the Bond Department. None of the men in this picture has been identified.

In the view of the Commercial Credit Department, below, the man on the high stool in the left foreground is WILLIAM H. HANDS. The author had the pleasure of talking with Mr. Hands several times in the spring of 1964. (He had retired as a manager of Brown Brothers Harriman & Co. in 1946, after 53 years of service in the bank.) Then 87 years old, he was a stocky, healthy-looking man with clear eyes, who walked with a brisk, firm step. He did his level best to educate me about commercial letters of credit, and if I have been able, elsewhere in this book, to give the non-banker any idea of how they function, the credit is chiefly his, though others now in the bank have patiently continued to educate me. He was terribly proud of the firm's distinguished place in the commercial credit field, and enjoyed telling how—after the establishment of the Federal Reserve—officers of the great commercial banks, and of such large corporations as Du Pont, Firestone, and Goodyear, came to Brown Brothers' Commercial Credit Department to find out how the credits worked. Mr. Hands had a phenomenally accurate and evaluative memory, and was as generous as can be about helping in the early stages of this project. It was a sad day when we heard that on August 24, 1964, he died of pneumonia.

MOREAU DELANO, whom we met earlier in the Maine Woods (p. 180), is shown here in a photograph taken about 1920 by Pach Brothers. Like his cousin, Thatcher Brown, he became a partner in the year with which this chapter opened, and was in charge of the firm's investment business (including, of course, the Bond Department pictured on the opposite page) throughout the period.

(Courtesy of Miss Caroline Delano Wadsworth)

In February 1929, two of the partners—Thatcher Brown and Ray Morris—made a business trip to Argentina, Chile, and Peru. The firm had distributed the bonds of a number of South American municipalities, and had banking relationships in all three countries. In Lima, Peru, Mayor Dasso gave a dinner in the Municipal Palace at which Thatcher Brown was the guest of honor. In this photograph (preserved in one of Mr. Brown's scrapbooks), Mr. Brown stands right of center with the Mayor's wife, and Mrs. Brown (just left of the painting on the wall) stands with the Mayor. Ray Morris is at far right. Mrs. Brown's diary records that it was "A most beautiful dinner—white & crimson—lovely table. The room a dream of flowers. The mayor charming."

A good many of the "undigested securities" on Brown Brothers' shelves after the stock market collapsed in 1929 (see p. 16) were South American bonds, though many of them later proved to be valuable reserves for the merged firms.

(Courtesy of Thatcher M. Brown, Jr.)

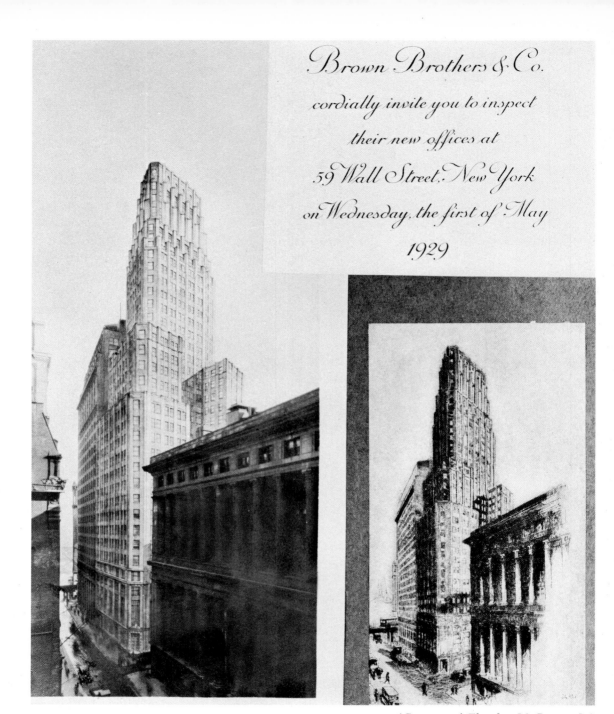

Brown Brothers & Co.

cordially invite you to inspect

their new offices at

59 Wall Street, New York

on Wednesday, the first of May

1929

(*Courtesy of Thatcher M. Brown, Jr.*)

The invitation and pictures reproduced above are shown just as Thatcher Brown pasted them onto a page of his scrapbook. Less than nine years after opening additional offices in a new building behind the banking house at 59 Wall Street (p. 194) the firm was inviting its clients and friends "to inspect their new offices" in a thirty-six story skyscraper—designed, as the 1920 building had been, by Delano & Aldrich (see p. 142). This was the only skyscraper William Adams Delano's firm ever designed.

It was a dramatic symbol of the booming 'twenties. But it was also symbolic in a special sense that Thatcher Brown must have been strongly aware of. For the plot of ground at the corner of Wall and Hanover Streets and the building thereon, which had been owned by the Brown family and Brown Brothers & Co. partners since 1843 (see pp. 73–74), was now in other hands.

The skyscraper, known as 61–63 Wall Street, was erected by Starrett Brothers, who bought the corner property and adjoining lots in 1928. It was, however, specially designed (on the exterior as well as the interior) to accommodate Brown Brothers & Co. in a separate unit with its own entrance (retaining the 59 Wall Street address) on the corner site they had so long occupied. And the paneling in the partners' room was the same that had been transferred from the 1865 building to the new wing in 1920. (The photograph in the scrapbook is by an unidentified photographer. The other picture was made from an etching by John A. Dix.)

On May 1, 1929—six months before the stock market shuddered and collapsed—Brown Brothers moved in. A year and a half later the sign above the corner entrance read: Brown Brothers Harriman & Co. (see p. 220).

196

Seventeen

NOT EVERYBODY'S BANK

The previous chapter brought us back to our starting point, when the Harrimans and their partners joined forces with the partners in Brown Brothers & Co. to carry on—with the increased efficiency and augmented resources demanded by modern conditions—a business with a century-old tradition. In that tradition there had been strong elements of pioneering enterprise, from the "cotton triangle" days, when the first generation of partners pioneered in the use of documentary sterling credits, up through the First World War, when the third generation pioneered as managers of the first syndicate to issue a commercial export acceptance credit in dollars. But there seems to be no doubt that in the years just prior to the merger the old firm was less enterprising and adaptable than it needed to be.

Men from both the Harriman and Brown Brothers sides remember the atmosphere at 59 Wall Street before the merger as "very old-fashioned," in spite of the new building. From their recollections one gets the impression of a sedate institution, where visitors encountered aloof English floor attendants and where the bank's employees were acutely aware of the remoteness of the partners. "We had no sense of being part of the business or responsible for it," one of them said not long ago. Once, to be sure, the staff was called together to hear a partner recommend "restraint in hiring people and in ordering equipment," but that was the only staff meeting he could remember in the pre-merger days.

The merger brought changes at every level. The partners became more accessible to staff and clients alike, and new and more efficient methods were introduced in all departments. Most importantly, there was increased emphasis on the firm's domestic banking business. Brown Brothers, as Thatcher Brown noted in his informal papers on the firm's history, had thought of itself chiefly "as a bank engaged in foreign business," and he did not recall their ever soliciting a purely domestic banking

account. "When we joined with the Harrimans, our point of view and emphasis changed," he wrote, "and we tried in every way to increase our domestic business, and with considerable success."

The firm's success in increasing its domestic business did not, of course, come during the first couple of years after the merger. Those were years of constantly deepening world-wide economic depression, and for three years or more, as Thatcher Brown frankly recorded, the firm's losses through loans and declining security values were so severe that the two wealthiest partners "postponed taking any profits on their capital and assumed all losses of the other partners, even deferring interest on capital, until certain partners (whose capital had become seriously impaired and, in certain cases, were owing to the firm) were in black figures once

HAROLD D. PENNINGTON, shown at his desk in this anonymous snapshot made about 1944, was one of the group of men from the old American Exchange National Bank who went with Knight Woolley when he organized the Harrimans' private banking house in 1927 (see p. 13). Though he did not become a partner in Brown Brothers Harriman & Co. until several years after the merger, he was from the start manager in charge of operations for the new concern. It was he who had charge of transferring the Harriman securities to the vault at 59 Wall Street—a rather casual episode as he recently recalled it. Four men simply wheeled them in handcarts down Broadway and Wall as Mr. Pennington walked behind with a pistol in his pocket.

more." Much the same situation had occurred after the panic of 1837, at which time William and James Brown assumed the losses which would otherwise have fallen heavily on the others, and Thatcher Brown took pleasure in telling of these two episodes "just about one hundred years apart but showing the same spirit of cooperation among the partners and of the placing of friendship ahead of profits."

The firm's decision, after the Banking Act of June 1933, to remain in the commercial banking business instead of becoming investment bankers as most private banking houses did, was the logical result of an analysis of the firm's business in the recent past. About 65% of it had been regular banking business—financing exports and imports by commercial letters of credit, receiving deposits, making loans, and buying and selling foreign exchange. Only 35% had been underwriting and distributing securities. Furthermore, a large majority of the partners was more interested in banking than in the issue business. The decision, therefore, was that the four partners who preferred investment banking —Ralph T. Crane, Laurence G. Tighe, P. Blair Lee, and Charles S. Garland—joined with a group of men who had been in the National City Bank's securities affiliate, the City Company, to form a new concern, unaffiliated with either of the banks.[1] Under the terms of the Banking Act, however, the firm could—like other commercial banks—continue to underwrite federal, state, and municipal bond issues, and, being a partnership, it was also able to retain its seat on the Stock Exchange and act as brokers for its clients, buying and selling stocks and bonds on a commission basis.

[1] This firm, headed by Joseph P. Ripley from the City Company, was at first called Brown Harriman & Co., Inc., but to avoid confusion the name was changed in 1938 to Harriman Ripley & Co., Inc. The Harrimans supplied the initial capital for the firm, their stock being placed in a voting trust of which they were not at any time trustees. After 1946 employees of Harriman Ripley owned the majority of the common stock, and by September 1953 the Harrimans were out entirely.

As Thatcher Brown said, the increased emphasis on domestic business after the merger was largely the result of the fact that the Harriman partners, "through their railroad and other interests, were well known in the West, and it was not difficult for them to build up excellent domestic industrial and banking connections." Only a few months after the merger, AVERELL HARRIMAN was elected chairman of the executive committee of the Illinois Central Railroad, and in July 1932 he succeeded Judge Lovett as chairman of the board of the Union Pacific. He is shown here looking through the window of one of the streamlined aluminum trains he introduced on the Union Pacific (with low-cost diner meals and trained nurse stewardesses), as a result of which the railroad's receipts from passenger traffic rose 66% in 1934, at the depths of the depression. (*Courtesy of the Harriman Estate Office*)

LAURENCE G. TIGHE (1894–1954) was one of the four Brown Brothers Harriman partners who elected, after the Banking Act of 1933, to go into investment banking (see above). He had been with the firm since 1924, when he was brought in to head the Bond Department of the Boston house. In 1930 he became a partner, remaining for two years in Boston with Louis Curtis, Jr., then transferring to New York in 1932. He was a vice-president of Harriman Ripley & Co., Inc., from 1934 until 1938, when he resigned to become associate treasurer of Yale University. In 1942 he became treasurer and served in that capacity until his death.

(*Courtesy of Mrs. Laurence G. Tighe*)

(Brown Brothers Harriman & Co. Historical File)

On October 21, 1934, the New York *Herald Tribune* reported that Brown Brothers Harriman & Co. would soon "embark on a campaign to increase its deposits and stimulate the various other branches of the banking business carried on by private bankers." Larger deposits, the paper said, were "the necessary offset to the enforced discontinuance of security underwriting," and the bank had therefore planned a series of advertisements calling attention to its commercial banking services. The first in the series, entitled "What the Private Banker Does," appeared in the *New York Times* and other papers on October 25th. The fourth, reproduced above, was published on December 6th, and emphasized the highly personal character of the banking services the firm provided.

Commenting on the bank's decision to advertise "the nature and governing principles of its business" the *Wall Street Journal* said: "Superficially, but superficially only, the firm thus makes a radical departure from the ways to which it has been accustomed since 1818. In other respects its practice of private banking still anchors upon the bottom principles which, by all reasonable inference, explain its survival. . . . A body of business precept and procedure which has outlasted the financial chaos of early America, the long struggle out of wildcat banking toward regularity and responsibility, the inauguration of the national banking system as an adjunct of government in the crisis of civil war, another series of depressions attendant upon the feverish 'winning of the West,' and finally the wrenching economic dislocations of a World War and its mad aftermath, must be conceded to have proved its permanent place in the commercial organism, if there is permanence in any part of it."

The development of the bank's investment management and investment advisory services is a good example of the way the revitalized firm adapted its services to changed conditions. In the 'twenties, when the stock market seemed only to go up, everyone thought he could manage his own investments, but—as the present head of the firm's Investment Advisory Department recently put it—"when the events of 1929 came along, people felt they needed assistance, to say the least." Both Brown Brothers & Co. and the Harriman firms had independently established research or statistical departments in the late 'twenties to evaluate stock investments, and after the merger these were put together as the Investment Management Department, designed to serve individuals, corporations, and institutions by supervising their investment portfolios, keeping their securities under the systematic review of the analytical and research staff and recommending purchases and sales that seemed advantageous in view of the client's particular objectives.

The work of this department was supervised by a committee consisting of partners and department heads, which met regularly to formulate general policy and to review the department's specific recommendations regarding particular accounts, each of which received individual attention. The first minute book of this committee, covering the meetings from February 2, 1931, to November 23, 1932, has fortunately been preserved, and shows how rapidly the new department expanded. By 1934, when the firm divested itself of its securities underwriting business and became a commercial bank, its investment management services had become one of the most important parts of the business.

Something of the exuberance with which the partnership operated in those days is reflected in the items reproduced below. At left is the title page of a booklet prepared in the fall of 1934, describing the new department's services and calling the attention of investors to the need for professional help in keeping track of the "scattered wealth" represented by the stocks and bonds they owned. At the right is the first page of a burlesque of the pamphlet, written by Prescott Bush with assists from Robert Lovett, and sent as a Christmas card to his partners by Bush, who had had charge of preparing the original. The text of the original began: "There is nothing about bonds and stocks that looks particularly hard to manage. Superficially they seem like a very simple means of conserving wealth. Probably you have experienced that sense of security which accompanies leaving some of them in a safe deposit box. As the gate of the vault closes behind you, you leave with the comfortable feeling that your wealth is safely locked up and cannot get away. Of course this is an illusion. Perhaps you have not been misled by it, but many investors have."

SCATTERED WEALTH

A Brief Discussion
of Investment Management

Banking Business Established 1818

BROWN BROTHERS HARRIMAN & CO.
PRIVATE BANKERS
59 WALL STREET, NEW YORK CITY

BOSTON: 10 POST OFFICE SQUARE ★ PHILADELPHIA: 1531 WALNUT STREET
CHICAGO: 135 SOUTH LA SALLE STREET

(*Brown Brothers Harriman & Co. Historical File*)

SHATTERED HEALTH

THERE is nothing about a book on investment management that looks particularly hard to write. Superficially it seems like a very simple thing. Probably you have experienced that sense of superiority which accompanies reading such a book written by some one else. As you yawn and close the book, you have a comfortable feeling that you could have done much better with one hand tied behind you.

Of course this is a joke. Maybe you have never tried to edit such a book, not to mention writing it; but I have. What you think is something pretty swell, turns out to be merely pieces of paper on which 18 different people think it is their God-given duty to scribble criticisms and sarcastic comments. Somebody in Chicago thinks it's too elementary and what is really needed is a 400-page Compendium of Universal Knowledge. Somebody in Boston or Philadelphia says it's too long and nobody will read it and what you ought to have is a one-page letter. Three of the partners in New York think the whole idea is lousy and should be abandoned in favor of a Christmas card.

Unposed snapshots of working members of the staff would have been unthinkable in the pre-merger days, but a good many have been taken since the 1930s and a number have found their way into the firm's Historical File. This one, probably taken by a member of the staff in 1939, is of Thomas McCANCE, then manager in charge of the research division of the Investment Advisory Department. Six years later McCance became a partner in the firm (see p. 216).

(Courtesy of Miss Gertrude A. Murphy)

(Both lower pictures from Brown Brothers Harriman & Co. Historical File)

Another manager in the Investment Advisory Department who later became a partner was DAVID G. ACKERMAN, shown here in a snapshot taken about 1945 by an unidentified photographer. Ackerman had been head of a branch office of Brown Brothers & Co. established in 1930 in Newark, New Jersey, to handle its securities business there. (There were such branch offices in a dozen or more cities when the firm was in the underwriting business.) After 1932 he was in the Investment Advisory Department at 59 Wall Street until in 1953 he became a partner. He retired in 1961, but continued with the firm in an advisory capacity for two more years in connection with various interests in the oil and gas industries.

The bank's commercial letters of credit department also expanded rapidly under the new regime. This snapshot, taken about 1945 in the Commercial Credit Department, shows JOHN KNOX (now a manager of the firm) at his desk conferring with ROY QUIBELL. Knox had been in the Commercial Credit Department since 1925, when he went to work there under William H. Hands (p. 194).

American Hens Cluck Defiance at German U-Boats

German long-range strategy counts on starving the British, in default of an all-out crossing of the Channel, which is a rough body of water. Here is the arrival of the first load of American food in England, with Lord Woolton, Food Minister; W. Averell Harriman, observer for the President, and Robert H. Hinckley, Assistant Secretary of Commerce from Washington, inspecting American eggs and American cheese.   *Herald Tribune—Acme*

Looking back over the history of the firm in 1950, Thatcher Brown was impressed with the extent to which it had been tacitly understood that public service "was more or less expected of the leaders of our business." Certainly Averell Harriman lived up to expectations. As James Reston recently wrote in his *New York Times* column, Harriman "has served longer in higher and more diverse posts than any other American official of his time."

His first public service jobs after becoming a partner in Brown Brothers Harriman & Co. were as a member of the Business Advisory Council of the Department of Commerce (of which he served as chairman from 1937 to 1939) and with the N.R.A.—first as administrator of the New York State division and later as national administrator. (He is shown, above left, with Postmaster General Farley at Floyd Bennett airfield August 11, 1933—the day thirty army planes were to take off carrying packages of N.R.A. Blue Eagle stickers to various Eastern and Southern cities for distribution.) In the months before Pearl Harbor

he served on the National Defense Advisory Commission, with the Office of Production Management, and as President Roosevelt's special representative in Great Britain to coordinate lend-lease aid. The picture above is from the rotogravure section of the *Herald Tribune,* June 22, 1941.

The pictures below show Harriman on two other occasions while he was still a general partner in the bank. (He became a limited partner in 1946 when he was appointed Secretary of Commerce in Roosevelt's cabinet.) At lower left he is shown (second from left) on H.M.S. *Prince of Wales* when President Roosevelt and Prime Minister Churchill met at sea to sign the Atlantic Charter, August 14, 1941. In the picture at right he is shown standing behind the President at the Teheran Conference, in November 1943, when he was Ambassador to Russia. The picture was taken as Stalin was introduced to Churchill's daughter Sarah.

Upper left: (*Photograph by International News Photos, Inc., courtesy of the Harriman Estate Office.*)
Upper right: (*Courtesy of the Harriman Estate Office*)
Lower left: (*Associated Press photograph, courtesy of the Harriman Estate Office*)
Lower right: (*Courtesy of the Harriman Estate Office*)

OFFICIAL PHOTO OF UNITED STATES NAVY.

We offer this as our feature picture. Its star, LT. COMDR. NORMAN KING, has labelled it - "Telling Him Why I Voted for Dewey". Actually, NORMAN, who was promoted last May to the Chief Engineer of the famous cruiser, USS AUGUSTA, is trying to make himself heard above the roar of the engine room machinery.

(*Courtesy of Wide World Photos, Inc.*)

During the war 86 members of the bank's staff, from the offices in New York, Philadelphia, Boston, and Chicago, served with the armed forces, and the firm kept in touch with them through the chatty pages of a house magazine called *The Fifty-Niner*. The picture and text reproduced here are from p. 10 of the fall, 1945 issue. (*Brown Brothers Harriman & Co. Historical File*)

Many of the firm's partners and executives devoted a good deal of time to war work. Roland Harriman was manager of the North Atlantic Area of the American Red Cross, and Prescott Bush in 1942 became national campaign chairman of the combined fundraising drives of the USO and other wartime charities. In June 1940, Robert Lovett was called to Washington as a Special Assistant to the Secretary of War, and from 1941–45 served as Assistant Secretary of War (for Air). In September, the Distinguished Service Medal was conferred upon him in recognition of his services as "the eyes, ears, and hands of the Secretary of War in respect to the growth of that enormous American air power which has astonished the world."

In the post-war years, also, these partners sustained the tradition of public service. In 1950 President Truman appointed Roland Harriman president of the American Red Cross, and he has been head of the national organization ever since, having been successively reappointed by Presidents Eisenhower, Kennedy, and Johnson. From 1952–62 Prescott Bush served as United States Senator from Connecticut. And Robert Lovett twice returned to Washington, from 1947–49 as Under Secretary of State, and from 1950–53 first as Deputy Secretary of Defense then (after September 1951) as Secretary in President Truman's cabinet. The photograph at left, captioned "Top Level Lineup," was taken at SHAPE headquarters near Paris on November 16, 1951. It shows Secretary of Defense Lovett and Averell Harriman (then director of the Mutual Security Administration) with Secretary of State Dean Acheson and SHAPE's commander, General Eisenhower.

While our legal and somewhat ancient address is 59 Wall Street, we have recently been spreading out in the general direction of 67 in the way of easing our growing pains. As you probably know, several of the heaviest thinkers of the I/A DEPARTMENT have been lodged in 67 for some years and the TAX DEPARTMENT has been paying rent there since 1937.

As matters now stand, there is quite a mixture of departments domiciled at 67 Wall Street and it might be that the recent moves will be of interest to those in the service and even to some of our co-workers who are quartered in the more remote corners of our Bank.

As soon as the new 67 territory was opened, the AUDITING DEPARTMENT staked its claim for the most desirable square footage obtainable. Art Smith now has two desks (both in good working order), one at 67 and the other on the bank floor at 59. As a matter of fact, the Auditors now have desk space in about every nook in the Bank except the Gents' Room (Al Colquhoun adds the caustic comment - "That's where they are usually found.")

In the way of assuring privacy and to add a touch of dignity, "Deacon" BEATTIE has a private office together with a reception foyer. Miss Leahy, his secretary, says that Brother Beattie's reaction has been fairly normal to date, but hints that he is showing some interest in winged collars.

The C/I and A/R DEPARTMENTS, which for months were as roomy as a Lexington Avenue Express at 5:30, are now in a spacious but somewhat gaudy office. The combined departments are linoleumed in a creamed-spinach green and walled with an indescribable tint of green. This fetching color combination is flooded with a battery of dazzling lights playing pretty effects on Nash's crew haircut and Barnet's bald dome.

The TRANSLATORS, Misses Dukas and Cortrell, are grouped with the C/I and A/R. Serious thought has been given to putting our linguists on wheels, for this is the 20th time they have moved in 22 years.

A glimpse of life on the home front at Brown Brothers Harriman during the war is given in these items from the same issue of *The Fifty-Niner* which carried the picture of Lt. Comdr. Norman King reproduced on p. 203. The bank's quarters in the new building at 59 Wall Street (see p. 196) had long since been outgrown, and it had been necessary to spread out into neighboring buildings where space could be rented. One reason for the Auditing Department's getting "the most desirable square footage" was that it handled all the reports and license applications in connection with the Treasury Department's Foreign Funds Control program, blocking the assets in the United States of nationals of countries that were invaded and occupied by the German armies. (*Brown Brothers Harriman & Co. Historical File*)

(Courtesy of Mrs. Grace Kline, St. Louis)

Expansion of the bank's investment management and brokerage business led in November 1941 to the opening of an office in St. Louis, Missouri. The first head of this office was HENRY DUNCKER, of an old St. Louis family, who had been resident manager of Fenner & Beane until that firm merged with Merrill Lynch and decided to give up its investment advisory services. Duncker is shown here (at left) with STEPHEN Y. HORD, resident partner in Chicago, in a photograph taken in September 1954 by the Illinois Central Railroad's photographer. Since Duncker's death in 1964 the St. Louis office has been managed by Edward P. Currier, Jr. (see p. 216).

In Boston, too, the firm's business was expanding rapidly. Soon after the merger the Boston house moved into handsome new quarters at 10 Post Office Square, designed by Coolidge, Shepley, Bulfinch & Abbott. This photograph, taken by Guy Gillette-Lensgroup in 1959, shows part of the main banking floor. The group of three men seated in the background at right includes (left to right) Louis Curtis, Jr., then managing partner in Boston, William F. Ray, a manager in the Banking Department (back to camera), and Ernest E. Nelson, a manager who has since retired. (*Brown Brothers Harriman & Co. Historical File*)

(*Brown Brothers Harriman & Co. Historical File*)

This photograph of a staff conference in the Chicago office, like the one above, was taken in 1959 by Guy Gillette-Lensgroup. Those in the group are (left to right) FRANK SOULE; JOHN S. SHUMWAY; RUSSELL J. EDDY (then an assistant manager, later a manager); STEPHEN Y. HORD, resident partner in charge of the office (see p. 215); and RICHARD A. HOOVER (then assistant manager, later a manager). (*Brown Brothers Harriman & Co. Historical File*)

Through all the changes in emphasis, in organization, and in personnel that resulted from the 1931 merger and from the decision in 1934 to continue the commercial banking activities of traditional merchant banking rather than its investment banking features, the business of Brown Brothers Harriman & Co. preserved a striking continuity with that of the antecedent partnerships. An interesting instance of this continuity, for which pictorial evidence happens to be available, is presented on these two pages.

In October 1964 announcement was made of the merger of the Bangor & Aroostook Corporation with the Punta Alegre Sugar Corporation. It was an unlikely-sounding merger from the layman's point of view, but it brought together two businesses with which the bank had had associations for many years. Back in John Crosby Brown's day, as we have seen (pp. 175–80), Brown Brothers had been instrumental in financing construction of the railroad, and as late as 1918–1920 a Brown Brothers partner, John Henry Hammond, had been acting president of the road. Though the association with Punta Alegre did not go back so far, it had begun in the 'twenties, as the prospectus below indicates.

JOHN HENRY HAMMOND (1871–1949), whom we first encountered on p. 166 as a recent college graduate visiting the Browns at Brighthurst, became a partner in Brown Brothers & Co. in 1916. Among his other responsibilities, he represented the firm's interests in the Bangor & Aroostook by serving on the executive committee of the railroad's board of directors, and from June 14, 1918, to February 29, 1920, he was acting president of the road. This photograph by Blackstone Studios was taken about a year after Hammond resigned from Brown Brothers Harriman & Co. at the end of 1931 to return to the practice of law.

This prospectus, dated September 1927, is the earliest extant evidence of Brown Brothers' connection with the Punta Alegre Sugar Co. The company owned or controlled more than 200,000 acres in the Providence of Camaguey, Cuba, where it grew sugar cane and manufactured raw sugar. (*Brown Brothers Harriman & Co. Historical File*)

(*Courtesy of Mrs. John Henry Hammond*)

$4,000,000
Punta Alegre Sugar Company
6% Gold Notes

Dated October 1, 1927   Due October 1, 1930

Interest payable April 1 and October 1 in Boston or New York City without deduction of Normal Federal Income Tax up to 2%. Pennsylvania and Connecticut 4 mills taxes, Maryland 4½ mills tax and Massachusetts taxes measured by income, not exceeding 6% per annum, will be refunded upon appropriate request. Coupon Notes in denominations of $1,000 and $500, registerable as to principal. Redeemable, at the option of the Company, as a whole or in part by lot, on 30 days' published notice at any time to and including October 1, 1928, at 102 and interest, thereafter to and including October 1, 1929, at 101 and interest, thereafter at 100 and interest.

THE FIRST NATIONAL BANK OF BOSTON, Trustee

CAPITALIZATION
(Upon completion of this financing)

6% Gold Notes (this issue)	$4,000,000
7% Convertible Debentures, due 1937	4,414,800
7½% First Mtge. Bonds of Baragua Sugar Co., due 1937	3,378,000
Purchase Money Mortgages, etc.	457,230
Total	$12,250,030
Capital Stock ($50) Authorized $25,000,000; Issued..	19,076,850
Preferred Stock of Subsidiary not owned	330,000

Mr. W. C. Douglas, President of Punta Alegre Sugar Company, has furnished us with the information contained in this circular and the accompanying balance sheet.

HISTORY AND PROPERTY: Punta Alegre Sugar Company, incorporated in Delaware in 1915, is engaged in the Province of Camaguey, Cuba, in the growing of sugar cane and the manufacture of raw sugar. The Company and its subsidiaries own approximately 105,000 acres of land, of which 38,500 are under cultivation, have leased land amounting to 92,000 acres, of which 57,000 are planted to cane, and control by contract or location 113,000 more acres of land, of which 37,000 are cultivated. This makes available for the Company the cane produced from 132,500 acres under cultivation, with 83,500 additional acres that can be planted to cane.

The Company and its subsidiaries own three sugar mills which have an aggregate annual capacity of over 1,500,000 bags of raw sugar. The lands and mills are served largely by company owned railroads and marine equipment, consisting of 240 miles of track, 27 locomotives, 1,336 cars, 2 tugs and 7 lighters.

The Company's properties, as a group, are among the lowest cost producers of raw sugar in Cuba.

PURPOSE: The proceeds from the sale of these Notes will be used to pay off $2,000,000 6% Gold Notes maturing November 1, 1927, to reimburse the treasury for capital expenditures made in the last two years, and for additional working capital.

FUNDED DEBT: These Notes will be a direct obligation of the Company and will rank equally with the Convertible Debentures. The consolidated funded debt, including the Baragua bonds, will amount upon completion of this financing to only $8.17 per bag of present total annual capacity including that of Baragua and only $10.19 per bag of the 1926-1927 crop as curtailed by government restriction.

The Indenture will contain provisions prohibiting the Company from placing any mortgage upon its property unless these Notes are ratably secured thereby, but such prohibition shall not apply to the execution of purchase money or refunding mortgages, the purchase of property subject to mortgage or to pledging or otherwise encumbering the sugar crops and other products.

ASSETS: An estimated consolidated balance sheet as of September 30, 1927, after giving effect to this financing, shows current and working assets including the growing cane and crop investment, of over $10,593,000, as compared with current liabilities of less than $2,056,000, a ratio of over 5 to 1 and a net position of $8,538,000; fixed assets of over $23,456,000; and net tangible assets of over $31,305,000 or over 2.5 times total funded indebtedness. The common stock, listed on the New York Stock Exchange, at present market prices shows a junior equity of approximately $14,000,000.

EARNINGS: Average earnings for the last five fiscal years (including estimated earnings for year ending September 30, 1927) before depreciation are 3.56 times the average of all interest charges, including interest on floating debt. For the year ending September 30, 1927, during which sugar conditions have been extremely unfavorable, such earnings are estimated to be 1.80 times all interest charges. After depreciation, earnings for the year ending September 30, 1927, are estimated to be 1.32 times all interest charges, and for the above five fiscal years the average of such earnings (year ending September 30, 1927, estimated), is 2.62 times the average of all interest charges.

All legal matters pertaining to this issue are to be approved by Messrs. Root, Clark, Buckner, Howland & Ballantine of New York City. The accounts of the Company and its subsidiaries are audited monthly by Peat, Marwick, Mitchell & Co.

We offer these Notes when, as and if issued and received by us and subject to the approval of Counsel. It is expected that delivery will be made in the form of Definitive Notes on or about October 7, 1927.

Price 99 and interest, yielding about 6⅜%

BROWN BROTHERS & CO.
59 WALL STREET, NEW YORK

The statements contained herein are not guaranteed but are based upon information which we believe to be accurate and reliable.

September, 1927.

The two pictures reproduced above, showing aspects of the Punta Alegre Sugar Corporation's operations in Cuba during the 1950s, were selected from a group that were fortunately saved when the company's property was confiscated by the Castro regime after the 1959 revolution. Engine No. 45, shown above in 1954 hauling sixty 35-ton cars of sugar cane to the company's Central Florida mill in Camaguey, was a 90-ton Baldwin steam locomotive that Punta Alegre bought in 1915 from the Panama Canal Co., who had used it during construction of the canal.

After processing at the company's mills, raw sugar was shipped from various ports, such as the one at Boca Grande, photographed in October 1955 by Giles S. Gianelloni. The railroad from the company's Central Baragua mill is shown at lower right. From the warehouse at the port, sugar was loaded on barges and towed by the company's tugboats down the "Estero," or inlet, at left, to deep water where seagoing vessels picked up the cargo. A battle between Che Guevara and the Batista forces was fought near Boca Grande during the Castro revolution.

After reorganization of Punta Alegre in 1931–32, Ray Morris of Brown Brothers Harriman & Co. (see p. 195) was elected to the board of directors. He served from 1933 to 1955 when he was succeeded by FREDERICK H. KINGSBURY, who had been a partner in the bank since 1949. Like Morris, Kingsbury kept in active touch with the company's operations. He is shown here at Punta Alegre's Central Macareno mill in February 1958, with Arthur Gianelloni, manager of the Central Macareno division.

Kingsbury continued to serve on Punta Alegre's board after the Cuban expropriation, when it began investing its remaining assets in a variety of industries in this country. By June of 1963 it had acquired a grain elevator, a metal foundry, and a textile converting firm. Then, in October 1964, came the merger with the Bangor & Aroostook. When Kingsbury went on an inspection trip over the railroad's system in July 1965, he was, therefore, renewing an old association as well as inaugurating a new one. He is shown above discussing mechanized track-maintenance equipment with P. H. Swales (left), chief engineer, and W. Jerome Strout (right), president of the railroad.

207

Perhaps in banking as in private life awareness of continuity with the past begets sensitivity to the future's challenges and possibilities. At all events, as the pictures on this page suggest, the firm has been as ready in recent years as at any time in its history to foster pioneering enterprises—public and private, foreign and domestic. What it will do in the future depends largely upon the character of those who inherit its traditions.

Some of these people appear in the portfolio of photographs that follows, including one of the bank's newest partners, Robert V. Roosa. When he resigned as Under Secretary of the Treasury for Monetary Affairs to join the firm, an editorial in the *American Banker* called him "one of the great innovators" in financial affairs, who typically "looked ahead to problems looming, and did not dwell upon the accomplishments of the past." Alexander Brown and his sons would, one imagines, have been pleased.

In 1959–60 the bank financed one of the first major enclosed-mall regional shopping centers—Cherry Hill Mall in New Jersey (at left, below). This was an early project of what is now the Rouse Company, which went on—under the leadership of James W. Rouse and with other financing —from shopping centers to residential projects, urban redevelopment, and most recently to the planning and building of an entire city. In 1963 ground was broken on the 15,000 acre site of Columbia, a new city for 110,000 people midway between Baltimore and Washington, recently described in *Harper's Magazine* as perhaps "the most imaginative attempt yet made to capture The Good Life for city dwellers." The model (below, right) shows the town center as envisioned for completion by 1980. (*Photograph at left by Molitor; at right by Ezra Stoller Associates. Both pictures courtesy of the Rouse Company*)

On July 24, 1958, the *New York Times* reported that "India's T.V.A.," the Damodar Valley Corporation had received a $25 million loan from the World Bank to finance enlargement of the Bokaro thermal power station (at top, above) in the region northwest of Calcutta where the D.V.C. was rehabilitating an uncultivated and eroded wilderness. "Brown Brothers Harriman & Co., without the guarantee of the World Bank, is participating in the loan," the *Times* reported. The participation was small by World Bank standards (only about a quarter of a million) but it was unique, and it would mean something in the lives of those who had been resettled by the D.V.C. in villages like Gouria Karma (above), "so planned as to bridge the gulf between the ancient ways and modern living." (*Both pictures courtesy of Consulate General of India, New York*)

BANKERS, AND EVANS, AND CHANCE

A PORTFOLIO OF PHOTOGRAPHS
By WALKER EVANS

A corner of the Foreign Investment Department, Nov. 2, 1966.

AUTHOR'S NOTE The first one-man show of a photographer's work ever given at the Museum of Modern Art was an exhibition of Walker Evans' pictures in 1938. For those who saw it, it was a revelation. It came at a time when photography seemed obsessed with being abstract or painterly, distorting actuality by blurring the focus of the lens, employing tricky "angle shots," and manipulating negatives. Evans would have none of that. He was—and is— a straight photographer, both in the sense that there is no trickery in his unhurried, almost casual craftsmanship and in the sense that his lens sees people and things squarely, head-on, not out of the corner of its eye. He has too much humor to care about creating effects. He is patiently and unsparingly interested in showing us the moral significance of whatever encounters his lens.

Four years ago, at my request, Evans was commissioned to take pictures for the firm's Historical File, from which some could be selected for a portfolio at the end of this book. The first were taken in March 1964, the latest in May 1967. (Data given in the captions is correct as of the specified date, and does not take account of subsequent promotions, resignations, or other changes.) Few of the picture-taking sessions were prearranged. Generally, Evans came and went at his convenience. He kept cameras, a tripod, and other equipment at the bank, and was free to take pictures wherever he wanted to go, of whoever or whatever interested him. And he alone selected, from the thousand or more negatives he made, those from which he would produce finished prints.

In choosing for this portfolio fifty-five of the several hundred prints in the file, I have tried to respect Evans' perceptions rather than provide "coverage" of the bank's functions or personnel, in order that the last episode in this historical portrait may be Brown Brothers Harriman & Co.'s encounter with a great photographer.

J.A.K.

The Personality of a Bank.

(Title of booklet published by Brown Brothers Harriman & Co., 1967.)

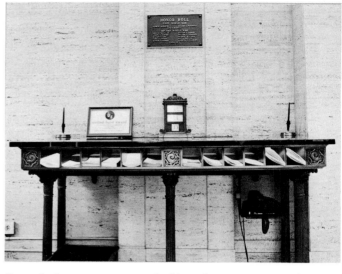

One of the two counters flanking the entrance to the Boston offices of the bank, July 13, 1965 (prior to the 1967 remodeling of the facilities at 10 Post Office Square).

Main banking floor at 59 Wall Street, looking from partners' hallway toward stairway leading to rotunda entrance, Oct. 13, 1966. Mrs. Diana Tadler, secretary in the Investment Department, turns toward camera while waiting for elevator. Guard Joseph Long stands duty left of entrance stairway.

James Ronan, elevator operator at 59 Wall Street, stops his car at main banking floor outside partners' hallway, Nov. 2, 1966.

"Imaginative banking calls for continuous probing to spot opportunities for profitable shifts in strategy or tactics."

(From *The Personality of a Bank,* published by Brown Brothers Harriman & Co., 1967.)

Scenes on the executive platforms at New York (above and at left) and Philadelphia (below right).

Above (Oct. 27, 1966): Counter-clockwise around table—Neil A. Morrison, Jr., assistant manager; James A. Harper, manager and a senior credit officer; John A. Knox (hidden); Frederick H. Kingsbury, partner; Walter W. Grist of Credit Department. In background Nancy Frescki, secretary to Mr. Knox.

Above left (Nov. 2, 1966): Foreground—John Madden, partner, and Mrs. Frances Wolfe, secretary to Thomas McCance. Background—Maarten van Hengel, manager in Foreign Investment Department, and John A. Knox, senior banking manager (see p. 201).

Left (Mar. 1, 1967): Arthur L. Nash (center), manager and chief credit officer, with John J. McCloy II (at left) and Robert H. Sanford, assistant manager.

Below left (Feb. 23, 1967): Walter H. Brown, manager in charge of business development, and Clarence F. von Glahn, deputy manager. In background, unidentified temporary secretary.

Below (Mar. 31, 1965): George F. S. Elder (center), assistant manager in charge of operations and personnel; George C. Brooke, Jr.; and Evelyn Smith, secretary to partner Moreau D. Brown.

Above (Mar. 3, 1967): Carol Morrison, investment officer in the Institutional Department. At right (Nov. 2, 1966): Laurence F. Whittemore, deputy manager and head of the Investment Department. Both at 59 Wall Street.

In 1895 a single wall telephone served partners and staff at 59 Wall Street.

At left (Mar. 31, 1965): Moreau Delano Brown, partner in charge of Philadelphia house. The picture on the wall at left is reproduced in color on p. 22.

At left (Nov. 2, 1966): Louis R. W. Soutendijk, manager in charge of assisting foreign and domestic companies in establishing international operations.

Below (Feb. 23, 1967): Merz K. Peters, of the Research Department.

Below (July 13, 1965): William R. Driver, Jr., partner in charge of Boston house.

Above left (Nov. 17, 1966): R. L. Ireland III. (The model on top of the rolltop desk is a Boeing 707.) Above (Nov. 17, 1966): John C. West.

"The partners own and operate the business. They have unlimited liability for the obligations of the firm. Our method of operation stems directly from these facts."

(From *The Personality of a Bank,* 1967.)

Below (July 28, 1964): The senior partners in a post-luncheon discussion. Left to right—E. Roland Harriman, Prescott S. Bush, Knight Woolley, and Robert A. Lovett. Former Senator Bush had just returned from the Republican National Convention in San Francisco. (See pictures on pp. 11–13 and p. 17.)

At right (Mar. 2, 1967): Frederick W. Kingsbury, Jr. (see p. 207) and Frank W. Hoch in Hoch's private office in the Foreign Investment Department. They were planning forthcoming trips to the Netherlands and Switzerland.

Above (Apr. 27, 1967): Stephen Y. Hord, partner in charge of the Chicago office (see p. 205), during one of his regular visits to 59 Wall Street. At right (July 28, 1964): former Senator Prescott S. Bush.

Above (Oct. 28, 1966): Herbert Gray, manager in charge of operations at 59 Wall Street, with Robert Bentivegna, the bank's purchasing agent.

Above left (Oct. 28, 1966): Hallway leading to Foreign Exchange Department, with Mrs. Joan Pollak at the Foreign Exchange window. Above right (Feb. 23, 1967): Part of the Research Department, with research analysts Robert Langen and Patrick Tatham in office beyond the department library.

Below (Dec. 1, 1966): Edward P. Currier, Jr. (at right), deputy manager in charge of the St. Louis office, with John C. Hanson, Jr. (at left), manager in charge of the Investment Advisory Department, and Thomas McCance, partner, in Hanson's office at 59 Wall Street.

"Our initiative and effectiveness are not restricted by organization charts. Each partner and executive officer is literally 'in on the whole business.'"

(*The Personality of a Bank,* 1967.)

Above (Nov. 2, 1966): Lester J. Newquist (at right), partner in charge of the Research Department, with Walter R. Good, manager, in Newquist's private office at 59 Wall Street.

Below (Feb. 23, 1967): Robert P. Bergin and Dr. Lester V. Plum of the Research Department.

"Evans is less concerned with the majesty of machinery than with the psychology, manners and looks of the men who make it work."

(Lincoln Kirstein, "Photographs of America: Walker Evans," 1938.)

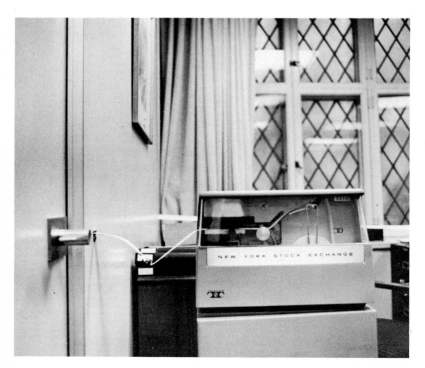

Above (Nov. 2, 1966): Four members of the Bond Department: Joseph N. Isolano (at left), Charles T. Foley, John E. Foster, and Charles J. McHugh. In the background is the Yield Board, indicating various rates of municipal bonds.

At left (Mar. 3, 1967): New York Stock Exchange high speed Teletype machine, feeding its tape through slot in wall at left into private office of Eugene Banks, partner in charge of Institutional Department.

"Most of the activities of the bank come under the direct supervision of managers, who are directly responsible to the partners."

(From *Introduction to Brown Brothers Harriman & Co.*, an employee handbook.)

Above (Mar. 31, 1965): At Philadelphia house, partner Moreau D. Brown (left) with William A. Hess, manager and senior loan officer, on the banking platform. Top left (July 13, 1965): At Boston house, George D. Rattray, deputy manager in charge of the Securities Department, with partner William R. Driver, Jr. (The picture on the wall is a copy of the one reproduced facing p. 1.) Center left (Nov. 17, 1966): Joseph R. Kenny, manager specializing in documentary credits and collections, welcomes Eric F. Southwood of the Australia and New Zealand Bank Ltd. In background, left to right: Mrs. Laura Kroemmelbein, secretary to partner John B. Madden; Agnes Sniechkus, secretary to Walter H. Brown, manager; Peter B. Bartlett, deputy manager (talking with a client whose back is to the camera); Hector P. Prud'homme, deputy manager; and Mrs. Joan Foy, secretary to Mr. Kenny.

Bottom left (Nov. 2, 1966): Elbridge T. Gerry, Jr., assistant manager in Domestic Banks Department and, with back to camera, Robert H. Chamberlin, manager in charge of the department (see also p. 226).

Below (Nov. 2, 1966): William C. Horn and Maarten van Hengel, managers in Foreign Investment Department.

At left (Feb. 1, 1967, 3:45 P.M.): Main entrance at 59 Wall Street. (See p. 196.) The men in foreground are wheeling one of the "securities buses" in which brokerage houses transport their securities to the banks at the end of a day's business.

At right (July 7, 1964, at noon): Part of the Hanover Street façade of 59 Wall Street, seen from Exchange Place, just west of William Street. The medallions above the fluted pilasters in Delano & Aldrich's design represent ancient coins. At the left is the back side of the old Merchants Exchange building (see p. 84), now the lower portion of the First National City Bank's building.

At left (Mar. 31, 1965): Brown Brothers Harriman & Co., 1531 Walnut Street (northeast corner of 16th Street), Philadelphia. This building, designed by the firm of Delano & Aldrich, was completed for the bank in 1927.

Below (July 30, 1964): Interior changes seem to be constantly occurring. The offices of the Boston house have been completely remodeled since Evans' visit. Here Evans records remodeling at 59 Wall Street, in the Investment Department area. Anthony J. Barberi (at right), assistant to Joseph C. Lucey, manager in charge of operations, talks with the representative of a rug and carpet company.

"Our buildings are impressive only in relation to the people who built and use them, and Evans knows this whether he puts people in front to give them scale, or not."

(Lincoln Kirstein, "Photographs of America: Walker Evans," 1938.)

"Our investment advisory services are as important to many of our customers as our banking facilities are to others."

(From *The Personality of a Bank,* 1967.)

At right (Mar. 31, 1965): George B. Llewellyn, assistant manager in charge of Foreign Department operations at the Philadelphia house, visits the office of Edward A. Doelp, secretary-treasurer of Irwin-Harrisons-Whitney, Inc., one of the oldest banking clients of the firm. The tea importing company still has its headquarters at 50 South Front Street (see the two Evans photographs above), and still uses the tea-making and tea-tasting equipment that was in use when the photograph on p. 168 was taken more than seventy years ago. Mr. Doelp's office and the Directors Room are on the second floor (reached by the stairs that show in right background of the 1895 picture).

Above (Feb. 17, 1967): Manager John C. Hanson, Jr. (at right, see p. 216) and Harold N. Howard (at far end of table), an account manager, at a luncheon meeting in one of the firm's private dining rooms with Mr. and Mrs. Frederick G. Frost, investment advisory clients. (It is interesting to note, by the way, that Mr. Frost, an architect, is president of the Citizens Housing and Planning Council of New York, which deals in contemporary terms with many of the problems that concerned the pioneering Citizens Association of which James M. Brown was chairman a century ago—see p. 132.)

At left (Mar. 3, 1967): J. Eugene Banks, partner in charge of the Institutional Department, talking in his private office with one of the department's clients, Mr. Chauncey L. Waddell, chairman of the board of Waddell & Reed, Inc., the management company for the United Fund group of mutual funds.

223

"A customer's feeling for his bank results from his dealings with many people—officers, tellers, account managers, and others."

(From *The Personality of a Bank,* 1967.)

Above (Nov. 2, 1966): Bookkeeping Department, 59 Wall Street. In group at far left, beyond open file drawer in foreground: Richard Grzymko (standing), Mrs. Sonia Maurrasse, Thomas Vargo, Mrs. Dorothy Romani, Mrs. Diane Del Negro, Rosemary Weaver. In center background: Susan Steinmetz, Arlene Brabyn, and, right of the post, Gloria Simmons. In foreground: Mrs. Noreen Malony, Carol Melesh, and (telephoning) Mary McCormack.

At left (Feb. 17, 1967): In Personnel Department Donald J. Petrie, personnel manager, discusses work with Linda Menake. At other desks: Carolyn Campbell and Elaine Camera.

Above left (Mar. 26, 1965): A corner of the mail room at 59 Wall Street.

Above (Mar. 1, 1967): Mrs. Elenore Paoli, secretary to James A. Harper, at her desk on banking platform.

At left (Feb. 23, 1967): On banking platform Armond Oneta of the mail room staff delivers mail to Andrea Gaulin, secretary to Terrence M. Farley, manager. Helen Fowler, secretary to partner R. L. Ireland III, is at desk beyond. In background are the tellers' windows.

Above (Nov. 17, 1966): In the partners' room, 59 Wall Street. Elbridge T. Gerry at left; L. Parks Shipley dictating to his secretary, Elizabeth Nixon.

"A Bank—But More Than a Bank."

(Title of a section in *The Personality of a Bank,* 1967.)

At left (Nov. 2, 1966): Robert H. Chamberlin, manager and head of the Domestic Banks Department.

At right (Mar. 31, 1965): Alan Crawford, Jr., deputy manager in charge of Investment Advisory Department in Philadelphia.

Above and at right (May 4, 1967): Robert A. Lovett and Robert V. Roosa talking in Roosa's office, adjoining the partners' room, just after the British lowered their bank rate.

Above (Oct. 6, 1966): In Robert A. Lovett's office.

At left (Nov. 17, 1966): Through the open door of the partners' room. The clock was presented to the partners by the staff in 1925, on the 100th anniversary of the founding of the New York house.

Above (Oct. 6, 1966): In Robert A. Lovett's office.

At left (Nov. 17, 1966): Through the open door of the partners' room. The clock was presented to the partners by the staff in 1925, on the 100th anniversary of the founding of the New York house.

PARTNERS IN BROWN BROTHERS

HARRIMAN & CO. AND ANTECEDENT FIRMS,

1818–1967

Section I

FOUNDING PARTNERS

Name	Became Partner	Ceased to be Partner		Comments
		By Death	By Retirement	
Alexander Brown (1764–1834)	1818	Mar. 4, 1834		Established Alexander Brown & Co. in Baltimore in Dec. 1800. In 1805, his eldest son William became his partner, and the name of the firm became Alexander Brown & Son. William ceased to be a partner in 1809, but the second son, George, had been admitted to partnership in 1808, and in 1810, when the third son, John A., was admitted, the firm was styled Alexander Brown & Sons. The fourth son, James, became a partner in 1811 or early 1812.
				Alexander Brown became a partner in both the American houses established by his sons (John A. Brown & Co. in Philadelphia, 1818, and Brown Brothers & Co., established by James Brown in New York, 1825). He was not, however, a partner in the firm William established in Liverpool in 1814, though William at that time again became a partner in Alexander Brown & Sons. In 1839, when Alexander's son George retired from his brothers' firms, Alexander Brown & Sons became an independent firm, no longer included in the interlocking partnerships.
William Brown (Sir William Brown after 1862) (1784–1864)	1818	Mar. 3, 1864		As noted above, William was a partner in his father's Baltimore house 1805–09 and after 1815. In 1810 William established his own firm, William Brown & Co., Liverpool, in which neither his father nor any of his brothers was a partner. In 1814 he established in Liverpool William & James Brown & Co. (later Brown, Shipley & Co.), in which his three brothers (but not his father) were partners. In 1818 he became a partner in John A. Brown & Co. Created Baronet in 1862.

Name	Became Partner	Ceased to be Partner		Comments
		By Death	By Retirement	
George Brown (1787–1859)	1818		1839	As noted above, George became a partner in his father's Baltimore house in 1808. He succeeded his father as its principal after the latter's death, and remained head of the firm until he died on Aug. 26, 1859. In 1814 he became a partner in his brother William's Liverpool house; in 1818 in John A. Brown & Co. (Philadelphia); and in 1825 in Brown Brothers & Co. (New York). From all of his brothers' firms he retired in 1839 (selling his interest to William and James for $1,150,000), and at that time his brothers ceased to be partners in Alexander Brown & Sons. From 1839 to 1859 he was, however, a silent partner, with his brother James, in Browns & Bowen, organized to take over the business of John A. Brown & Co. in Philadelphia.
John A. Brown (1788–1872)	1818		1837	As noted above, John A. became a partner in his father's Baltimore house in 1810. In 1814 he became a partner in William's Liverpool house. And in 1818 he established at Philadelphia the firm of John A. Brown & Co., whose business was taken over after his retirement by Brown Brothers & Co., which James Brown had established in New York. The date of the founding of John A. Brown & Co. is, therefore, taken as the date of the establishment of the business now carried on by Brown Brothers Harriman & Co.
James Brown (1791–1877)	1818	Nov. 1, 1877		As noted above, James became a partner in Alexander Brown & Sons in 1811 or 1812. In 1814 he became a partner in William's Liverpool house, which was styled William & James Brown & Co., and in 1818 of John A. Brown & Co. (see comments on John A. Brown, above). In 1825 he established Brown Brothers & Co. in New York, in which his father and all three of his brothers were also partners.

Section II

Generally, the partners in each of the firms established by Alexander Brown and his sons, on both sides of the Atlantic, were partners in all the others from 1818 through 1917, except that Alexander Brown & Sons, of Baltimore, became independent of the other concerns in 1839. At the end of 1917 the transatlantic partnership ceased. A few individual exceptions to the usual arrangement are noted in the comments below.

ALPHABETICAL LIST OF PARTNERS ADMITTED SINCE 1818

Name	Became Partner	Ceased to be Partner By Death	By Retirement	Comments
David Greenlie Ackerman (1895–)	Jan. 1, 1953		Dec. 31, 1961	Resident in New York.
J. Eugene Banks (1908–)	Jan. 1, 1962			Resident in New York.
William Ezra Bowen (1797–1866)	1837		Dec., 1859	Resident first in Liverpool, then after 1839 in Philadelphia as partner in Browns & Bowen.
Alexander Hargreaves Brown (afterwards Sir Alexander Hargreaves Brown, Bart.) (1844–1922)	Jan. 1, 1875		1920	Grandson of Sir William Brown. Resident in London. Created Baronet in 1902.
Clarence Stewart Brown (1840–1875)	Jan. 1, 1867		1868	Fifth and youngest son of James Brown. Resident in New York.
Edward Clifton Brown (1870–1944)	1899	Nov. 1, 1944		Great-grandson of Sir William Brown. Resident in London.
George Hunter Brown (1835–1900)	Jan. 1, 1858		Dec. 31, 1862	Son of James Brown. Resident in New York.
James Brown (1863–1935)	1901		Jan. 1, 1934	Son of George Hunter Brown. Resident in New York.
James Crosby Brown (1872–1930)	1904	Apr. 1, 1930		Son of John Crosby Brown. Resident in Philadelphia.
James Muncaster Brown (1820–1890)	Jan. 1, 1847	July 19, 1890		A half brother of Stewart Brown. Resident in New York.
John Crosby Brown (1838–1909)	1864	June 25, 1909		Fourth son of James Brown. Resident in New York.
Moreau Delano Brown (1905–)	Feb. 1, 1939			Son of Thatcher M. Brown. Resident in Philadelphia.
Stewart Brown (1802–1880)	Jan. 1, 1827 (of New York house) Jan. 1, 1836 (of other houses)	Jan. 30, 1880		First cousin of James Brown. Resident in New York. From 1827 to 1836 was partner only in New York house.
Stewart Henry Brown (1831–1905)	Jan. 21, 1856		Dec. 31, 1888	Son of Stewart Brown. Resident in Liverpool. He retired when the Liverpool office was closed.
Thatcher Magoun Brown (1876–1954)	1907	May 2, 1954		Son of John Crosby Brown. Resident in New York.
Waldron Post Brown (1848–1915)	Jan. 1, 1887		Dec. 31, 1914	Son of James Muncaster Brown. Resident in New York.
Walter Hargreaves Brown (1881–1936)	1915	June 1, 1936		Son of Sir Alexander Hargreaves Brown. Resident in London.
William Benedict Brown (1825–1854)	Jan. 1, 1853	Sept. 27, 1854		Second son of James Brown. Resident in New York.
Prescott Sheldon Bush (1895–)	Jan. 1, 1930 (of Harriman Bros. & Co.) Jan. 1, 1931 (of B B H & CO.)			Resident in New York. On leave of absence from the firm, he filled the unexpired term of the late Brien McMahon, as U. S. Senator from Connecticut, Nov. 1952–55. He was elected to serve a full term in 1956. Resumed active participation as a general partner in 1963.

Name	Became Partner	Ceased to be Partner		Comments
		By Death	By Retirement	
Frederick W. M. Chalmers (1836–1898)	1869	Dec. 28, 1898		Brother-in-law of Sir Mark W. Collet. Resident in London.
Lawrence Edlmann Chalmers (1863–1924)	1898	1924		Son of Frederick W. M. Chalmers. Resident in London.
Mark Wilks Collet (afterwards Sir Mark Wilks Collet, Bart.) (1816–1905)	July 1, 1851	Apr. 25, 1905		Resident in Liverpool and London. Established London office of Brown, Shipley & Co., 1863. Became Director of the Bank of England, 1866; Deputy Governor, 1885–87; Governor, 1887–89. Created Baronet in 1889.
Ralph Thompson Crane (1878–1938)	June 1, 1929		June 9, 1934	Resident in New York. Resigned to join Brown Harriman & Co., Inc. in the investment banking business after Banking Act of 1933.
Louis Curtis, Sr. (1849–1931)	1911		Dec. 31, 1930	Son of Thomas B. Curtis, who had established the Boston agency of Brown Brothers & Co. in 1844. Resident in Boston.
Louis Curtis, Jr. (1891–)	Jan. 1, 1922		Sept. 1, 1962	Resident in Boston. After retirement became a limited partner. (See Section III.)
Eugene Delano (1843–1920)	Jan. 1, 1894	Apr. 2, 1920		Brother-in-law of John Crosby Brown. Resident partner in Philadelphia, 1894–96—the first since William E. Bowen. Resident in New York after 1896.
Moreau Delano (1877–1936)	1907	Dec. 4, 1936		Son of Eugene Delano. Resident principally in New York, but for a time in Philadelphia.
Charles Denston Dickey, Sr. (1818–1897)	Oct. 1, 1859	Aug. 13, 1897		Great-nephew of Mrs. Alexander Brown (Grace Davison). Resident in Mobile, Alabama, 1859–60; Liverpool, 1861–62; New York thereafter.
Charles Denston Dickey, Jr. (1860–1919)	Jan. 1, 1889	Feb. 3, 1919		Resident in New York.
Charles Denston Dickey III (1895–)	Jan. 1, 1922		Dec. 31, 1931	Resident in Philadelphia. Retired to become a partner in J. P. Morgan & Co.
William Raymond Driver, Jr. (1907–)	Jan. 1, 1961			Resident in Boston.
James May Duane (1851–1912)	Jan. 1, 1896	Dec. 2, 1912		Resident in Philadelphia, 1896–98, in New York after Aug. 1, 1898.
George Harrison Frazier (1867–1934)	Jan. 1, 1898		Jan. 1, 1921	Resident in Philadelphia. Retired to become president of American Sugar Refining Co.
Ellison Frodsham (no. b. or d. dates available)	1816		1830	Not a partner in any of the American houses. Shared only in the profits of the Liverpool house.
Charles Stedman Garland (1898--)	Jan. 1, 1933		June 9, 1934	As a manager of Brown Brothers & Co. established Chicago office in 1929. Resident partner in Chicago, 1933–34. Resigned to join Brown Harriman & Co., Inc., in the investment banking business after Banking Act of 1933. Since 1939, a partner in Alex. Brown & Sons, Baltimore.

Name	Became Partner	Ceased to be Partner		Comments
		By Death	By Retirement	
Elbridge Thomas Gerry (1908–)	Jan. 1, 1956			Nephew of Averell and Roland Harriman. Resident in New York. (See Section III—Gerry Bros. & Co.)
Francis Alexander Hamilton (1814–1907)	July 1, 1845		Dec. 31, 1903	Resident in Liverpool, 1845–66, and London after 1866.
John Henry Hammond (1891–1949)	Jan. 1, 1916		Dec. 31, 1931	Resident in New York. Retired to become a member of the law firm later known as Dorr, Hammond, Hand & Dawson.
Edward Roland Noel Harriman (1895–)	Oct. 30, 1926 (of W. A. Harriman & Co.) Jan. 1, 1931 (of B B H & CO.)			Co-founder with his brother Averell of W. A. Harriman & Co., the banking partnership which later became Harriman Bros. & Co., and which merged with Brown Brothers & Co. Jan. 1, 1931. Resident in New York.
William Averell Harriman (1891–)	Oct. 30, 1926 (of W. A. Harriman & Co.) Jan. 1, 1931 (of B B H & CO.)		Oct. 31, 1946	Founder of W. A. Harriman & Co., Inc., in 1919, and in 1926 co-founder with his brother Roland Harriman of W. A. Harriman & Co., the banking partnership which later became Harriman Bros. & Co., and which merged with Brown Brothers & Co. Jan. 1, 1931. Resident in New York. Retired to become Secretary of Commerce in Oct. 1946. Has been a limited partner since then. (See Section III.)
Frank William Hoch (1921–)	Jan. 1, 1960			Resident in New York.
Stephen Young Hord (1897–)	Jan. 1, 1945			Resident in Chicago.
Herman Hoskier (1832–1904)	1866		1880	Resident in London.
Robert Livingston Ireland III (1920–)	Jan. 1, 1960			Resident in New York.
Ellery Sedgewick James (1895–1932)	Jan. 1, 1925	Nov. 25, 1932		Resident in New York, 1925–31, and in Philadelphia in 1932.
John E. Johnson (no. b. or d. dates available)	Jan. 1, 1875		Dec. 31, 1886	Resident in New York.
Frederick Hutchinson Kingsbury, Jr. (1907–)	Jan. 1, 1949			Resident in New York.
P. Blair Lee (1897–)	Oct. 1, 1930 Jan. 1, 1935 (rejoined)		June 9, 1934 Feb. 1, 1939	Resident in Philadelphia. Resigned to join Brown Harriman & Co. Inc., in investment banking business after the Banking Act of 1933. Rejoined B B H & CO. in 1935. Resigned to become president of the Western Savings Fund Society, Philadelphia.
Robert Abercrombie Lovett (1895–)	Jan. 1, 1926 rejoined: June 1, 1946 Apr. 1, 1949 Mar. 1, 1953		Dec. 16, 1940 May 15, 1947 Oct. 3, 1950	Son-in-law of James Brown (1863–1935). Resident in New York. From Dec. 1940–Apr. 1941, served in Washington as special assistant to Secretary of War. From April 1941–45, served as Assistant Secretary of War for Air. From July 1947–Jan. 1949 was Under Secretary of State; from Oct. 1950–Oct. 1951, Deputy Secretary of Defense; and from 1951–53, Secretary of Defense.

Name	Became Partner	Ceased to be Partner		Comments
		By Death	By Retirement	
Thomas McCance (1902–)	Jan. 1, 1945			Resident in New York.
Johnston McLanahan (1794–1855)	Probably 1818		June 1, 1839	Bachelor brother of Isabella McLanahan, the wife of George Brown of Baltimore. From 1818–39, he appears to have been a partner only in the Philadelphia house.
John Beckwith Madden (1919–)	Jan. 1, 1955			Resident in New York.
Ray Morris (1878–1961)	Jan. 1, 1921		1956	Resident in New York.
Lester John Newquist (1910–)	Jan. 1, 1960			Resident in New York.
Samuel Nicholson (1795?–1857)	1826		Dec. 31, 1856	In 1826, he became a partner in the New York house; in 1836 in the other houses. Resident in New York, excepting winters spent at New Orleans from 1838 (when the New Orleans agency of Brown Brothers & Co. was established under the name of Samuel Nicholson & Co.) to 1850.
Montagu Collet Norman (later Lord Norman) (1871–1950)	1900		1915	Grandson of Sir Mark W. Collet. Resident in London. He became Director of the Bank of England in 1907. After retiring from Brown, Shipley & Co., he served as Deputy Governor, 1918–20, and then Governor, 1920–44, of the Bank of England. Created a Baron in 1944 and took title of Lord Norman of St. Clere.
Harold Douglas Pennington (1891–)	Jan. 1, 1930 (of Harriman Bros. & Co.) Jan. 1, 1945 (of B B H & CO.)	Dec. 31, 1930 Dec. 31, 1956		After Harriman Bros. & Co. merged with Brown Brothers & Co., he served as a manager at B B H & CO. until he became a partner. Resident in New York.
Herman Henry Perry (1809–1853)	1836		1839	Resident at Baltimore, interested only in the Baltimore business until 1837 when he appears to have acquired an interest in the Liverpool house as well. It is possible that from 1837–39 he may also have been a general partner in all American houses. In 1852–53 he acted as Brown Brothers & Co.'s agent in Baltimore.
Howard Potter (1826–1897)	1863	Mar. 24, 1897		Son-in-law of James Brown. Resident in New York, 1863–83; in London after 1883.
John Moore Priestman (? –1846)	1830	1846		Was a "salaried partner" in Liverpool house only.
Charles James Rhoads (1872–1956)	Jan. 1, 1921		June 30, 1929	Resident in Philadelphia. Retired to become Commissioner of Indian Affairs under President Herbert Hoover.
Robert Vincent Roosa (1918–)	Jan. 1, 1965			Resigned from his post as Under Secretary of the Treasury for Monetary Affairs to become a partner, resident in New York.

Name	Became Partner	Ceased to be Partner By Death	By Retirement	Comments
Joseph Shipley (1795–1867)	1826		Oct. 31, 1850	Resident in Liverpool, first as partner only in W. & J. Brown & Co., but after 1836 as a partner in all of the houses.
L. Parks Shipley (1905–)	Jan. 1, 1953			Resident in New York.
Laurence Gotzian Tighe (1894–1954)	Jan. 1, 1930		June 9, 1934	Resident in Boston, 1930–32 and in New York, 1932–34. Resigned to join Brown Harriman & Co. Inc., in the investment banking business after the Banking Act of 1933.
John Cristy West (1908–)	Jan. 1, 1956			Resident in New York.
James Leigh Wood (later Sir J. Leigh-Wood) (1870–1949)	1907		1936	Resident in London.
Knight Woolley (1895–)	Jan. 1, 1929 (of Harriman Bros. & Co.) Jan. 1, 1931 (of B B H & CO.)			Had been general manager of Harriman Bros. & Co. from its founding in 1926 until he became a partner. Resident in New York.

Addendum

PARTNERS ADMITTED SINCE THIS BOOK WENT TO PRESS

Name	Became Partner			Comments
Walter Henderson Brown (1923–)	Jan. 1, 1968			Resident in New York.
William Felix Ray (1915–)	Jan. 1, 1968			Resident in New York.
Maarten van Hengel (1927–)	Jan. 1, 1968			Resident in New York.

Section III

LIMITED PARTNERS

Name	Became Limited Partner			Comments
Louis Curtis, Jr.	Sept. 1, 1962			See Section II.
Gerry Bros. & Co.	Nov. 1, 1955			Gerry Bros. & Co. was organized in New York in 1953 to acquire the assets of Gerry Estates, Inc., and to handle investments of the Gerry family. The general partners are Elbridge T. Gerry (see Section II), Edward H. Gerry, and Henry A. Gerry.
W. Averell Harriman	Oct. 31, 1946			See Section II.

ACKNOWLEDGMENTS

I owe a very special debt to Thatcher M. Brown (1876–1954), the first senior partner of the merged firms, for a comment he made in a letter I found among his papers early in my work as director of the Historical File. The letter was written on April 23, 1951, to his cousin, William Adams Delano, architect of the buildings occupied by the firm in New York and Philadelphia and himself the son of a partner in the firm. Mr. Delano had commented appreciatively about the informal history of the bank which Mr. Brown had written covering the years 1900–1950. There was only one thing, Thatcher Brown wrote, of which he was proud, "and that is that I tried to be honest and related our failures, as well as our successes. I'm fed up with anniversary books, particularly in the banking field, which always make everything look rosy. We made plenty of mistakes and they are duly recorded in my booklet." I have felt those words both as a challenge and as a kind of benediction during the four years of work on this book.

To the present partners I am grateful not only for the freedom of operation described in the Preface but also for facilitating my work in other ways. First of all, they enabled me to have the resourceful help of Sarah B. Brown as a research assistant. A former teacher of history at the Brearley School in New York, Mrs. Brown brought well-disciplined interest and skill to the job. The fact that she is a granddaughter of James Crosby Brown (partner in Philadelphia 1904–1930) and that her husband Thatcher M. Brown III, is the grandson and namesake of another partner might have been embarrassing—to me, if not to her—had she not been gifted with humor and a pleasantly irreverent kind of intellectual curiosity. As it was, her help was invaluable.

The partners also provided me with the full-time assistance of Miss Patricia C. Hoban. With no prior experience in historical projects, Miss Hoban has become, in effect, the assistant director of the Historical File, and I have been able to rely on her for sedulous attention to innumerable details at every step of the way. For her patience and care in typing and checking the manuscript of this book while continuing the work of indexing and filing the growing collection of historical documents I am quite humbly grateful.

Many other acknowledgments are due—far more than I shall be able to call to mind in the brief interval before this manuscript goes to the publisher. Certain books—some of which are referred to in the text—have been repeatedly consulted. The most important of these is John Crosby Brown's *A Hundred Years of Merchant Banking,* privately printed in 1909 but available in most large libraries. The anonymous *Experiences of a Century 1818–1918* (probably written chiefly by James Crosby Brown), which was privately printed for Brown Brothers & Co. in 1919, includes important material relating to the years prior to and during the First World War and provides some additional data on the Philadelphia house, whose hundredth anniversary it celebrated. Frank R. Kent's *The Story of Alexander Brown & Sons,* privately printed at Baltimore in 1925, focuses specifically on the Baltimore firm but contains some valuable extracts from the early correspondence of the other houses as well. Aytoun Ellis's *Heir of Adventure. The Story of Brown, Shipley & Co., Merchant Bankers,* issued privately by Brown, Shipley & Co., Ltd. in 1960, draws heavily on the earlier books, but adds fresh details on the early period from English sources and carries the history of the London firm up to the recent present.

I have left out of its chronological position in this list Thatcher M. Brown's unpublished historical booklet. It had no title page. Stamped on the cover were the words: "Brown Brothers & Co. Brown Brothers Harriman & Co. 1900–1950," and the first page was in the form of a letter addressed "To my Partners" and signed "T.M.B." Mr. Brown referred to his work as "these informal papers, . . . written without any idea of their publication at the present time," in continuation of his father's (John Crosby Brown's) book.

Sometime, perhaps in the future years, what I've written may have use as a basis for our Firm's story at some anniversary period, [he concluded]. Then it can be decided what part of it—if any—can be used for publication and circulated among our customers and friends.

A number of copies were, in fact, distributed in 1951, but the booklet should someday be published. The few excerpts included in this "historical portrait" barely suggest the value and interest of these frank and charming papers.

I have consulted many other books, some of which are mentioned in the text, but have made no attempt to equip myself to write a proper history of the firm

236

comparable, for example, to Ralph W. Hidy's *The House of Baring in American Trade and Finance* (Harvard University Press, 1949), or to Merrill Denison's *Canada's First Bank,* the two-volume history of the Bank of Montreal, published in 1966–67—models of what such a history should be. I can at best hope that publication of my book, with its sampling of the primary source material in our Historical File, will tempt qualified scholars to undertake the special studies out of which such a history may ultimately come.

Many of my obligations to individuals, to libraries and museums, and to various firms whose records have been made available to me are indicated in the text and in the credit lines accompanying the pictures. But it is pleasant to be able to express my special thanks to the following people: my colleagues at Barnard College, Columbia University, including especially Professor David A. Robertson and Professor Raymond Saulnier; Mr. Charles D. Dickey III, Mr. James R. Brugger, and Mr. Warren Paul of the Morgan Guaranty Trust Co.; Mr. John Prideaux of Arbuthnot Latham & Co., Ltd.; Mr. Ion Garnett-Orme and Mr. Bernard S. Wheble of Brown, Shipley & Co., Ltd.; Mr. Franklin B. Tuttle and Miss Celia Lambert of the Atlantic Mutual Insurance Co.; Mr. Joseph P. Ripley of Drexel Harriman Ripley, Inc.; Mrs. Evelyn Knowlton of the Federal Reserve Bank of New York; Mr. Francis F. Randolph and Mr. Henry C. Breck of J. & W. Seligman & Co.; Mr. Ross Muir of Tri-Continental Corporation; Mr. Charles Garland and Mr. Charles M. Schneider of Alex. Brown & Sons; Mr. Berkeley D. Johnson and Mr. James Lyall of the United States Trust Co.; Mr. Thatcher M. Brown, Jr., of G. H. Walker & Co.; Mr. Mungo Conacher and Mr. Geoffrey R. Kelly of Martins Bank, Ltd.; the late Mr. James Crosby Brown and Mr. Eric J. Guthrie of the Royal Globe Insurance Co.'s; Mr. Wesley Parker of the Ulster Bank, Ltd., Belfast; and Mr. Robert McLean Stewart of the Austral Oil Co., Inc.

Also to: Mr. A. K. Baragwanath of the Museum of the City of New York; Mr. John L. Lochhead of the Mariners Museum, Newport News, Va.; Miss Grace Mayer of the Museum of Modern Art; Mr. Harry S. Parker III, of the Metropolitan Museum of Art; the late Mr. Arthur B. Carlson of the New York Historical Society; Miss Elizabeth Roth of the Prints Division, and Mr. Robert W. Hill of the Manuscript Division of the New York Public Library; Dr. George Chandler of the Brown, Picton and Hornby Libraries of Liverpool; Mrs. Carter Smith of the Historic Mobile Preservation Society; Mr. Jonathan Fairbanks of the Henry Francis du Pont Winterthur Museum; Mr. John D. Kilbourne of the Maryland Historical Society; Mr. Donald C. Ringwald of the Steamship Historical Society of America; Miss Helen Ruskell of the New York Society Library; and Mr. Randolph H. Dyer of the Union Theological Seminary.

Also to: Mr. Alexander Crosby Brown, Mrs. Arthur Burkhard, Mr. John C. B. Moore, Mrs. Harold T. White, Mrs. John Crosby Brown II, Mrs. May deForest McCall, Miss Mary Elizabeth Johnson, Mrs. Patience Lee-Steere, and Mr. and Mrs. Moreau D. Brown for contributions to the Historical File; and, for help of various kinds, Mrs. M. S. W. Cullen, Mr. William Ward of Sigman-Ward, Inc., Mr. Allan Titley of Caru Studios, Mr. Samuel G. Stoney, the late Mr. Carl C. Cutler, Professor David B. Tyler, Mrs. W. H. Hagan, Mr. Walter Lord, Mr. Aubrey Toulmin, Jr., Mr. and Mrs. Frederick G. Frost, Jr., and Mr. Gordon S. Hargraves.

To the staff my individual obligations are too numerous to list, but I owe special thanks to the following: at 59 Wall Street, the partners' secretaries; Mr. Clarence F. von Glahn; Mrs. Marion Warner; Miss Joan Maloney; and Mr. Arthur R. Flannery. At the Philadelphia office, Miss Evelyn Smith and Mr. George F. S. Elder; at the Boston office, Miss Catherine Hanley and Mr. William E. Thrasher; Miss Delsa Priestley of the Chicago office, and Mrs. Ada A. Vidakovich of the St. Louis office. A number of the "alumni" of the firm were generously helpful, including Mr. Harold D. Pennington, Mr. Harold B. Norris, Mr. Howard P. Maeder, the late Mr. Willet C. Roper, Mr. Hudson A. Beattie, and Mr. Joseph C. Lucey. And finally a special word of appreciation is due to Miss Catherine Barrett, formerly of the Tax Department, whose scrapbooks are a valuable adjunct of the Historical File and whose interest in this project from the beginning has been heartwarming to us all.

If the book had a dedication page, it would be inscribed to my wife, Joan Vatsek Kouwenhoven, with wondering delight and love.

J.A.K.

INDEX